Library of
Davidson College

Robert T. Green • James M. Lutz

THE UNITED STATES AND WORLD TRADE

Changing Patterns and Dimensions

PRAEGER PUBLISHERS
Praeger Special Studies

New York • London • Sydney • Toronto

Library of Congress Cataloging in Publication Data

Green, Robert T   1943-
   The United States and world trade.

   Bibliography: p.
   1. International economic relations. 2. United States—Foreign economic relations. 3. Commercial policy. I. Lutz, James M., joint author. II. Title.
HF1411.G693   382'.0973   78-19762

ISBN 0-03-045351-8

PRAEGER PUBLISHERS
PRAEGER SPECIAL STUDIES
383 Madison Avenue, New York, N.Y. 10017, U.S.A.

Published in the United States of America in 1978
by Praeger Publishers,
A Division of Holt, Rinehart and Winston, CBS, Inc.

0123456789   038   98765432

© 1978 by Praeger Publishers

All rights reserved

Printed in the United States of America

PREFACE

For all the concern that has been expressed about the changing U. S. position in the international economy, very few studies at the macro level have been undertaken that would indicate the nature of these changes. It was our purpose to attempt to do just that: to provide some estimation of U. S. relationships with the rest of the nations of the world and some indication of the changes that have occurred in these relationships over time. Part way through the project, we realized why so few attempts at this type of venture had been made in the past. It is an ambitious venture, to say the least, and it is fraught with numerous ambiguities and contradictions that make the interpretation of findings sometimes seem impossible. Such are the problems of dealing with huge data bases. Nonetheless we persevered and the finished product is one that we feel will be of interest to professionals and scholars from many fields, since the findings are of both economic and political significance. Many of the findings of the studies that are presented in the book would have been anticipated, but some of the findings came as surprises to us, since they would not have been predicted from past information.

We feel that it is important for the reader to bear in mind that the nature of the analyses reported in this book, and of the book itself, is basically descriptive. It is not prescriptive, even though some portions of the book consider the policy implications that arise from the findings. It does not build any new theory, even though some of the relationships indicated by the data might be used by others for theory-building purposes. It does, in a systematic way, describe the changes that have occurred in the United States' position vis-a-vis the rest of the world as both a market for world goods and services and as a supplier of high technology goods. The book describes these changes within the framework of existing theory and methodology, although the methodology has not been frequently used for this purpose. We further believe that the way in which the data are analyzed and presented will be useful as a source of information concerning the changes that have occurred in the international economy in general.

Several individuals deserve recognition for the contributions they made during the four years that this project took to complete. We are particularly grateful to Dean George Kozmetsky and Dr. David L. Huff of the Graduate School of Business at The University of Texas at Austin. Dean Kozmetsky provided several ideas that became integral to the project as well as support and encouragement throughout the duration of the project. Dr. Huff was instrumental in the conceptualizing stages of the project, in providing the ideas for methodological techniques employed in the studies, and in numerous other ways during all stages of the project.

In addition, there were several other individuals who played an integral role in the conduct of this project who deserve special thanks for their contributions. Dr. Diana DeAre of the U. S. Bureau of the Census helped to operationalize the methods associated with the hierarchies employed in Part I of the book, and Dr. Randall Batsell of the University of Pennsylvania wrote the associated programs for the data analysis. Susan Flaggert and John Lewis, both graduate students at The University of Texas at Austin, contributed in multitudinous ways during the completion stages of the book, and Mary Fisher provided the cartography work. Appreciation is also expressed to the typists, Mary Lou Swanson of The University of Texas and Susan Steve and Lauren Heidelbach of West Virginia University for their patience, understanding, and editorial suggestions throughout the drafts of the book. We are also grateful to the students from The University of Texas who were involved in the collection, coding, verification, compilation, and tabularization of the huge amount of data involved in the study: Vanessa Agnew, William Black, Karen Huff, Lisa Kohl, Jerry Kotecki, Cynthia Toles, Kiki Walsh, and Alice Wightman.

Finally, we would like to thank the College of Business Foundation, the University Research Institute, and the Department of Marketing Administration, all of The University of Texas at Austin, as well as the Department of Political Science of West Virginia University, for the provision of support during the various stages of the project.

Notwithstanding all of the above assistance, we remain responsible for the results and any errors in the study.

Robert T. Green
James M. Lutz

CONTENTS

	Page
PREFACE	iii
LIST OF TABLES	x
LIST OF FIGURES	xv

Chapter

1 THE POSITION OF THE UNITED STATES IN WORLD TRADE ... 1

    Objectives of the Study ... 2
    Organization of the Study ... 3
        Part I ... 3
        Part II ... 5
        Part III ... 7

PART I: THE HIERARCHY OF INTERNATIONAL TRADE

2 WORLD TRADE, HIERARCHIES, ECONOMIC DEPENDENCE, AND PATTERNS OF INTERNATIONAL INFLUENCE ... 11

    Studies of World Trade Patterns ... 12
    Cores and Peripheries ... 14
    Large States and Small States ... 16
        Dependency Theory ... 17
        Political Compliance of Small States ... 24
    Hierarchical Studies ... 27
    Flow Analysis ... 30
    Summary ... 31

3 THE DEVELOPMENT OF TRADE HIERARCHIES ... 33

    The Hierarchy of World Trade ... 33
    Methodology ... 35
        Data and Nations ... 35
    Construction of Trade Hierarchies ... 38

Chapter		Page
	Trade Flow Index	38
	Hierarchical Structure	40
	Hypothetical Example	40
4	OVERVIEW OF INTERNATIONAL TRADE HIERARCHIES	44
	Cartographic Presentations	44
	1951	44
	1961	47
	1971	49
	1976	51
	Principal Hierarchies Over Time	51
	The United States Hierarchy	53
	United Kingdom Hierarchy	55
	Japanese Hierarchy	64
	West German Hierarchy	65
	French Hierarchy	69
	Soviet Union Hierarchy	72
	Conclusions	72
5	DEPENDENCY PATTERNS AMONG NATIONS	75
	Proportionate Trade with Dominant Nations	76
	United States	77
	United Kingdom	83
	Japan	87
	West Germany	89
	France	89
	Summary	95
	Dependency of National Economy on Dominant Nations	95
	United States	97
	United Kingdom	102
	Japan	106
	West Germany	108
	France	110
	Dependency and Interdependency in International Trade	112
	Proportionate Trade: A Global View	112
	Proportionate GDP: A Global View	114
6	INTERNATIONAL HIERARCHIES: CONCLUSIONS AND IMPLICATIONS	118
	International Hierarchies	118

Chapter		Page
	The Methodology	118
	The Major Hierarchies	119
	Decreasing Number of Hierarchical Nodes	121
	Dependency Theory	122
	Exports and Development	122
	Hierarchical Shifts	124
	Political Compliance: Unanswered Questions	125
	The Role of the EEC	126
	Summary	127

PART II: THE TECHNOLOGY-INTENSIVE EXPORT POSITION OF THE UNITED STATES

Chapter		Page
7	THE ROLE OF TECHNOLOGY IN EXPORT TRADE	131
	The Position of the United States in Technology-Intensive Trade	131
	Leontief's Paradox and the Search for Answers	132
	Technology Factors in Trade	133
	Technology Inputs and Trade	134
	Product Life Cycle	136
	Human Capital of Skill Intensity	139
	Other Factors	141
	Scale Economies	141
	Natural Resource Industries	142
	Open and Hidden Tariffs	143
	Nature of Markets	143
	Country Findings	144
	United States	144
	United Kingdom	145
	European Economic Community	145
	Japan	146
	Summary	147
8	ANALYSIS OF TECHNOLOGY-INTENSIVE TRADE	148
	Description of the Study	148
	Nations and Trade Data	150
	General Analytical Method	151
	Organization	156
	The United States and Technology-Intensive Trade	156
	Other Major Trading Nations and Technology-Intensive Trade	158

Chapter		Page
9	UNITED STATES TECHNOLOGY-INTENSIVE EXPORT POSITION	159
	World Overview	160
	Market Share Analysis	164
	Net Shift Analysis	168
	Summary	173
	Industry-Specific Export Positions	174
	Industrial Trade Patterns of Major Trading Nations	175
	Shift Share within Industrial Groupings	179
	Shift Shares at the Two-Digit SITC Level	184
	Shift Shares at the Four-Digit SITC Level	190
	Summary	197
	U. S. Imports of Technology-Intensive Products	197
	U. S. Imports versus Other Major Trading Nations	198
	U. S. Import Shares within Industry Groups	200
10	TECHNOLOGY-INTENSIVE EXPORT POSITION OF OTHER MAJOR TRADING NATIONS	206
	German Export Position	206
	One-Digit SITC Analysis	207
	Two-Digit SITC Analysis	210
	Japanese Export Position	216
	One-Digit SITC Analysis	216
	Two-Digit SITC Analysis	220
	United Kingdom Export Position	225
	French Export Position	230
	U. S., German, and Japanese Export Positions Compared	233
	Summary	237
11	IMPLICATIONS FOR U. S. TECHNOLOGY-INTENSIVE TRADE	239
	Technology Intensity and Comparative Advantage	240
	The United States	240
	Other Countries	242
	World Trends	244
	Explanations of Shifts in Technology-Intensive Export Markets	244
	The Product Life Cycle	245
	Other Possible Causes	246
	Policy Areas	251

Chapter		Page
	PART III: CONCLUSIONS AND IMPLICATIONS	
12	EXPORT PATTERNS AND U.S. ECONOMIC INFLUENCE	255
	Technology Intensity and Export Markets	255
	Competitive Positions	256
	Dependence and Political Compliance	258
	Hierarchical Positions and Export Shares	259
	Prospects for the Future	261
Appendix		
A	COUNTRIES EMPLOYED IN HIERARCHY STUDY	267
B	PERCENTAGE OF EXPORTS TO LARGEST MARKETS	277
C	PERCENTAGE OF GDP REPRESENTED BY EXPORTS TO LARGEST MARKETS	285
D	FOUR-DIGIT SITC PRODUCT CATEGORIES AND UNITED STATES MARKET SHARES AND PERCENT NET SHIFTS, 1963 TO 1974	291
REFERENCES		302
DATA SOURCES		317
ABOUT THE AUTHORS		319

LIST OF TABLES

Table		Page
5.1	UNITED STATES: Export Percentages from Attached Nations	78
5.2	UNITED STATES HIERARCHY: Historical Export Percentages	82
5.3	UNITED KINGDOM: Export Percentages from Attached Nations	84
5.4	UNITED KINGDOM HIERARCHY: Historical Export Percentages	86
5.5	JAPAN: Export Percentages from Attached Nations	88
5.6	WEST GERMANY: Export Percentages from Attached Nations	90
5.7	WEST GERMAN HIERARCHY: Historical Export Percentages	91
5.8	FRANCE: Export Percentages from Attached Nations	92
5.9	FRENCH HIERARCHY: Historical Export Percentages	94
5.10	UNITED STATES: Exports as a Percentage of GDP from Attached Nations	98
5.11	UNITED STATES HIERARCHY: Historical GDP Percentages	101
5.12	UNITED KINGDOM: Exports as a Percentage of GDP from Attached Nations	104
5.13	UNITED KINGDOM HIERARCHY: Historical GDP Percentages	106
5.14	JAPAN: Exports as a Percentage of GDP from Attached Nations	107
5.15	WEST GERMANY: Exports as a Percentage of GDP from Attached Nations	109

Table		Page
5.16	WEST GERMAN HIERARCHY: Historical GDP Percentages	110
5.17	FRANCE: Exports as a Percentage of GDP from Attached Nations	111
5.18	Regional Export Percentages to Largest Markets	113
5.19	Regional Exports to Largest Markets as a Percentage of GDP	115
5.20	Increases in World Trade: 1971-1976	116
9.1	1963 to 1974 Technology-Intensive Export Shifts of Major Trading Nations	169
9.2	1972 to 1974 Technology-Intensive Export Shifts of Major Trading Nations	171
9.3	1963 to 1974 Nontechnology-Intensive Export Shifts of Major Trading Nations	172
9.4	1972 to 1974 Nontechnology-Intensive Export Shifts of Major Trading Nations	173
9.5	Percentage of Technology-Intensive Exports from Industry Groups for Major Trading Nations	176
9.6	Percentage of Nontechnology-Intensive Exports from Industry Groups for Major Trading Nations	178
9.7	1963 to 1974 United States Technology-Intensive Export Shifts by Industry Group	180
9.8	1972 to 1974 United States Technology-Intensive Export Shifts by Industry Group	181
9.9	1963 to 1974 United States Nontechnology-Intensive Export Shifts by Industry Group	184
9.10	1972 to 1974 United States Nontechnology-Intensive Export Shifts by Industry Group	184
9.11	1963 to 1974 United States Technology-Intensive Export Shifts Within Two-Digit SITC Classifications	186

Table		Page
9.12	1972 to 1974 United States Technology-Intensive Export Shifts Within Two-Digit SITC Classifications	187
9.13	1963 to 1974 United States Nontechnology-Intensive Export Shifts Within Two-Digit SITC Classifications	189
9.14	1972 to 1974 United States Nontechnology-Intensive Export Shifts Within Two-Digit SITC Classifications	191
9.15	U.S. Technology-Intensive Exports: 1963 to 1974 and 1972 to 1974 Market Share Changes of Four-Digit SITC Categories	193
9.16	U.S. Nontechnology-Intensive Exports: 1963 to 1974 and 1972 to 1974 Market Share Changes of Four-Digit SITC Categories	195
9.17	Associated Volumes and Percentages of U.S. Exports Which Gained, Lost, and Maintained Constant Market Share, 1963 to 1974 and 1972 to 1974	196
9.18	1963 to 1974 Technology-Intensive Import Shifts of Major Trading Nations	199
9.19	1963 to 1974 Nontechnology-Intensive Import Shifts of Major Trading Nations	199
9.20	1972 to 1974 Technology-Intensive Import Shifts of Major Trading Nations	201
9.21	1972 to 1974 Nontechnology-Intensive Import Shifts of Major Trading Nations	201
9.22	1963 to 1974 United States Technology-Intensive and Nontechnology-Intensive Import Shifts by Industry Group	202
9.23	1972 to 1974 United States Technology-Intensive and Nontechnology-Intensive Import Shifts by Industry Group	204
10.1	WEST GERMANY: 1963 to 1974 Technology-Intensive and Nontechnology-Intensive Export Shifts by Industry Group	208

Table		Page
10.2	WEST GERMANY: 1972 to 1974 Technology-Intensive and Nontechnology-Intensive Export Shifts by Industry Group	209
10.3	WEST GERMANY: 1963 to 1974 Technology-Intensive Export Shifts Within Two-Digit SITC Classifications	211
10.4	WEST GERMANY: 1963 to 1974 Nontechnology-Intensive Export Shifts Within Two-Digit SITC Classifications	213
10.5	WEST GERMANY: 1972 to 1974 Technology-Intensive Export Shifts Within Two-Digit SITC Classifications	214
10.6	WEST GERMANY: 1972 to 1974 Nontechnology-Intensive Export Shifts Within Two-Digit SITC Classifications	215
10.7	JAPAN: 1963 to 1974 Technology-Intensive and Nontechnology-Intensive Export Shifts by Industry Group	217
10.8	JAPAN: 1972 to 1974 Technology-Intensive and Nontechnology-Intensive Export Shifts by Industry Group	219
10.9	JAPAN: 1963 to 1974 Technology-Intensive Export Shifts Within Two-Digit SITC Classifications	221
10.10	JAPAN: 1963 to 1974 Nontechnology-Intensive Export Shifts Within Two-Digit SITC Classifications	222
10.11	JAPAN: 1972 to 1974 Technology-Intensive Export Shifts Within Two-Digit SITC Classifications	223
10.12	JAPAN: 1972 to 1974 Nontechnology-Intensive Export Shifts Within Two-Digit SITC Classifications	224
10.13	UNITED KINGDOM: 1963 to 1974 Technology-Intensive and Nontechnology-Intensive Export Shifts by Industry Group	227
10.14	UNITED KINGDOM: 1972 to 1974 Technology-Intensive and Nontechnology-Intensive Export Shifts by Industry Group	229

Table		Page
10.15	FRANCE: 1963 to 1974 Technology-Intensive and Nontechnology-Intensive Export Shifts by Industry Group	231
10.16	FRANCE: 1972 to 1974 Technology-Intensive and Nontechnology-Intensive Export Shifts by Industry Group	232
10.17	1963 to 1974 U.S. Net Shifts Correlated With German and Japanese Net Shifts	234
10.18	1972 to 1974 U.S. Net Shifts Correlated With German and Japanese Net Shifts	236
A.1	Countries Employed in Hierarchy Study, 1951	269
A.2	Countries Employed in Hierarchy Study, 1961	271
A.3	Countries Employed in Hierarchy Study, 1971	273
A.4	Countries Employed in Hierarchy Study, 1976	275
B.1	Percentage of Exports to Largest Markets	279
C.1	Percentage of GDP Represented by Export to Largest Markets	287
D.1	Market Share and Percentage Net Shift for United States Technology-Intensive Exports, Four Digit SITC Level	293
D.2	Market Share and Percentage Net Shift for United States Nontechnology-Intensive Exports, Four-Digit SITC Level	297

LIST OF FIGURES

Figure		Page
4.1	World Trade Hierarchy, 1951	45
4.2	World Trade Hierarchy, 1951	46
4.3	World Trade Hierarchy, 1961	48
4.4	World Trade Hierarchy, 1971	50
4.5	World Trade Hierarchy, 1976	52
4.6	United States Hierarchy, 1951	54
4.7	United States Hierarchy, 1961	56
4.8	United States Hierarchy, 1971	58
4.9	United States Hierarchy, 1976	60
4.10	United Kingdom Hierarchy, 1951	63
4.11	West German Hierarchy, 1951	65
4.12	West German Hierarchy, 1961	66
4.13	West German Hierarchy, 1971	68
4.14	West German Hierarchy, 1976	70
4.15	French Hierarchy, 1951	71
4.16	U.S.S.R. Hierarchy, 1951-1976	73
9.1	Technology-Intensive Exports	161
9.2	Nontechnology-Intensive Exports	163
9.3	Technology-Intensive Export Market Shares	165
9.4	Nontechnology-Intensive Export Market Shares	167

1

THE POSITION OF THE UNITED STATES IN WORLD TRADE

International trade is an important component of an increasingly complex and interactive world. The United States, as the world's largest trader, has a critical role in the international economic system. The energy crisis, as well as international concern over dollar devaluations and the recent U. S. trade deficits, all point to the importance of trade and the key position of the United States. The present study concentrates on the position of the United States in the international economy and the changes that have occurred in its position over time.

The tenure of the United States as the dominant economic power in the world may be one of the shortest in history. It has lasted only about a quarter of a century, from the end of World War II to the 1970s. This time span is a brief one compared to the period of economic dominance held by England, Holland, Spain, and Portugal, or even Venice and Genoa. While there can be little doubt that the United States continues to be the single most dominant economic nation in the world, its supremacy appears to be on the wane. This nation no longer enjoys the position it once occupied in the international economy. West Germany and Japan, while not yet the economic equals of the United States, have obtained positions from which they can exert considerable economic influence on the United States. In the past, this type of influence was largely unidirectional from the United States to the rest of the world, except for the communist countries for which the Soviet Union has maintained a virtually closed economic system. The recently enlarged European Common Market is a good example of multi-directional influence and also represents an economic challenge to the United States. If economic unification, with or without political cohesion, is ever achieved in the European Economic Community (EEC), this group of nations could surpass the highest level of influence ever achieved by the United States.

The loss of world economic supremacy by the United States need not be viewed with total alarm. In essence, it represents the achievement of goals that were established during the peak of U. S. power in the world. The present economic competition from Europe and Asia for world markets and resources is the natural outgrowth of the postwar economic recovery to which the United States contributed so heavily. Even the formation of the Common Market was encouraged by the United States. The present competition in international trade also suggests that world income is becoming more evenly distributed; perhaps not as evenly as might be desirable, but more evenly than in the period immediately following World War II. Finally, the loss of economic supremacy, or at least its lessening, means the loss of some of the responsibilities that are associated with such supremacy. For many years the saying was that "when the United States sneezes the rest of the world catches cold." Saddled with the burden of world economic trusteeship, the United States was not always free to pursue economic policies in its own interest, particularly domestic economic policies. The partial release from this burden, signified in part by the 1971 discontinuation of the dollar's tie to gold, has given the United States more economic flexibility, both domestically and internationally.

OBJECTIVES OF THE STUDY

The underlying premise of the previous remarks is that the United States no longer occupies the supreme position it once held in the international economic system. While in many respects this premise seems obvious, its parameters have never been established. It is possible to look at several individual measures of lost influence, such as the declining value of the dollar and the decreasing share of world trade held by the United States, and then to rely on these surrogate indicators. No attempt has been made, however, to establish the extent to which the position of the United States has changed with respect to all of the nations in the world. Nor has the extent of changes in the positions of the main competitors of the United States in world markets been clearly established.

The present study consists of two related components that attempt to provide a reasonably comprehensive picture of the changing position of the United States in international trade. The first part of the study analyzes the position of the United States as a market for international products. The method of analysis involves the construction of international trade hierarchies which depict the dominant nations in the international economy together with the nations that rely upon these dominant nations as markets for their products. The analysis is undertaken in a comparative framework in that it depicts the U.S. position relative to the positions of the other major trading nations through time. The detailed analyses provide a basis for determining the changes in the role of the United States as a major economic power. Thus, it is possible to ascertain whether the United States has lost its economic supremacy, and if it has, to what extent. It might also be possible to identify potential causes for any changes that have occurred over time.

The second part of the study investigates the changes that have occurred in the position of the United States as a supplier of manufactured products for the rest of the world. The major emphasis in this portion of the study is on U.S. exports of technology-intensive products, a broad category of goods in which the United States has traditionally had a strong competitive advantage. The changes in the U.S. shipments are compared over time, and again the positions of major competitors are compared. These analyses provide additional inputs for determining whether or not the U.S. position in world trade is deteriorating. If its share of those exports for which it has had an historical comparative advantage has significantly decreased, then its world trading position has clearly declined. If, on the other hand, this export sector has remained competitive, the outlook for the future may be brighter.

ORGANIZATION OF THE STUDY

Part I

This portion of the study reports the findings of the longitudinal study of international trade ties using analyses of derived trade hierarchies for the years 1951, 1961, 1971, and 1976. Briefly, the hierarchical analysis employed analyzes the linkages of greatest international trade association for all the individual countries and territories of the world for which trade data were available. Through the identification of each nation's largest market, chains of association are developed between nations, with the nations at the top of the structure considered the nodal or dominant nations in the hierarchies. The study identifies three major hierarchies that existed throughout the time frame—one associated with the United States, a second associated with West Germany, and the third dominated by the Soviet Union. The structures of these hierarchies show varying degrees of change over the time period, and it is these dynamic aspects and the directions they portend with which the study is primarily concerned.

The analysis of trade ties begins with a consideration of some of the key elements of international trade theory that are important to the analysis. Chapter 2 discusses previous global studies and highlights the main points of previous work on dependency theory, the connection between economic ties and political compliance, and trade flow studies. Attention is focused upon previous analyses of international hierarchies since the hierarchical concept is central to the whole work. While these works are not as comprehensive as the present study, and few of them provided a longitudinal perspective, many of the past studies did have as an objective the identification of underlying relationships that exist between nations at different levels of economic or political hierarchies.

Chapter 3 presents the background for and the specific methodology used to derive the trade hierarchies. The data used for the study are also discussed, including comments on the sources, data limitations and data availability.

The derived hierarchies for the four years are presented in cartographic form in Chapter 4, together with a detailed discussion of the major hierarchies. Particular attention is paid to the changes that have occurred over time within each of the major hierarchies. While the individual shifts of states between hierarchies are mentioned, detailed analyses of individual countries' changing associations are not undertaken since the emphasis of the study is on global patterns. Also, shifting trade patterns of some countries would require individual volumes to explain the underlying pressures for such changes.

Chapter 5 focuses on questions of economic dependency relationships within the major hierarchies and their evolution over the years of the study. The hierarchies of the United States and West Germany, as well as those associated with the United Kingdom, Japan, and France, are analyzed in terms of the concentration of exports to these markets from the nations in each hierarchy. As a further measure of dependency, the portions of Gross Domestic Product (GDP) accounted for by exports to these countries are also discussed. Additionally, comments on regional trends and concentration levels through time are presented. While it was anticipated that such dependence has been decreasing, the findings indicate that this is not necessarily the case. Although nations are tending to show less concentration in their export markets, there has been less of a tendency to decrease their economic reliance upon their major markets.

A summary of the findings of Part I is contained in Chapter 6. An evaluation of the results provides an opportunity to assess the implications of the existing trade structures of U.S. policies. The main concepts from the previous literature discussed in Chapter 2 are evaluated within the context of the findings. Additionally, an attempt is made to extrapolate the findings of Part I to a consideration of future trends and implications for the position of the United States in the international economy. An integral part of this discussion will be the increasing impact of the EEC on future trading relationships.

Part II

Throughout the period of its economic supremacy, the United States has held a wide lead in advanced technology. This lead encompassed both the development of new technology and the production of products for export which incorporated such technology. Exports of technology-intensive products have been a mainstay of U. S. comparative advantage since World War II. Changes in this aspect of international trade might explain some of the changes that have been occurring in the hierarchies derived in Part I as well as in the overall U. S. trade position. The identification of those nations that are assuming central positions in technology-intensive export markets could be another indication of future trends in the international economic system.

Chapter 7 discusses the previous literature that has considered technology inputs into export trade and comparative advantage. By far the largest segment of this body of work has concentrated on the United States, although there have been some comparative studies. An additional theoretical perspective which must be considered when analyzing technology-intensive exports is the concept of a product life cycle. Since this concept is particularly relevant to the trading position of the United States, it is discussed in some depth. Other ideas are discussed which have also been put forward to explain U. S. comparative advantage, and most have a direct or indirect relationship to technology intensity.

The discussion of the past studies of U. S. comparative advantage is followed in Chapter 8 with a presentation of the methodology employed in Part II to analyze the export flows of technology-intensive products. For this portion of the study, the primary methodological technique consists of a shift share routine that determines the changes that have occurred in export market shares of the major trading nations. Chapter 8 presents the three main indicators that are employed in the study to analyze the changes that have occurred in export markets for technology-intensive goods: market share, growth rate, and net shift. These indicators are explained in terms of their relevance to the study, and the formulas used to calculate these indicators are derived in the chapter. In addition, the limitations of the methodological approach and the source and limitations of the data are discussed in Chapter 8.

Chapter 9 is the first of two chapters that present the findings of the study of technology-intensive export trends. The chapter begins with a presentation of the changes that have occurred in the level of total technology-intensive exports by the five major trading nations, the United States, the United Kingdom, West Germany, Japan, and France. While the emphasis is upon exports of technology-intensive products, the study also analyzes exports of a selected group of manufactured goods that are not considered technology intensive. The inclusion of these nontechnology-intensive goods provides a type of control group against which the results for the technology-intensive exports can be compared. In addition, these analyses take place over two time periods, 1963 to 1974 and 1972 to 1974. The latter period is included to provide an indication of the effect of the realignment of currencies which occurred after 1971, while the former provides an indication of the longer term trends in technology-intensive exports of the major trading nations.

The remainder of Chapter 9 provides an in-depth analysis of the United States' position with regard to technology-intensive exports. The analysis of the U.S. position considers the technology-intensive exports of this country at decreasing levels of product data aggregation. First, technology-intensive exports are analyzed within broad industry groups, followed by an analysis of technology-intensive exports within 12 specific industries. At the highest level of disaggregation, U.S. exports of technology-intensive goods within specific product groups are analyzed. The findings presented in this chapter generally show that although U.S. losses of technology-intensive export markets are more concentrated in certain industries, selected products from all of the industries have been adversely affected. The analyses of the changes that have occurred in the U.S. technology-intensive export position are then followed by an analysis of the corresponding changes that have occurred in U.S. imports of the same products. When the export and import findings are compared, they suggest that perhaps the United States has not lost its comparative cost advantage in the production of many technology-intensive goods, but that other factors are involved in the United States' loss of export market share.

Chapter 10 focuses upon the changes which have occurred in the technology-intensive export positions of the United States' four major competitors in international trade—West Germany, Japan, the United Kingdom, and France. The discussion in the chapter is particularly concerned with the positions of West Germany and Japan, since the analyses indicate that these two nations are most responsible for the associated U.S. losses in market share. The findings presented in this chapter show that despite the currency revaluations undergone by West Germany and Japan since 1971, these two nations have continued to maintain or increase their export market shares in many cases. The chapter concludes with a presentation of the results of a correlation analysis run on the changes which have occurred in the United States, Japanese, and West German export market shares within the product categories employed in the study.

The last chapter of Part II, Chapter 11, assesses the implications of the previous findings for the competitive advantage of the United States. The chapter also presents an evaluation of the overall position of the United States in the technology-intensive export market. Since the findings strongly suggest that U. S. losses in the technology-intensive export market are not due to economic factors alone, Chapter 11 also presents some policy suggestions that are related to the improvement of the present situation.

Part III

The last chapter of the book provides an integration of the results from Parts I and II of the work. Since the study has included longitudinal analyses of the positions of the major trading nations both as markets for international goods and as suppliers of these goods, it is possible to present a reasonably comprehensive evaluation of the trends which are occurring in international trade. The discussion focuses upon the changing role of the United States within the international economic system relative to the other major trading nations. The chapter assesses the future prospects for the United States and presents policy alternatives that will probably be faced in the near future if the current trends continue.

PART I

THE HIERARCHY OF INTERNATIONAL TRADE

2

WORLD TRADE, HIERARCHIES, ECONOMIC DEPENDENCE, AND PATTERNS OF INTERNATIONAL INFLUENCE

The recognized importance of international trade has been reflected in the large body of existing literature on the subject. The literature in this area can conveniently be separated into a number of basic, although not entirely distinct, categories, some of which contributed to the theoretical framework for portions of the present analysis. This body of literature also provides the necessary background for the interpretation of the results of the present study. The most relevant works from these general categories will be discussed in this chapter.

The first group of works contains a relatively limited number of studies that analyzed overall trade patterns in the world. While not usually as comprehensive as the present study, they have contributed knowledge of basic trade patterns over time. A second group has dealt with trade relations between the "core" and "periphery" areas of the world. A third category, more voluminous than the first two, has been concerned with economic relations between large and small states. Prominent among these works are those that have formulated and tested various aspects of dependency theory. This multifaceted theory has provided an important perspective for analyzing trade relations between the large and small nations. Another, related portion of the literature in this area has explicitly attempted to link the existence of economic ties with the ability of large states to bring about or influence political actions of the smaller states.

The existing body of literature dealing with world trade has also provided support for two important methodological components of the present work. First, since hierarchies are a key portion of this part of the study, it is important to note the few studies that have either directly considered the idea of hierarchies existing in the international system or have attempted to derive such hierarchies. Secondly, the analysis of international trade flows as indicators of relationships between states has been undertaken by a number of scholars to achieve different goals.

STUDIES OF WORLD TRADE PATTERNS

Previous efforts have been made to analyze overall world trade patterns. Most of these works gave a central position to the United States in the world trade system, notwithstanding their different approaches to the topic. One of the early works, as well as one of the more ambitious in regards to time covered, was that of P. Lamartine Yates (1959), who used then existing data to describe world trade patterns and changes over time. He used longitudinal data, with the key years being 1913, 1937, and 1953. These particular years were chosen as being representative of different eras while not being directly affected by extraordinary events such as the Korean conflict or the onset of the Great Depression. Much of the description that he provided was based on large world areas rather than on individual countries. The United States, however, was usually dealt with as an individual nation due to its importance in the system.

Herbert B. Woolley (1966) and Richard S. Thoman and Edgar C. Conkling (1967) also dealt with international trade patterns. Woolley only used eight world areas in his analysis, ranging from single countries such as the United States and the United Kingdom to much larger areas such as Latin America. Clearly, his work was at a very aggregated level, although he also dealt with the United States separately. He noted that the importance of the largest trader in the international economic system had decreased in the last century. The United States, as the largest market in 1959, accounted for 18 percent of world imports, whereas in 1860 Great Britain accounted for 31 percent of all imports (pp. 1-2). The work by Thoman and Conkling was similar to those of Yates and Woolley in that large regions were used, although the number of individual countries included was larger. Thoman and Conkling were particularly interested in the geographic aspects of trade; therefore, their use of regions was generally appropriate to their purposes. Similarly, Rene Condoni et al. (1971), being interested in regional economic groupings, aggregated their data at a scale well beyond that of the individual country. The resulting comparisons in this work were generally interregional in scope.

Andreas Grotewold and Lois Grotewold (1957) analyzed world trade patterns for those territories for which statistics were available in the early 1950s. They noted that the larger traders were usually less dependent on a single commodity in terms of exports (pp. 259-60).

They also found that France, the United Kingdom, the United States, and the Soviet Union were the only countries that consistently accounted for a large proportion of the total exports of other territories (p. 263). Grotewold (1961) applied similar analyses to data for 1957-58. The analyses and results were basically similar, except that country links were not included in this later work. These two studies, while hampered by a lack of data for many areas of the world, did provide an overview of world trade patterns in these two time periods.

Two other works dealt with international trade in some detail. Simon Kuznets (1964) was interested in various interrelationships between the economic growth of nations and international transactions, particularly trade. His analyses included data for 104 countries or territories in 1958, but for the various analyses he divided the countries into groups based on size and GNP per capita. As a result, his findings were on the aggregate level. In addition, they were not directly based on trade relations between individual states. Another study is important for the present work since it emphasized the central role of the United States. Joseph D. Coppock (1962) undertook an analysis of the international economic system after World War II. He placed a major emphasis on the role of the United States as the most important trading entity in the system. He concentrated on export instability as a sign of weakness within the system and attempted to determine if instability in the system resulted from economic problems in the United States. He found that the impact of the United States on the international economic system was less than had been previously assumed. He concluded that one country, or even a few countries, were incapable of spreading instability throughout the system (pp. 89-90). Coppock's findings would seem to indicate that the American role in international economics may be overrated, although its importance still cannot be doubted. It is also possible that Coppock's findings were related to the fact that the role of the largest trading nations had declined relatively over time.

Others have concentrated on specific aspects of international trade rather than overall patterns. The increasing importance of trade between industrial countries as opposed to trade between the industrial countries and the developing nations has been noted (Maizels 1963, pp. 43-4; Kuznets 1964, p. 34). Others have noted general trends in the trade of the developing countries, such as an increased commodity concentration and a decreasing relative share of overall trade (Tinbergen 1962, p. 66; Maizels 1963, p. 46; Ingram 1966, pp. 79-81; Chou 1967, p. 281). While these studies considered overall patterns and noted some significant trends that had been occurring, they constituted only preliminary steps in terms of understanding relations between specific nations and changes in those relations over time.

One recent study did include a large number of individual nations in an analysis that included trade as a variable. Donald B. Freeman (1973) sought to identify linkages between different international economic flows, including trade, and commercial attributes of the various nations in the world. His study included 108 nations, but he was forced to exclude about thirty states, including the People's Republic of China and other communist states as well as many Third World countries, due to lack of data for some of his indicators (p. 84). In the latter part of his work, his country set was reduced to 74 nations due to additional data limitations, thus restricting the scope of his work even further in regards to the number of nations involved. Also, for purposes of analysis, he combined indicators through factor analysis.

These previous studies of international trade at the world level have provided the background for many of the more specific works dealing with some aspect of international trade. The general works have also identified particular patterns and problems. In the case of studies that also included longitudinal analyses, changes over time—or lack of change—in various world areas or types of change have been detailed. As a result, these studies, even when on a regional level, have provided basic inputs for further research into international trade.

In addition to the above works, there have been studies that have commented upon or speculated about world trade patterns, but their main emphasis was on other topics. Many of these works are discussed where relevant in later sections of this chapter. The observations in some of the works that will not be discussed, moreover, were either for aggregate areas, specific countries, or small groups of countries. On the whole, the previous work on world trade patterns has not provided analyses of specific country interactions for the whole world. Also, in many cases the longitudinal analysis has not been present.

CORES AND PERIPHERIES

One approach to studying international trade flows has been to distinguish between core areas and peripheries. The works cited in the previous section tended to implicitly follow this pattern in their aggregation of states into regions. A. Predohl (1949) in his study of the spatial organization of world trade was one of the first to use this twofold distinction. He observed that the international economy at one time could have been considered to be unicentric, with the United Kingdom (and later Western Europe as a whole) as the singular core with the rest of the world as the periphery. Over time, the core area evolved into a multicentric one. The majority of world trade occurred between core areas, while areas in the periphery traded with the cores as well, rather than interacting with other parts of the periphery. Thus, Predohl, in essence, suggested a two-tiered hierarchy of international trade, accompanied by periphery reliance on the core areas.

The core-periphery dichotomy developed by Predohl has become more widely used in recent times under either the same terms or in equivalent ones. Works associated with the International Peace Research Institute at Oslo that have dealt with international economic ties have tended to rely on a nominal distinction between center and periphery (Senghass 1975; Senghass-Knoblock 1975). Johan Galtung (1971), who is associated with the institute, also used this distinction in his efforts to define imperialism in structural terms, both at the center and in the periphery. He characterized the existing structural ties between the two areas as being part of a feudal relationship. Christopher Chase-Dunn (1975) also used the same dichotomy. He felt that this distinction required a reorientation of thinking about economic development from individual nations to an emphasis on the world system (p. 720). Lawrence R. Alschuler (1976) used similar terminology in his discussion of Latin American economies. He termed the industrialized countries as the center and interchangeably used satellite and periphery for the other countries in the world. He identified states in the center as those having the most exchange linkages with other countries. Nations on the periphery were those that had the fewest exchange linkages. In his view periphery nations interacted only with one center nation, thus becoming satellites. He also noted that in the typical pattern of center-periphery relationships there were more nations in the peripheral areas than in the center (p. 46).

Variations on the core-periphery dichotomy have been used by others. Osvaldo Sunkel (1973) as well as Anibal Pinto and Jan Knakel (1973) used the center and periphery terms in their discussions of the economic problems of the Third World nations. Pinto and Knakel made an important distinction in their study. They observed that center countries did not correspond with industrialized countries. While all center states were industrialized, not all industrialized states were part of the center (p. 36). They also noted that the United States was the major state in the center (p. 35). J. F. Rweyemamu (1969) also used the center-periphery terminology in his study of trade relationships, occasionally substituting metropole for center. Similarly, Giovanni Arrighi (1970) divided the world into developing and industrialized states and analyzed economic relations between the two areas.

The distinction between core (center, metropole, developed, industrialized) and periphery (satellite, developing, Third World) has been well established in the literature on international trade. This distinction has been important for the work of the dependency theorists, which will be discussed below. In fact, the literature on dependency to a large extent has its base in this distinction. Also, to the extent that other studies have concentrated on regions, there is an implicit use of this dichotomy in many respects. This distinction and the studies originally exploring the concept are thus central to much of the work done in international trade.

A basic, two-level hierarchical view, notwithstanding the lack of the use of the term "hierarchy," has obviously been prevalent in much of the literature dealing with international trade. Studies using such a dichotomy contain a basic weakness for understanding the structure of hierarchies in international trade, in that the twofold division assumes the relative equality of the nations in each class. As some of the studies on hierarchy included below have noted, however, hierarchies can exist within both the core and periphery areas. The identification of such hierarchies can thus provide an enhanced understanding of the international trade system and the role of the United States in that system. It should be possible for a particular hierarchy to include states from both classes of nations or only one.

LARGE STATES AND SMALL STATES

Another dichotomy that has often been used in considering international relations and international trade has been the distinction between large and small states. Large and small usually has not referred to population size or area, but rather has been referenced in terms of total Gross National Product (GNP), military power, or level of industrialization. It has been stated that if all other things are equal, "the bigger the state, the greater its influence capability" (McGowan and Gottwald 1975, p. 476). This statement has been the essence of the dichotomy, and since the United States, by whatever criterion, is a large state, it is relevant to the background for the present study. This large state-small state distinction is related to that of core and periphery, since the majority of the small states are Third World countries that are normally considered part of the periphery. The large states may be equivalent to center states, particularly if Pinto and Knakel's caution against including all industrialized countries in the center category is remembered. While states such as India or the Peoples' Republic of China may not fit in the small category for most definitions, most other peripheral countries cannot be considered large in comparison with the United States, West Germany, or France in terms of GNP or industrial output.

This section will briefly consider general studies of small and large state relations, but the majority of such studies in the area will be discussed under two subfields. First, various aspects of dependency theory that have been developed in regard to economic ties between large states (core states) and small states (peripheral states) will be considered. This theory as propounded by various advocates has usually assigned a central role to international trade. The second aspect of the large state-small state distinction has been covered in studies that attempted to link political behavior to economic relationships.

There are a few studies that primarily dealt with the relations among small and large states and also discussed economic relations. Peter J. Lloyd (1968) was specifically interested in the trade problems of small nations. His study included sixty non-communist nations, including the smaller European states and some of the Third World countries. Due to lack of data availability, many developing countries were not included. One of his conclusions was that small states cannot be considered as a homogeneous group. They lack uniform trade characteristics, and thus they could not be expected to exhibit similar behavior under similar circumstances (p. 127). Marshall R. Singer (1972) was also interested in the role of small states in the international system. He considered both economic and political ties in an effort to describe and understand the position of weakness in which many states found themselves. David Vital's (1967; 1971) works are typical of those that were principally concerned with the political aspects of relations between large and small states in the international system although he did discuss the implications of economic relations, which he considered to be important. The international politics literature on the role of the small state is quite extensive, but since they emphasize political factors, these studies will be mentioned only to the extent that they deal with either dependency or economic pressure brought to bear to gain political ends.

Dependency Theory

Lloyd (1968, p. 36) observed that small states were quite often "dependent" on international trade. Similarly, Coppock's tests as to the importance of the United States in the international economic system were related to ideas put forward suggesting that the system and many states in it were dependent on the health of the American economy. These general ideas of dependency have been refined and formalized as a theory to explain much of the present circumstances of international economics, particularly in regard to links between large, developed states and small, developing ones. Actually, dependency theory consists of a number of overlapping tenets and concepts, but since they all specify the weakness of the small or Third World states compared to the large, industrialized ones, the singular will be used in discussing the various ideas put forward under this general theoretical perspective.

A relevant starting point for a discussion of dependency is to distinguish it from interdependency. Every nation in an increasingly integrated world is forced to rely on other states in some way. In the economic realm, the existence of international trade indicates the presence of needs that can be filled by activities in other states. In some cases, at least in the short term, these needs can only be met by activities in other states. A total breakdown of international trade would create problems for all the states in the system, from the largest to the smallest and from the richest to the poorest. Interdependence, however, refers to a situation of near equality, while dependency reflects an unequal relationship. When states are approximately equally dependent on each other, in terms proportional to their size, interdependence exists. When one of the states is more reliant, dependency results (Singer 1972, p. 223; Hveem 1973, p. 321). It has been claimed, moreover, that the interdependent status is characteristic only of links between the developed countries (Stallings 1972, p. 6). Thus, dependency theory has not usually been totally critical of international economic connections, only those that are considered to be unequal.

The idea that the smaller states in the Third World might be suffering from international trade inequalities is a relatively recent concept. Raul Prebisch (1959), in considering the development problems of Latin America, proposed the idea that the present system of international trade had created many difficulties in individual states. He was principally concerned with deteriorating terms of trade, as well as the fact that the Latin American countries were generally in a dependent economic position in the world, particularly in relation to the United States. Other social scientists in the Third World, as well as some in the industrial countries, have supported this theme and refined it.

There are a number of basic propositions that have been put forward by most of the proponents of dependency theory. One of the most basic tenets, which includes aspects of international trade, is the denial of the traditional doctrine of comparative advantage. In essence, dependency theorists have claimed that comparative advantage hurts the weaker states that are in a dependent position. The advantages gained are not reciprocal, but rather the industrialized countries derive the major benefit (Senghass 1975, p. 257). Arghiri Emmanuel (1969) considered trade to be primarily a means whereby workers in the industrialized countries were pacified by the high incomes resulting from trade exploitation of the Third World. Theotonio Dos Santos (1971, p. 225), one of the leading Latin American dependency theorists, felt that trading relations in a dependent situation were designed to drain surpluses from the dependent countries for the benefit of the dominant states. Other theorists have noted that international trade contributes to an unequal international division of labor where the developing countries in essence perform the low-paid "menial" tasks, with the benefits accruing to the industrialized nations (Gantzel 1973, p. 209; Rweyemamu 1969, p. 205). The advantages gained from this unequal exchange go primarily to the developed states, making comparative advantage more advantageous for these nations. David P. Rapkin (1976, p. 3) has summarized the suspected problems with the comparative advantage theory well.

> The comparative advantage doctrine, however, purports only that trade augments total output; it does not address the question of how the gains from trade are distributed among trading countries. Hence, the universality of the benefits derived from specialization for trade cannot be taken as axiomatic.

T. Baumgartner and T. R. Burns (1975) also denied the claimed benefits of comparative advantage. They used the classic textbook example of comparative advantage—British textiles for Portuguese wine—to demonstrate in some detail how dependency can develop and how it can be maintained at the expense of the weaker state. They presented an historical evaluation of this trade, demonstrating how British interests and the British government manipulated the situation to help the British economy and keep the Portuguese economy in a subordinate underdeveloped position.

Another recurring tenet of the theory is related to an idea that Baumgartner and Burns referred to, namely, that development is hindered by a situation of dependency. The failure of Latin American and African nations to develop fully has been blamed on their integration into the world market system in a dependent position (Bodenheimer 1971, p. 158; Girvan 1973, p. 23; Amin 1973, p. 179). Dependent relations have also been cited as a factor that "deepens and aggravates" the basic problems of Third World peoples (Dos Santos 1971, p. 225). Others have felt that underdevelopment could not be properly understood simply by looking at individual national economies. Rather, it was the dependent status of the peripheral states in the international system that generated many of the problems of underdevelopment (Furtado 1973, p. 122; Alschuler 1976, p. 77). Barbara Stallings (1972, p. 5) felt that dependency was "an explanation of the <u>failure</u> of Third World countries to develop."

Other studies have also contained the argument that a dependent status has hindered development in the Third World (Senghass 1975,

p. 267; Sunkel 1969, p. 25; Bechin 1963, p. 231). This aspect of dependency theory has been tested empirically in a number of studies. Of interest to the present work is the fact that all the empirical studies used trade ties as at least one indication of the level of dependency. These empirical tests have had mixed results. Robert R. Kaufman and his associates (1975) had indeterminate findings in their analysis of Latin America. They concluded, however, that enough results were supportive of the dependency theory to prevent the rejection of the presumption that dependence hindered development (p. 321). Alschuler (1976, p. 77-8) in his study of Latin America found that the more dependent a state was, the lower had been its rate of development. The findings of the work by Chase-Dunn (1975) on many developing countries also cannot be considered definitive. He found some indications that dependence slowed growth, but in others the opposite effect seemed present (pp. 733-5). David P. Rapkin (1976, p. 5) found support for the tenet that "trade dependency retards development." James Lee Ray and Thomas Webster (1977, p. 16), on the other hand, found that dependency levels did not have much relation to levels of development, although they did caution against a premature rejection of this basic proposition of the dependency theory, given the crudeness and incompleteness of their variables. It is obvious from the differing empirical results that recent work has failed to resolve the issue of the link between dependency and development. The varying results could be ascribed to different measures of dependence and development, different study areas, and different time periods. The resolution of the controversy is an important issue that remains in dependency theory. Subsidiary questions that also remain are related to determining the appropriate measures of a dependent relationship as well as appropriate measures of development, questions that are not important or unique only to the dependency theorists. Sufficient disagreement exists at present to permit advocates and opponents of the dependency-underdevelopment thesis to cite support for their own views and to ignore conflicting evidence.

In most areas of the world the present dependency relationship has been ascribed at least in part to the previous existence of colonial empires, including those of Spain and Portugal in the Western Hemisphere. It has also been noted that the occupation of Africa by the European powers led to grave distortions of the local economies under the colonial administrations. These distortions of the local economies have persisted to the present time, even though the colonial empires have disappeared (Dos Santos 1971; Amin 1972; Senghass 1975, p. 258; Senghass-Knoblock 1975, p. 276). Rweyemamu (1969) noted in a similar vein that the problems of the developing countries resulted from their original integration into the world system as satellites of existing powers. This position has continued after independence, and he noted that international trade was one of the key factors in its persistence (p. 212). Thomas Birnberg and Stephen Resnick (1973) sought to identify forces active in the period from 1900 to 1939 that eventually led many Third World countries to become dependent on international trade. They determined that the decisions and activities of colonial administrations had been critical. Colonial expenditures were designed to develop export industries at the expense of indigeneous manufacturing in order to provide the quickest returns for the investments and the overhead costs of the administrations (p. 576). Sidney Dell (1970, p. 348) and Frederick Arkhurst (1970, p. 372) also commented upon the distorting effects of the decisions made during the colonial era. The end result of these practices was the shaping of the economies in these areas to respond to outside economic demands, usually in the industrialized countries, and primarily in the metropole. Birnberg and Resnick included not only directly controlled colonies in their analysis but also states such as Chile, Egypt, and Thailand "where foreign influence and control were perhaps more subtle but no less important in determining economic activity" (p. 572). Even the governments of independent states faced the problems of financing administrative functions and gaining quick tax returns on investments.

While the activities of colonial and national administrations seeking to generate revenues for government services may have inadvertently created situations leading to dependency, arguments have been raised in the dependency literature that claim continued dependence has been actively sought. It has been argued that indirect control through dependency relations is cheaper than imperial control of the periphery directly (O'Conner 1970, p. 116; Hveem 1973, p. 325). Some theorists have also noted that investment policies from the industrialized countries have been designed to reinforce the export sectors serving foreign markets, and, thus, the perpetuation of dependency is being encouraged (Rweyemamu 1969, p. 213; Senghass-Knoblock 1975, p. 282). Leland L. Johnson (1965, pp. 440-1) also noted that foreign investment policies _might_ lead to increasing dependence.

Dependency theorists have often incorporated the role of the multinational corporation into the pattern of overall dominance of the Third World by the industrialized countries. The multinationals are seen as agents of economic imperialism or neo-colonialism. For example, it has been stated that the elites of the new African states are too weak to be able to control the foreign firms that dominate their economies (Okumu 1971, p. 149). Dieter Senghass (1975, p. 268) and Alschuler (1976, pp. 51-5) have also emphasized the negative impacts of the operations of the multinationals in the Third World. While John D. Esseks (1971, p. 1056) noted that the activities of foreign entrepreneurs could bring about modernization, he felt that the economies so influenced were excessively dependent on trade. Robert E. Smith

(1974) also considered the role of multinationals in the international economic system, noting the difficulties facing any nation in dealing with these entities. While small Third World states may have more difficulties with multinationals, he did not view them as a problem for only small or developing nations.

There are a number of additional tenets in the dependency theory that are often put forward and should be briefly mentioned. They will not be considered in any detail since their relationship to trade is indirect. Foreign investment, both public and private, has often been seen as furthering dependence, regardless of whether or not that is the intent (Gantzel 1973, p. 207; Sunkel 1973, p. 161). This view has not been accepted by all theorists in the area. Some writers have acknowledged the possibility of positive effects arising from such investment (Ray 1973, p. 11; Pinto and Knakel 1973, p. 64; Blake and Walters 1976, p. 170). It has been postulated that quite often a client class in the state of the periphery is part of the dependency relationship and necessary for the exploitation of the weaker countries (Arrighi 1970, p. 222-3; Galtung 1971; Hveem 1973, p. 322; Ray 1973, p. 9; Sunkel 1973, p. 146). The association of internal dysfunctions and societal problems within the dependent countries has also been noted (Furtado 1973, p. 122; Senghass 1975, p. 267; Alschuler 1976, p. 42). Another facet of the theory is that industrialization may not break dependency since the new industries are channeled to products that require foreign machinery, parts, and raw materials (Frank 1970; Sunkel 1969, pp. 29, 37; Berg 1971, p. 222; Stallings 1972, p. 38; Girvan 1973, p. 22). These themes, as well as the others already discussed, form the core of the various portions of dependency theory as put forth by a number of writers.

While the various aspects of dependency theory have been well expounded, in many cases these ideas have not been uncritically received. Some studies with non supportive results were cited above. Some more basic theoretical fallacies were pointed out by David Ray (1973), although he did not seek to attack the basis of the dependency theme as such. First, he was one of those who disagreed with the assumption that foreign investment was always negative. Second, he pointed out that dependency theory was too often tied to capitalism (p. 15). Reginald H. Green and K. G. V. Krishna (1967, p. 14) also noted that the more ideological definitions of dependence excluded the Soviet Union. For example, Klaus J. Gantzel (1973, pp. 203, 208-9) and Bodenheimer (1971, p. 164) explicitly called for the establishment of socialism (Marxism) in the Third World as a means of ending dependency. Susanne Girvan (1973, p. 23) identified dependency as resulting from "integration into a system of global capitalism" (emphasis added), as did Samir Amin (1972, p. 179). Gantzel (p. 210) actually did consider the possibility that the Soviet Union might be in a position to benefit from dependency relationships, but he discounted it. Uwe Stehr (1977) also considered the possibility of unequal exchange between the USSR and Eastern Europe, but he concluded that dependency was not present. Galtung (1971, p. 113n) was more ambivalent about the possibility, but he did emphasize capitalist impacts. Most of the other dependency theorists concentrated on the western nations or on the United States. Ray, on the other hand, felt that powerful nations have always imposed economic dependence on weaker states (p. 7), and he also thought that Soviet economic imperialism has been no less a reality than the capitalist variety (p. 8). Brzezinski (1967, pp. 287-8) also felt that the USSR sought to place the Eastern European states in a dependent position. Finally, Ray pointed out another problem—the expression of dependency as a dichotomous variable rather than a continuous one (p. 7). Ray argued that total nondependence could not be achieved. Kaufman et al. (1975, p. 315) also noted that dependency was an ideal type and that varying levels of dependence could be present. While these three criticisms seem to be warranted, they do not destroy the main premises of dependency theory.

One other aspect of dependency should be noted. While many writers and Third World leaders do not doubt the existence of dependency, they are not all totally opposed to it. A. K. Cairncross (1966, p. 423) felt, contrary to dependency theorists, that foreign trade was necessary for economic development and that economic dependence was the price. Vital (1967, p. 39) thought that trade was necessary for progress and would ultimately lead to both economic and political independence. Esseks (1971, p. 1064) noted that most African countries had "realized a surplus of benefits over costs" by remaining in an essentially dependent position in the early years of independence. Gottfried Haberler (1968, p. 92) and Carol Ann Cosgrove (1972, p. 150) were in agreement. Others have noted that many leaders of developing countries apparently subscribe to this view since they have maintained what may be termed dependent ties (Weinstein 1967; Johnson 1967, pp. 165-6; Cosgrove 1972, p. 151). It should be noted, however, that these leaders could well be considered the clientele classes mentioned in dependency theory.

Notwithstanding the problems that Ray mentioned in regard to dependency theory, he still considered the concept to be "important and useful" and that it "contains a large element of truth" (p. 6). Even if the theory were discovered to have basic flaws, it would still be important since many political leaders believe it to be true (Uri 1976, p. 8). Since trade is often considered an important aspect of dependency, the theory is important to the present work. In keeping with one of Ray's criticisms, the analysis in this study will not be restricted to capitalist states. Since the present study will identify key trading relationships over time, the hierarchies derived may also provide some basic input for later testing of various aspects of dependency theory.

Political Compliance of Small States

"[I]nternational economic relations among private and public actors necessitate profound alterations in contemporary American foreign policy and in political relations among states everywhere" (Blake and Walters 1976, p. 3). This relationship of economic and political activities has been one aspect of relations between large and small states that has often been considered in the literature. It has been hypothesized that small states can be forced or persuaded to be politically compliant to the desires of the large states through economic pressure. Economic ties, including trade, are often seen as one form of pressure. Belief in this possibility has been widespread in much of the work dealing with international relations and international economics.

Political compliance has often been considered to be one outcome of a dependency situation. Galtung (1971, p. 90) observed that the most important facet of dependent structures was political in that the center was protected from the periphery. James O'Conner (1970, pp. 117-8) noted that economic dependence was designed to keep independent states from consolidating their political independence. The possibility of political dependence as a general or theoretical phenomenon associated with economic dependence has been noted by other dependency theorists (Hveem 1973, pp. 320, 328; Gantzel 1973, p. 205), particularly in the specific context of different Third World regions such as Africa (Rweyemamu 1969, p. 215; McGowan and Gottwald 1975, pp. 471-2) and Latin America (Alschuler, 1976, p. 60). John J. Okumu (1971, p. 151) noted that African states maintained close ties with their former metropoles because they were forced to rely on them for economic security. In the case of Latin America, Annette B. Fox (1971, p. 163) observed that the United States was so economically dominant that it could use very subtle techniques to bring about compliance. Esseks (1971, p. 1067) felt that dominant partners in an economic relationship could seek the compliance of a weaker state by threatening or practicing economic sabotage.

Two recent efforts to test the effects of economic dependency on political behavior were made by Neil R. Richardson (1976) and Richardson and Charles W. Kegley, Jr. (1977). Richardson felt that smaller nations that were dominated economically by a larger state would exhibit cooperative political behavior (p. 1099). Operationally, he considered those countries that had more than a specified minimum level of their GNP accounted for by exports to the United States to be economically dependent. He then compared their voting behavior on General Assembly roll call votes dealing with Cold War issues (that is, votes on which the United States and the Soviet Union opposed each other) with the voting patterns of non dependent states. He discovered that the dependencies were, in fact, more likely to vote with the United States on Cold War issues than were the other countries (p. 1106). In the Richardson and Kegley study this approach was continued, encompassing a longer time span and using 4.6 percent of GNP as the minimum figure. The results of Cold War votes were similar to the first study (p. 48). Perhaps more important, they also found that compliance did not vary directly with the level of dependence (pp. 48-9). Thus, trade ties may be important regardless of their level, or there may be some threshhold level at which trade ties become important. While the results of these two studies are supportive of political compliance ideas and dependency theory, they have to be viewed with some caution. First, included among American dependencies were states that had stronger trading ties with other nations. In a hierarchical system these states would be cross-pressured to take cues from the most dominant state rather than from the United States. Secondly, if the original premise of voting compliance being forced by economic dependency was correct, these studies need to take into account and control for other dependent relationships (such as countries consistently voting with the Soviet Union that had strong trade ties with that state).

Others have analyzed the impact of foreign ties on political activity. Albert O. Hirschman (1969), in a book originally published at the end of World War II, was one of the first. In his study of German trade patterns in the 1930s, he noted that trade could be a source of power (p. 15). He felt that for a large state it would be "an elementary principle of the power policy to <u>direct its trade away from the large to the smaller trading states</u>" (p. 31, author's emphasis). Thoman and Conkling (1967, p. 137) made a similar point in their study. In comparing Germany to the other major powers, Hirschman found a greater preference on the part of Germany for smaller and weaker trading partners. This preference, already present under the Weimar Republic, was increased after the National Socialists came to power (pp. 92-5). This early work concerned with trade and politics constituded an important and clear historical case study that demonstrated the connections between international economics and politics. In keeping with later dependency theory, Hirschman also noted that Germany used its trading power to inhibit industrialization among the Danubian countries, thus maintaining Germany's initial advantageous position in trade (p. 36).

Later researchers other than dependency theorists have supported Hirschman's ideas. Lloyd (1968, p. 18) noted that there were political and economic risks involved in producing for a foreign market. Richard N. Cooper (1972-73) observed that trade policy was part of foreign policy. Blake and Walters (1976, pp. 197-8), Thoman and Conkling (1967, p. 6), and Joseph Nye, Jr. and Robert Keohane (1967, p. 379) presented similar views. Hugh Corbet (1971, p. 79) felt that American trade policy was primarily directed to political goals rather than to economic goals. Richard Rosecrance and Arthur Stein (1973, p. 12) observed that it was impossible for political leaders to ignore the impact of outside economic forces. In regard to Third World states, one writer felt that the former colonial powers "in their structuring of the external economic ties of the colonies taught the successor states a lesson they are unlikely to forget—that external economic ties must reflect, indeed be part of, the state's total foreign policy" (Ojedokum 1972, p. 536). Analysts concerned with the situation of small states in the international system have also noted the importance of trade. Vital (1967, p. 55) found that trade could be an effective weapon for large states since "the weakest spot in a nation's armor is the economic one." It should be noted that, notwithstanding the potential power of economic pressure, political compliance does not always result. Despite heavy economic pressure by both the United States and the United Kingdom in World War II, the Irish government consistently refused to accede to political requests for rights to bases in the Republic, even though Ireland was heavily dependent on trade with these two countries (Vital 1971, p. 103).

Discussions of political effects resulting from economic ties have been present in works dealing with the Soviet Union. Soviet willingness in the past to use Finnish reliance on Soviet markets to influence actions of that state's government has been noted (Vital 1971, pp. 110-1). Similar activities occurred in the case of Poland after World War II (Brzezinski 1967, p. 288). The long-standing Soviet goal of autarchy, only recently modified, was originally designed to avoid dependence on the capitalist states for critical goods (Smith 1973, p. 26; Brzenk 1964, p. 27). Michael Hudson (1972, p. 83) noted that the Soviet leaders after World War II feared integration into the international economy dominated by the United States because such a situation "might threaten Russian security itself." On the other hand, he noted that the United States feared the entrance into the international economy of a potential rival that "would seek to capture selected U. S. satellites by dominating their foreign trade" (p. 89). Trade between Eastern and Western Europe after the war was limited for a number of years for much the same reasons, since leaders on both sides feared becoming vulnerable to its sudden stop (Dell 1963, p. 325). This fear has persisted as is evidenced by a suggestion that the recent increases of this trade have been assymetrical, with Eastern Europe becoming dependent on the West (Gantzel 1973, p. 209).

These works on various aspects of the economic and political ties all point to the importance of trade and the possibility of political compliance resulting from economic ties. While many different theoretical perspectives were present in these works, the conclusions were remarkably similar. As a result, for yet an additional reason, the specification of these economic linkages in the present study becomes important.

HIERARCHICAL STUDIES

Although the previous works that have emphasized relationships between the core and periphery nations or the existence of political and economic dependency have implicitly recognized the inherent hierarchical nature of the international trade system, there have been only a few studies that have directly dealt with or analyzed the concept, and some of these studies have not included international trade as a variable. Richardson (1976, p. 1098) in his study of political compliance assumed that a hierarchy did in fact exist. He concluded from his study that a continuing focus on hierarchies in the international system was necessary. Since hierarchies in the international system are an essential portion of the present study, the previous work that either derived hierarchies or discussed them in a more theoretical context are worth noting.

Stephen J. Brams (1966) used international trade flows as one of three critical inputs in his study of ties between states. He employed a model of international transaction flows based upon an earlier work of I. Richard Savage and Karl W. Deutsch (1960), constructing the hierarchy based on data for trade, diplomatic relations, and shared memberships in intergovernmental organizations. The Deutsch and Savage model relied on a relative acceptance index that was based on the expected level of interactions based on total flows sent by each state and total flows received. The model identified those flows that were larger than expected. For Brams these larger than expected ties were deemed to be the most salient ones (p. 884). These salient links were then the basis for the hierarchy that he derived. This hierarchy, however, was not of the same type as the ones that will be derived in the present study. His was, in effect, a clustering of nations into increasingly smaller subgroups according to the level of salient ties between them. The resulting hierarchies (as Brams used the term) actually represented the level of interaction between the 119 nations in his analysis rather than relative positions in the international system or identification of dominance patterns. Some of the states in the study group, moreover, were not included in various hierarchies at any group level since they lacked salient links. Notwithstanding the differences in approach, Brams did reach one relevant conclusion for the present study. He observed that trade relations between states were more erratic than the other two forms of international transactions. He felt that this erratic pattern suggested that trade relations were "probably [more] reflective of changes or disturbances in the international system [than] diplomatic or organizational relations between nations" (p. 898). He thought changes in trade relationships were more likely to reflect changes in political relationships between countries than his other two measures (p. 887). As a result, any changes that are found in the trade hierarchies which will be derived may indicate changing political patterns as well as economic ones.

Brams (1969) later utilized another technique for deriving an international hierarchy. This hierarchy was based on using directed graphs to determine important linkages between countries. Kegley and Eugene R. Wittkopf (1976) used the same method in a later effort to both replicate and expand Bram's original study. Both of these studies noted the presence of an international hierarchy, and they assumed that a state's actions would be affected by its position in this hierarchy. The basis of determining the influence hierarchies were visits by key members of governments. The state being visited was assumed to be exerting influence. If more than a miminal assymetry (more than a difference of one between visitors sent to another state and visitors received from that state) was involved, the visited state was assumed to be exerting influence. If the number of visits were not assymetrical, then both states exerted equal influence on each other. The digraph method joins together states on the basis of shared links (visits), but it does so without regard to the total number of visits that an individual state receives from all foreign dignitaries. Thus, in all the years under consideration there were various small countries that had dominant positions of influence vis-a-vis the United States, for example, while the United States was at an equal level with a large number of states. Kegley and Wittkopf did analyze the relative position of the United States and the Soviet Union in this influence hierarchy, but this was on an ad hoc basis. The resulting hierarchies did not clearly identify these two states as relevant for detailed treatment. The methodology used in the present study might have been more appropriate for determining these types of influence hierarchies.

Steven L. Spiegel (1972) attempted to develop a tiered hierarchy of the international system. He assigned nations' rankings in the international order. The inputs for the assigning process did not include international trade. Indicators of resource availability, levels of economic and human development, military strength, size, and motivational attitudes were used to create a seven-tiered hierarchy based on the "power" of individual states. Spiegel's hierarchy will not be directly comparable to the ones derived in this work for a number of reasons. First, the inputs do not overlap. Second, the methodology used by Spiegel involved both empirical and subjective approaches. Third, there are no relationships specified between the state in different levels of the hierarchy. Spiegel did make some relevant observations in his analysis. He noted that when there are only a few powerful states, they have almost complete control over the weaker countries in the system (p. 117). He also noted that the more important states in a given area could be influential locally (pp. 97, 102-3).

Helge Hveem (1973) and Gantzel (1973) considered the international system to be hierarchically structured, and they both linked the existence of this hierarchy to the existence of dependency relationships. Hveem theorized three components to the hierarchy—actors, agents, and objects (p. 321). This hierarchy was particularly important in the economic realm with the greatest advantages accruing to the actor nations. The nations on the periphery of the international economic system corresponded to the object class, while some of the larger regional states could fulfill the agent function, thereby gaining some of the rewards (p. 322). Fox (1970, p. 157), Sunkel (1973, pp. 146-7), and Galtung (1971, pp. 104-5) all commented on the possibility of regional actors being influential, although their respective terminologies were not the same as Hveem's. Gantzel had a somewhat different view of the hierarchy. His division was in part based on a separation of the world into socialist and capitalist systems. The United States was dominant overall, even having limited dominance over the socialist states through Western Europe. Other states were similarly dependent upon the United States, either directly or through other states (pp. 204-5). He emphasized the need to consider indirect links as well as direct ones, since the United States dominated parts of the Third World only through other nations (p. 207). He also observed that time was an important component of these relations and that by observing temporal trends it would be possible to understand changes in the positions and structures of the system as a whole (p. 205).

Both Hveem (pp. 326, 331-3) and Gantzel (pp. 206-8) provided some examples of where states were placed in the international hierarchy. As a result, their ideas can be compared with the trade hierarchies that will be derived in this study. The derived hierarchies, however, will not include a priori assumptions that some states are not dominating ones in the economic sphere. That determination will be made empirically. Thus, both capitalist and socialist states can occupy any positions in the trade hierarchies. Some Third World or periphery states could also prove to be in dominant positions.

FLOW ANALYSIS

The literature on international trade has also included a group of studies that concentrated on trade flows. These flows are essential to the present study, and, moreover, they have been important in other areas discussed above. For example, the emphasis in the dependency writings on flows between centers and between a periphery and only one center was mentioned. Also, as was mentioned, Alschuler explicitly defined a center nation as one that had a large number of links with other states in the international economic system. The previous studies of flows have sought to determine various aspects of international economic and political relations. Thus, the utilization of trade flows in the present work will build upon the previous literature, although it will be carried further in that the flows that are identified will be used to structure trade hierarchies.

The Deutsch and Savage study mentioned earlier attempted to determine which countries were trading with each other in a preferential fashion. The study set consisted of fifteen nations in Western Europe and North America. Expected trade flows between each set of states was generated for 1928 on the basis of the relative acceptance index and geographic proximity. The use of geographic proximity has often been considered relevant to this type of analysis, although its exact importance is a matter of some debate (Beckerman 1956; Kuznets 1964, pp. 31-4; Pen 1967, p. 77; Wolf and Wernschrott 1973, p. 23; Freeman, 1973, p. 182). The actual flows in the Deutsch and Savage study that were larger than expected were assumed to indicate the most salient links in the system for the countries involved. The results of their analysis were difficult to interpret at the individual country level. There was no detectable pattern and no apparent explanation for some of the larger than expected trade flows. On a regional level (such as Scandinavia or Anglo-America) results were more readily interpretable. Possible difficulties in the results may have had a number of sources. If other countries and their trade flows had been included, as well as their respective distances, the predicted levels of trade would have been different. For example, the inclusion of the Soviet Union in the study might have changed the results. Also, the fifteen nations did not include the nations of Southeastern Europe, exactly those smaller states Hirschman found to be the preferred trading partners for Weimar Germany. Also, the analysis could not take into account the possibility that states close to each other might have competing economies rather than complementary ones (although the regional comparisons were partially a response to this problem).

Various efforts have added to the Deutsch and Savage effort. Jan Tinbergen (1962) and Hans Linneman (1966), building upon Tinbergern, applied econometric analyses to flows. While both studies

PATTERNS OF INTERNATIONAL INFLUENCE / 31

analyzed flows in some depth and looked at the spatial structure of international trade, they made no effort to analyze the overall structure of trade in hierarchical terms. F. P. Jansen and L. H. Janssen (1969) used similar methods to study the United States, the EEC, and the European Free Trade Association (EFTA) as the major markets in the world trade system, particularly in regard to the developing nations. In essence, they were using a core-periphery dichotomy as the basis of their study. Norman D. Aitken (1973) used the Linneman techniques to determine the trade creation and trade diversion effects of the EEC and EFTA. He found that trade was created in the sense that levels between states in each group increased. This increase, however, tended to be at the expense of trade between states in the two groups.

Maurice H. Yeates (1969) utilized a similar approach to the study of international trade. He analyzed trade flows on the basis of a gravity model. The key variables input into the model were national income and the distance between the countries in the trading system. In addition, a variable was included to represent preferential trading groups such as the EEC and EFTA. The results of his work explained individual flows between countries fairly reliably. He did not, however, attempt a hierarchical arrangement of the trading pairs. Also, he did not attempt to explain what effects might have resulted from the flows and inequalities in the relationships between trading partners.

The first part of the present work will use trade flows in a somewhat different manner than the above studies since it will not attempt to generate expected flows to compare to the actual patterns. These flow studies remain important in the context of the other portions of the literature discussed in this chapter. Dependency theorists could derive conclusions from trade patterns that deviated from the expected, as could those interested in the political implications of economic links (or the economic implications of political relations). The present study will integrate many of these concepts and could provide a base for further works.

SUMMARY

The background for various portions of the first part of this study has been well established in many ways by existing literature on international trade. As the above discussions have indicated, the different categories are interrelated with specific works and often contain comments germane to more than one area. Most of the overall analyses of world trade that have been undertaken gave the United States a key position in the structure of world trade. While not as comprehensive in terms of areas covered at a detailed level or overall comprehensiveness in comparison over time, they do form a solid base for the present work. The core-periphery studies implied a hierarchy in world trade, as has much of the work of dependency theorists. The dependency theorists also have emphasized trade as one of the important indicators of a dependent relationship. The United States has also often been a center of the attention of dependency theorists, particularly those interested specifically in Latin America. The works dealing with hierarchies, while limited in number, have indicated the importance of this facet of the present study. In the few cases in which hierarchies were derived, trade flows were not used. The work on trade flows themselves has become highly sophisticated, but this area of study has moved in a somewhat different direction than the present work. As a consequence, the present analysis of trade hierarchies provides an integrating focus for much of this previous work. In that sense, it can have positive feedback in the future for research in all the above areas.

3

THE DEVELOPMENT OF TRADE HIERARCHIES

The notion of a hierarchy is well established in the literature of international trade and international politics, as discussed in the preceding chapter. This chapter will provide a discussion of the hierarchical analysis employed in the present research and an overview of the hierarchies that have been derived from four representative years of world trade data. The chapter will begin with a presentation of the operational definition of a trade hierarchy used in the study, and of the specific methodology used to structure the hierarchies. The methodological discussion will be followed by a presentation of the hierarchies of world trade identified in each of the years of the study, including analyses of the changing composition of the hierarchies with particular attention paid to the United States.

THE HIERARCHY OF WORLD TRADE

The notion of a hierarchy of trade existing among the nations of the world is based on the fact that nations are not equal in their trading relationships. Variations in absolute size, the availability of resources, and several other factors combine to create basic inequalities in the trading relationships that exist among nations. In fact, most of the nations of the world have their closest economic ties with nations that are economically more powerful than themselves. In addition, the strength of the economic ties that exist between nations is often not reciprocal. In terms of their international trade, larger nations are typically not tied as closely to the smaller nations whose trade they support. An extreme example of such an inequality would be the case of Niger and that nation's largest trading partner, France.

In 1976 Niger's exports to France accounted for 82.6 percent of its total exports, while France's exports to Niger accounted for only .1 percent of France's total exports. In this case Niger is clearly more dependent on the French market than vice versa. A less extreme case may be that of the United States and the United Kingdom. Here the United States accounts for approximately 10 percent of the United Kingdom's exports (1976), although the United Kingdom receives only 4 percent of the United States' exports. Both of these cases illustrate the inequalities that exist between nations in their international trade relationships. France would be considered "above" Niger in an international trade hierarchy, and the United States would be considered "above" the United Kingdom, since France and the United States quantitatively dominate the trading relationship in their respective cases.

The preceding cases of France and Niger and of the United States and the United Kingdom illustrate the direct ties that exist among trading nations, and the manner in which hierarchies can be constructed based upon these direct ties. As some theorists, such as Hveem (1973) noted, however, dominant-subordinant trading relationships need not always be direct. It is possible that these relationships can exist through third nations. As a hypothetical example, the United Kingdom may receive 17 percent of Denmark's exports while the United States receives 10 percent of the United Kingdom's exports. Under these conditions Denmark may be indirectly tied more closely with the United States than it is with the United Kingdom, even though Denmark's direct exports to the United States are less than those to the United Kingdom. A decrease in the demand for British goods in the United States could precipitate a drop in the United Kingdom's demand for Danish goods due either to the diminished national income in the United Kingdom or to the possibility that Danish exports provide inputs into the United Kingdom's subsequent exports to the United States. In this case, therefore, Denmark's trade may be more closely tied to the United States than to the United Kingdom, albeit indirectly.

The hierarchies of international trade that are developed in the present study are conceptually based on the inequalities that exist between nations in their trading relationships. The hierarchies also take into account the possibility of strong indirect trading ties that can exist between trading nations, as discussed above. Some nations are economically dominant (in a quantitative sense) with virtually all of their major trading partners, and thus would be placed at the top of a hierarchy, for example, the United States. Other nations are dominant in trading relationships with some of their major partners, but are subordinate in others, for example, the United Kingdom. The hierarchy extends down to those nations that do not dominate the trading relationship with any of their primary trading partners, for example, Niger.

METHODOLOGY

Data and Nations

The international trade hierarchies developed in the present study are based on the exports of the nations of the world. The hierarchies therefore represent the structure of trade relationships with respect to the markets (or demand) for nations' products and services. A "dominant" nation would be one that provides the major market for a smaller nation's products. Hierarchies could also be constructed based on nations' imports (thus the supply side of the equation). Exports, however, are felt to provide a better indication of dominant-subordinate trading ties.

The primary reason underlying the conclusion that exports are more reflective of dominant-subordinate trade relationships is that nations are generally more dependent on their existing markets for goods and services than upon their suppliers. This is particularly the case for manufactured goods, since in very few cases does any single nation have a monopoly in the production of a specific manufactured item. It is generally less difficult, therefore, to find alternative suppliers than it is to find new markets. This idea would also apply to most commodities and raw materials. The obvious exceptions would be oil and other raw materials that are in short supply or for which strong cartels exist.

The importance of exports in determining levels of interaction at the international level has been recognized in the previous literature discussed in Chapter 2. Coppock (1962) and Lloyd (1968) concentrated on exports in their analyses of international trade. Dependency theorists have also emphasized exports in their writing. Alschuler (1976, p. 62) noted that a measure of feudal interaction patterns in international economics was the percentage of exports that each country sent to its most important trading partner. In addition, he used partner concentration for exports as one variable in his analysis of dependency relationships. William G. Tyler and J. Peter Wogart (1973), Rapkin (1976), and Ray and Webster (1977) used the same measure in the empirical portions of their studies of dependency. It is noteworthy that none of them used import concentrations as an appropriate measure of dependency. Sunkel (1969, p. 29) observed that Latin American countries had become extremely dependent on foreign markets and thus extremely vulnerable to changes in these markets. Condoni et al. (1971, p. 281) viewed heavy concentrations of markets in only a few nations as a sure sign of dependency, and Singer (1972, p. 210) observed that industrial states could easily suffer a loss of a market in a developing country, but that an underdeveloped country could be gravely hurt by a loss of a major market. Others have commented on the importance of markets, and thus exports, to developing states (Reno 1970, p. 87; MacFarlane 1971, p. 100; Esseks 1971, p. 1056; Lupton 1972, p. 177; Senghass 1975, p. 264; Dos Santos 1971, p. 229). In another vein, Richardson (1976) and Richardson and Kegley (1977) used export concentration in their studies of political compliance.

Most of the works noted above did not even mention imports as a factor in dependency or as an important indicator of economic ties. Coppock (1962) felt that exports were the best single variable. He noted that import data suffer from the possible intrusion of outside factors such as donations, capital imports, and earnings from exports. Import levels could thus reflect the effects of policies undertaken to limit the use of outside goods due to fluctuations in export earnings. Import fluctuations could also reflect the "choices of buyers and governments rather than externally imposed necessities" (p. 18). Lloyd (1968) observed that imports show much less variation across countries, and therefore, do not "have the important implications that concentration of export trade has" (p. 14) and that receipts from exports are the "best variable in considering the effects . . . of instability arising in the trade sector" (p. 46). O'Conner (1970, p. 147n) noted that the United States could no longer chastise a "satellite" by threatening to cut off supplies. "Thus the United States must threaten to damage other economies by curtailing access to markets which it controls." Even in the case of a critical product, such as petroleum, the markets are important. Zuhayr Mikdashi (1974) noted that the Organization of Petroleum Exporting Countries (OPEC) members have had difficulty in cooperating on economic issues. The pressure for price-cutting is great (p. 30). He also noted that the industrialized countries have the ability to develop alternative sources of energy (pp. 29-30). Recourse to this last possibility has been evident in the industrialized states in recent years.

The trade hierarchies based on each nation's exports were constructed for four years, 1951, 1961, 1971, and 1976. These years were selected to provide an adequate basis for a longitudinal evaluation of the evolution of world trade patterns since World War II. Of these four years, 1951 is the least representative in terms of world trade. In 1951 total world trade was high due to the export boom associated with the Korean war, and trade in the years immediately following 1951 decreased somewhat. No single country or particular group of countries, however, absorbed a disproportionate share of this increased level of trade. This year also represents a time when the major economic dislocations of World War II were beginning to recede into the past, and international trade was stabilizing. Finally, 1951 precedes any attempt at economic union, both in Western Europe and in other areas of the world, thus providing a base from which to analyze the effects of the EEC and other trade groups that have been organized since that time. It was for these reasons that 1951 was selected as the initial year in the analysis.

The years 1961 and 1971 are reasonably representative insofar as world trade is concerned. In each case, total world trade was less in the preceding years and greater in the following years. In addition, the individual areas of the world (such as Europe, Latin America, Asia) did not experience any wide fluctuations in their trade during the immediately preceding or following years. Trade for these areas increased from 1960 to 1961 and increased again from 1961 to 1962, although not all at the same rate. Similarly, none of the major trading nations were subject to wide variations in their trade in the immediately preceding or following years, although some of the smaller countries or territories show substantial variations. Further, 1971 was the year in which the United States was forced to devalue the dollar, and thus represented the low point in the long-term trend which led to this event. Finally, trade data from 1961 and 1971 provide a means to gauge the impact of the EEC on international trade patterns, with 1961 suggesting the immediate effects and 1971 perhaps showing some of the long-term effects (together with 1976).

The last year for which data were gathered and analyzed, 1976, was selected primarily because it is the most recent year for which data were available at the time of this writing. It was considered desirable to ascertain the directions that international trade patterns have taken since 1971 when the dollar surrendered its role as the key currency. The five years that elapsed between 1971 and 1976 should provide some initial indications of the directions that the world economy is taking and of the changing role the United States has assumed in the international economy.

Hierarchical structures have been developed on the basis of trade data for a varying number of nations and territories—164 for 1976, 168 for 1971, 158 for 1961, and 130 for 1951. The specific nations and territories employed in each year are presented in Exhibits I, II, III, and IV of Appendix A. The territories chosen for inclusion in the four years are highly varied in some respects. Included are independent nations, colonial territories, a few special status areas, and detached segments of individual nations such as the overseas departments of France and the Netherlands. As Yates (1959, pp. 22-3) noted in his early study, there is no definitive criteria for trade reporting areas other than an area "which has come <u>by convention</u> to be regarded as a separate unit for international trade purposes." The use of all available territories does permit comparability over time. The colonies of 1951 were often the independent states of later years. The variations in the number of nations used in each year are due to changes in national and territorial boundaries that resulted from independence, joint reporting in some years (for example, British West Indies), integration (United Arab Republic), or disintegration (Malaysia and Singapore), as well as the availability of data in each of the years.

The primary source of the trade data is the International Monetary Fund and International Bank for Reconstruction and Development publication <u>Direction of Trade</u> for each of the four years considered in the study. Supplementary sources were used for data not found in the preceding source, such as trade for the Council for Mutual Economic Assistance (COMECON) nations. A complete listing of the supplementary sources used in the study is presented in the bibliography at the end of this volume. The specific data employed in the analysis were the dollar volumes of exports (f.o.b.) from each nation to every other nation. In a few cases export data were not available since trade data for a few countries were not reported in either the primary or supplementary sources. Where possible, the imports of partner countries were used to provide data on the exports of these non reporting countries.

CONSTRUCTION OF TRADE HIERARCHIES

To formally construct the trade hierarchies a method was used which is capable of quantifying the degree of association between each pair of countries in such a way that the networks of strongest association could be identified. These associations are in terms of trade flows that occur directly between two countries, or indirectly through one or more intermediary countries. The magnitude of the combined direct and indirect trade flow associations was measured by an index that is related to certain concepts of graph theory and has been employed by geographers for spatial analysis (Nystuen and Dacy 1961). Not only does this index identify the degree of trade flow contact between pairs of countries, but it also provides a quantitative basis for grouping the countries in an hierarchical structure.

Trade Flow Index

The first step in deriving the index, which accounts for both direct and indirect trade flows, is to transform the m x n raw data matrix (where m = n = number of countries) so that the direct trade flows between each pair of countries is some proportion of the total trade among all countries. This is accomplished by summing all of the cell entries of the matrix and then dividing every x_{ij} cell element (where i is the row country, or exporting country, and j is the column country or importing country) by this summation. That is,

$$y_{ij} = \frac{x_{ij}}{\sum_{i=1}^{m}\sum_{j=1}^{n} x_{ij}} \qquad (1)$$

where y_{ij} possesses the following properties:

$$0 \leq y_{ij} < 1 \qquad (2)$$

$$\sum_{i=1}^{m}\sum_{j=1}^{n} y_{ij} = 1.0 \qquad (3)$$

This new matrix containing positive decimal loadings is denoted as Y and represents all of the direct trade flow associations between pairs of countries.

The second step in deriving the trade flow index is to perform a series of power expansions of Y. Since the direct or first-order trade flows between pairs of countries are expressed as decimals, attenuated values are obtained for the indirect trade flows, that is, second-order, third-order, and so forth, derived from these expansions. Thus, it is postulated that the increment of indirect trade flow association decreases as the number of orders increase. For example, the matrix Y^2 which is obtained by $Y \cdot Y$ through standard matrix multiplication, denotes second-order trade flow associations between pairs of countries. The sum of all such two-step sequences from country i to country j is the value of all possible indirect second-order trade flows. That is,

$$a_{ij} = \sum_{k=1}^{n} ky_{ik}y_{kj} \qquad (4)$$

where a_{ij} is an element in Y^2. Continued power expansions of Y decrease the value of all possible indirect higher-order trade flows even further, and ultimately they approach zero.

The third step in deriving the index that reflects both direct and indirect trade flow associations is to add the matrix of direct flows to the matrices of indirect flows to form a new Matrix B. That is,

$$B = Y + Y^2 + Y^3 + \cdots + Y^n + \cdots \qquad (5)$$

The element b_{ij} of B is the index value representing the total direct and indirect trade flow association between country i and country j.

A more convenient computational method that was employed in the present study to compute the Matrix B is presented below.

$$(1 - y)^{-1} = 1 + Y + Y^2 + Y^3 + \cdots + Y^n + \cdots \tag{6}$$

Thus:

$$B = (1 - Y)^{-1} - 1 \tag{7}$$

where the 1 is the identity matrix.

The Matrix B does not represent a perfect measure of the total direct and indirect trade flows. It is essentially a measure of chance indirect contact. The distribution of actual indirect trade flow associations is probably not random but rather concentrated in certain flow channels, in which case the Matrix B would be a conservative estimate of indirect influence. It does, however, have a greater appeal than the Matrix Y which incorporates only the direct influences.

Hierarchical Structure

The hierarchical structure of Matrix B is established on the basis of the notion of largest trade flows. The following procedure has been employed in deriving the hierarchical structure from Matrix B. First, identify the jth country that has the largest trade flow index value associated with a given country i. Second, determine if the column total for this jth country is larger or smaller than the column total for the ith country. Third, if the column total of j is less than i, then i is considered to be dominant; that is, its largest flow is to a smaller country. Conversely, if the column total of the jth country is larger than the column total of i, then i is considered to be subordinate to j. Fourth, repeat steps 1-3 for all of the ith countries. Fifth, portray graphically the structural relationship derived from the dominant countries and then link all the remaining countries to the countries to which they are subordinate. The resulting graph will reflect the hierarchical nature of these structural relationships.

Hypothetical Example

A simple case will provide an illustration of the analytic procedures that were used to derive hierarchical trade structures. Consider a hypothetical international trade network comprised of four countries, A, B, C and D. The directional flow of trade between these four countries is depicted in the following di-graph.

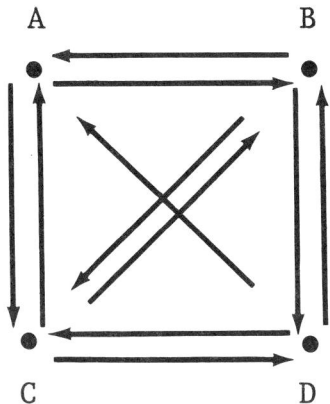

The Values (expressed in millions of dollars) associated with these direct trade flows are enumerated in the following "raw data" Matrix R.

$$R = \begin{array}{c} \\ \text{Exports} \end{array}$$

		\multicolumn{5}{c}{Imports}			
		A	B	C	D	Total
	A	0	4	12	0	16
	B	12	0	8	8	28
	C	12	12	0	40	64
	D	4	8	80	0	92
	Total	28	24	100	48	200

The total value of trade among these four countries amounts to $200 million. Country C constitutes the largest market for the exports of these countries amounting to 50 percent of the total trade.

The Matrix Y is derived next in which the cell values in Matrix R are expressed as proportions of the total trade. This matrix is shown at the top of the next page.

		Imports				
		A	B	C	D	Total
Exports	A	0	.02	.06	0	.08
	B	.06	0	.04	.04	.14
Y =	C	.06	.06	0	.20	.32
	D	.02	.04	.40	0	.46
	Total	.14	.12	.50	.24	1.00

In order to derive a trade flow index value for each pair of countries that reflects direct as well as indirect trade flows, power expansions of Matrix Y are performed and such matrices are summed to obtain the Matrix B below.

		A	B	C	D
	A	.0058	.0247	.0671	.0144
B =	B	.0645	.0074	.0656	.0534
	C	.0748	.0761	.0965	.2023
	D	.0527	.0713	.4426	.0914
	Total	.1978	.1795	.6718	.3615

The hierarchical structure of trade among these four countries reflected in Matrix B is portrayed graphically below.

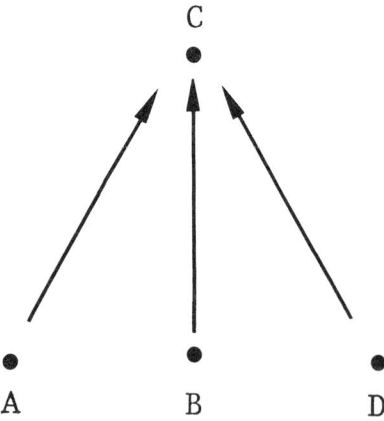

Thus, among these four countries, A, B, and D are most closely associated with country C as a market, when direct and indirect trade flows are considered.

If only the direct trade flows as reflected in Matrix Y are incorporated, the hierarchical structure among these four countries would be as follows.

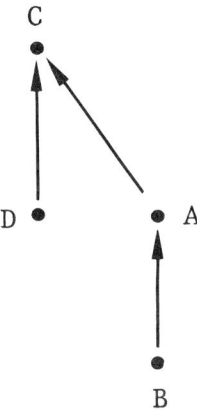

Country B is shown as being most closely associated with Country A when only direct effects are considered. However, as the hierarchy developed from Matrix B indicates, this may not be a true indication of Country B's position. Thus, the calculation of the indirect effects provides a useful extra dimension in the development of the trade hierarchies, although the method used to calculate these effects can only be considered a rough approximation of the actual indirect effects that occur.

The foregoing method will provide the framework for the analysis of the changing pattern of international trade. It serves to structure international trade data into coherent groupings based upon each nation's largest trading partner, that is, the nation with which it has the closest international economic ties. The hierarchies that have been derived through the application of this method are presented in Chapter 4, with further analyses of the hierarchies presented in Chapter 5. Chapter 4 presents the hierarchies first in cartographic form and then discusses the changes that occurred in the specific hierarchies during the years of the study. Chapter 5 analyzes the composition of the hierarchies more from the standpoint of the dependency theorists. Each hierarchy is examined from the perspective of the degree of dependency of the subordinate nations upon the dominant nations, with dependency operationally defined as the percentage of total exports and the percentage of each nation's Gross Domestic Product represented by exports to the dominant nation.

4

OVERVIEW OF INTERNATIONAL TRADE HIERARCHIES

CARTOGRAPHIC PRESENTATIONS

Global overviews of the international trade hierarchies, which were constructed through the application of the method discussed in Chapter 3, are presented on the world maps in Figures 4.1 through 4.5. The maps have been shaded to identify the nations that compose each of the hierarchies. The discussion of these hierarchies will first be composed of a general description of the hierarchies in each of the years. This discussion will be followed by a more detailed discussion of each principal nation's hierarchy as it progressed over the time frame of the analysis.

1951

The trade hierarchies that existed in 1951 are presented in Figures 4.1 and 4.2. The maps indicate five hierarchies associated with the United States, the United Kingdom, West Germany, France, and the U.S.S.R. This year could be considered part of the "End of Empire" period, with the United Kingdom and France still closely associated in terms of trade with their colonial empires. In 1951 both France and the United Kingdom had smaller nations as their largest export markets (and thus their positions at the top of a hierarchy), and both exported heavily to their colonies. The United Kingdom's three largest export markets in 1951 were all members of its commonwealth: Australia, South Africa, and Canada. Algeria was the largest export market for French goods, receiving more than $466 million worth of goods from France (United Nations 1953). France's next larg-

FIGURE 4.1

World Trade Hierarchy, 1951

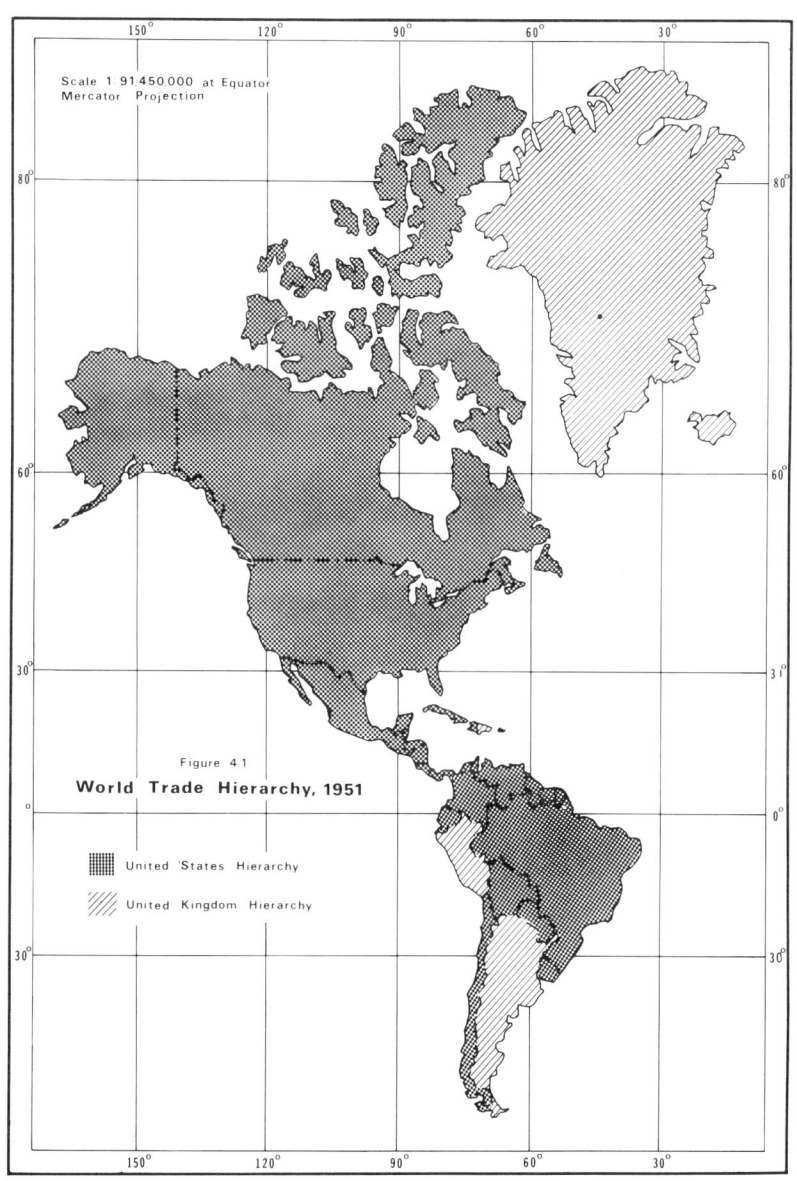

Source: Constructed by Mary Fisher based on information compiled by the authors.

FIGURE 4.2 World Trade Hierarchy, 1951

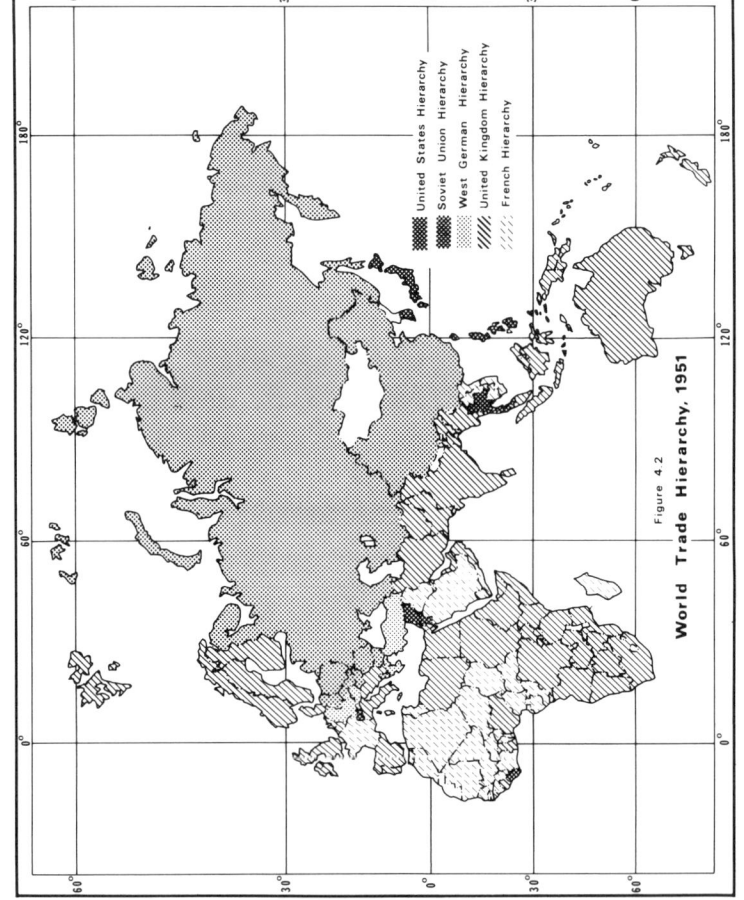

Source: Constructed by Mary Fisher based on information compiled by the authors.

est export market, the United Kingdom, received considerably less French exports ($360 million). France also had heavy export markets throughout the rest of its African and Southeast Asian empires.

The hierarchies that existed in 1951 reflect the transitional economic nature of this time period. Western Europe was still heavily engaged in reconstruction following World War II. Most European nations maintained strict exchange controls, thus limiting the amount of trade that could be done with other industrialized nations. West Germany was just beginning to re-emerge as an economic power, with only three geographically proximate nations and the Free Territory of Trieste linked closely to its market. The United States provided the principal market primarily for Latin American nations, but also for a few other nations scattered around the world. The Soviet Union's hierarchy consisted of only its newly-acquired dependencies in Eastern Europe and the Communist nations of Asia.

The 1951 maps, therefore, suggest a considerable amount of fragmentation in the world trade system at that time. The dominant nations in the hierarchy tended to be reasonably independent of each other, trading mainly with their traditional "periphery" nations and colonies. In addition, geographic proximity appears to have been a major determinant of trade patterns, particularly for those nations that did not have colonial empires.

1961

Figure 4.3 depicts a substantially different set of trade hierarchies for 1961 than those that existed in 1951. By 1961, the map indicates that the economic superpowers had emerged—the United States, West Germany, and the Soviet Union. In terms of the method employed to construct the hierarchies, the former two nations had subsumed the previous hierarchies of the United Kingdom and France.

By 1961 West Germany had established itself as the dominant economic power among the countries of the European Economic Community. West Germany now provided the major market for French exports. Approximately 15 percent of all French exports went to West Germany in 1961, as opposed to 5.5 percent in 1951 (International Monetary Fund 1963). In addition, West Germany had become the principal market for several other nations not associated with France.

The United States' hierarchy in 1961 had expanded to include virtually the entire Western Hemisphere, with the exception of Cuba. By this time the United States had become the principal market for British exports, thus bringing Scandinavia and most of the British Commonwealth into the United States' hierarchy.

FIGURE 4.3 World Trade Hierarchy, 1961

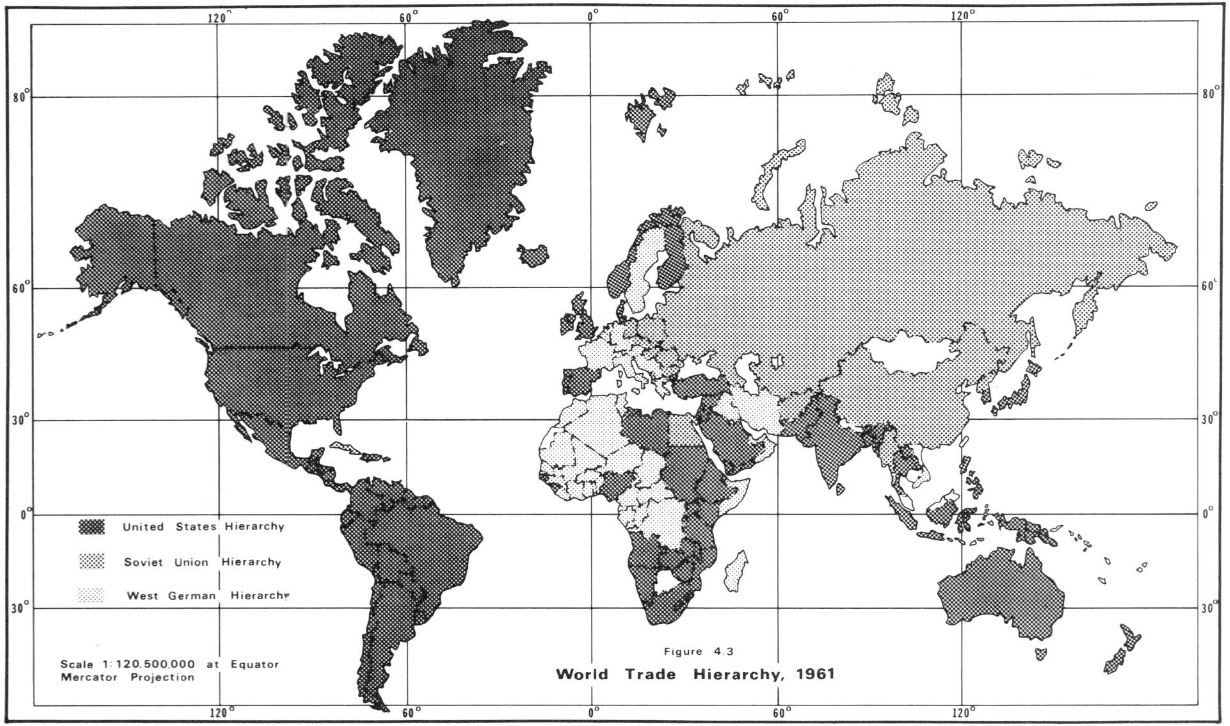

Source: Constructed by Mary Fisher based on information compiled by the authors.

OVERVIEW OF TRADE HIERARCHIES / 49

The hierarchy associated with the Soviet Union showed very little change between 1951 and 1961. It continued to consist primarily of European and Asian nations with communist governments. Cuba and the United Arab Republic had been added to the hierarchy. However, both of these additions were largely due to political, rather than economic, forces.

The most apparent trend that can be seen by comparing the 1951 and 1961 hierarchies is the tendency toward greater economic integration among the industrialized nations in 1961. These nations had begun to trade more with each other than with their past or present periphery nations or colonies. In fact, the proportion of total world trade represented by trade among the industrialized nations has increased steadily since World War II. The reasons for this change in trade patterns are manifold. Economic recovery among the European nations and Japan meant the dissolution of exchange controls and increased consumer incomes. The inauguration of the European Economic Community meant a reduction or discontinuation of trade barriers among those nations. Private enterprise had begun to move heavily into foreign direct investment, primarily in the industrialized nations. The end result appears to be the greater international economic integration depicted on the 1961 map.

1971

Between 1961 and the U.S. dollar devaluation in 1971, several changes had occurred in the international trade hierarchies (see Figure 4.4), although the principal hierarchies were still associated with the United States, West Germany, and the Soviet Union. Many of these changes occurred within the hierarchies themselves and will be discussed in detail in the next section of this chapter. However, there were also shifts that took place between the major hierarchies.

A few major nations that had previously been part of the United States' hierarchy had shifted to the West German hierarchy, notably Argentina and Turkey. In terms of territory covered, however, the United States' hierarchy remained approximately the same. The major addition, surprisingly, was the People's Republic of China. This addition reflects the importance of trade ties through intermediate states. Due to the Sino-Soviet split that occurred between 1961 and 1971, China began to rely primarily on Hong Kong and Japan rather than the Soviet Union as outlets for its exports. The importance of these third nations, both tied to the United States, cannot be ignored. For political reasons, China could not undertake direct trade with the United States. Thus, the intermediate markets of Hong Kong and Japan became crucial. Hong Kong and Japan's exports relied on American mar-

FIGURE 4.4 World Trade Hierarchy, 1971

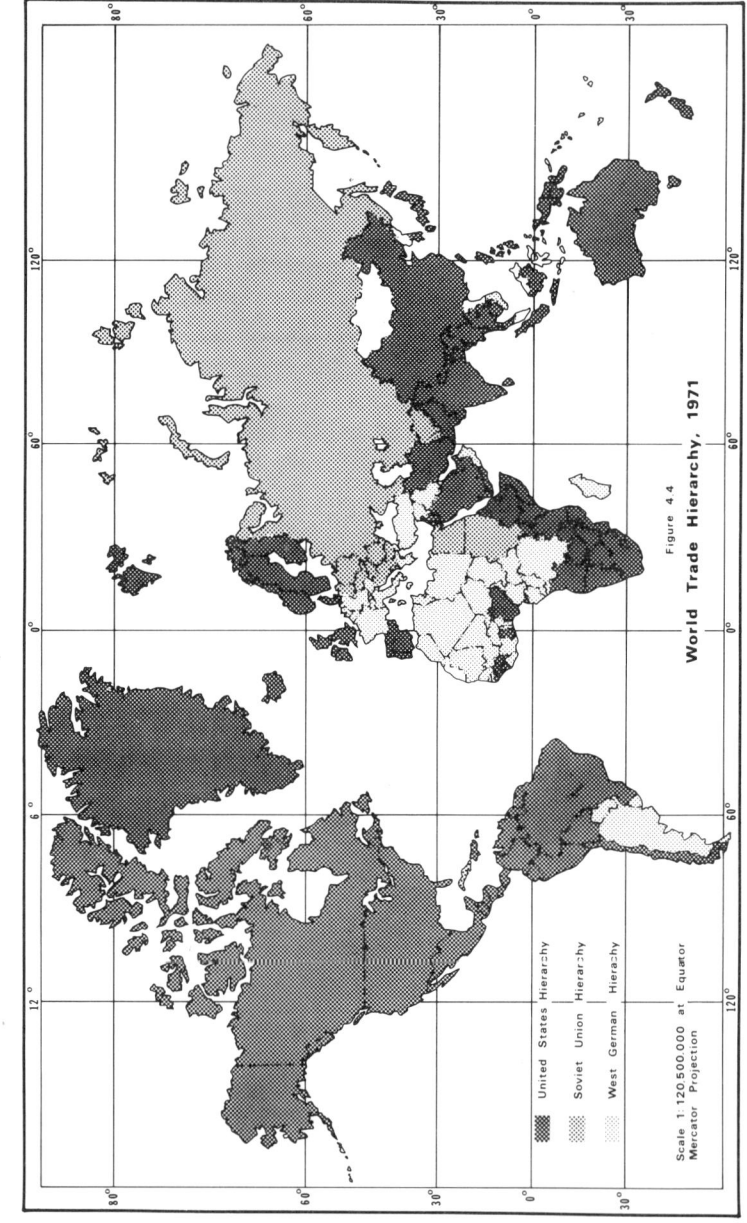

kets, and China relied on Hong Kong and Japan. In the case of Hong Kong, it is because of the city's importance as an export market that the government in Peking has been willing to maintain the status quo and has not actively sought to bring about a British withdrawal from the city (Lupton 1972, pp. 176-80). The reliance of China overall upon its export trade, however, is small relative to other nations. Further analyses that take into account the variation of hierarchy "members" reliance upon their trading partners are presented in Chapter 5.

1976

It should be expected that after the 1971 devaluation of the U.S. dollar, the hierarchy associated with the United States would shrink. The devalued dollar would have reduced U.S. demand for imports, and thus made the U.S. market less dominant for other nations' exports. Conversely, the hierarchies of nations with revalued currencies would probably have expanded, since the dollar value of their exports should have expanded. Figure 4.5, however, indicates that the United States experienced very little loss in its overall hierarchy between 1971 and 1976, at least not in terms of the global view offered through the maps. In fact, the U.S. hierarchy appears to have gained in territory through the addition of such nations as Argentina, Algeria, Libya, and the People's Republic of the Congo. Nor did the West German hierarchy expand, as might have been predicted. The overviews afforded by the maps of the hierarchies do not indicate even a minor shift in the U.S. position with regard to other nations' reliance upon the United States as a market for their exports.

PRINCIPAL HIERARCHIES OVER TIME

The overviews provided by the preceding maps give an initial indication of the hierarchies associated with the major world economic powers. In the following section each of the major hierarchies is analyzed over time with respect to the notable changes that occurred in them. In addition, the hierarchies attached to the major trading nations of Japan, the United Kingdom, and France will be analyzed over the time frame of the study. These three nations were part of either the German or U.S. hierarchy, but each had its own attached hierarchy throughout the period. It should be remembered that any comparisons of the hierarchies over time must take into account the fact that in the later years, data was available for more states and territories.

FIGURE 4.5 World Trade Hierarchy, 1976

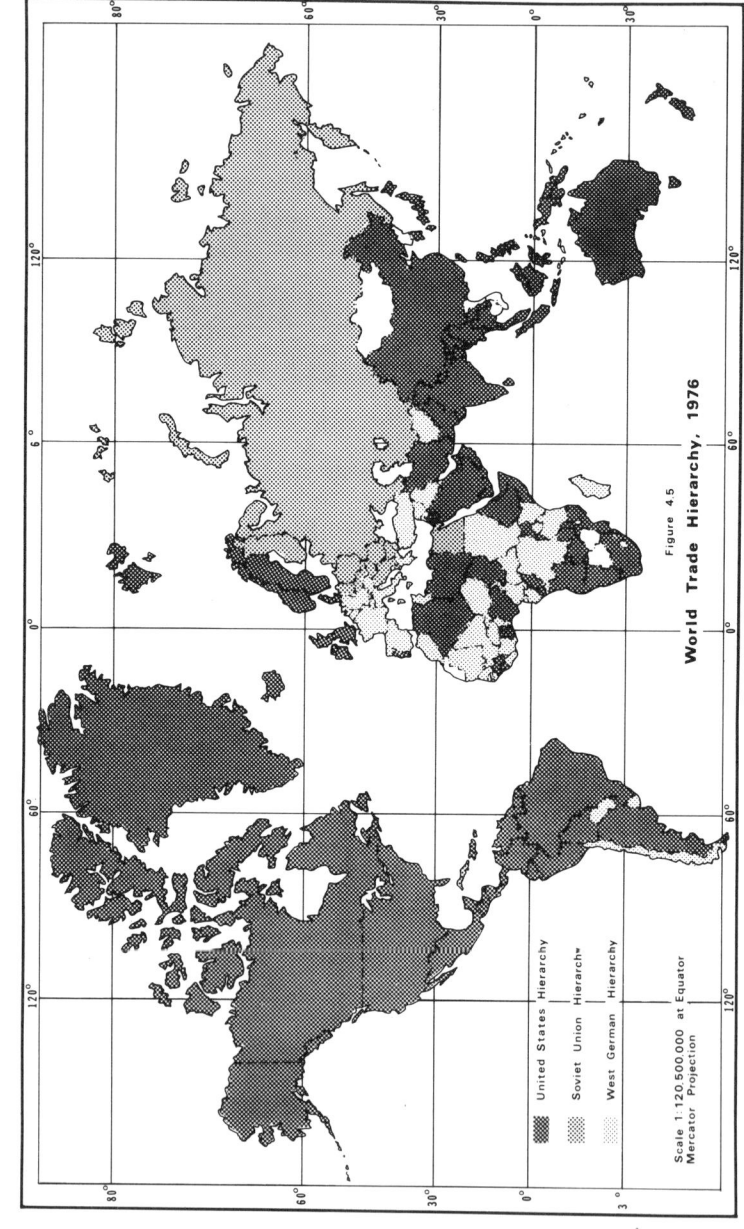

Source: Constructed by Mary Fisher based on information compiled by the authors.

OVERVIEW OF TRADE HIERARCHIES / 53

The United States Hierarchy

The United States hierarchy in 1959, shown in Figure 4.6, indicates that U.S. economic influence was centered primarily in the Western Hemisphere. The vast majority of nations that had the United States as their largest trading partner were located in North or South America. Outside of the Western Hemisphere, only Japan, Switzerland, Lebanon, the Philippines, Liberia, and Thailand had the United States as their largest export market.

The great expansion that occurred in the overall U.S. hierarchy between 1951 and 1961 came mostly as a result of the inclusion of the United Kingdom (see Figure 4.7). The addition of the United Kingdom to the U.S. hierarchy resulted in the addition of all the nations and territories that had the United Kingdom as their largest export market. These British trading partners were located throughout most areas of the world: Northern Europe, Africa, South America, South Asia, and Oceania.

In addition to the gains the United States received through the United Kingdom between 1951 and 1961, several other nations had become directly linked through trade to the United States. Most of these nations had been linked to the United Kingdom in 1951. The area from which many of these nations came was Latin America, and thus represents an increased presence of the United States trade in the Western Hemisphere. New Latin American nations linked directly to the United States in 1961 included Peru, the Dominican Republic, and Trinidad and Tobago. However, two other Latin American nations that had been linked directly to the United States in 1951, Bolivia and Uruguay, had switched to the United Kingdom in 1961. In addition, some of the island territories in the British West Indies were directly tied to markets in the United States in 1961, where as a group they shipped most to the United Kingdom in 1951. Other nations that switched from the United Kingdom to the United States between 1951 and 1961 included Ethiopia, Israel, Indonesia, and Angola, while Hong Kong came from Mainland China and Turkey from Germany. The French Somali Coast also shifted from Japan to the United States.

The losses that the United States incurred between 1951 and 1961, with the exception of Uruguay and Bolivia, appear to represent shifts attributable to geographical proximity or to political factors. With respect to the latter, Cuba's largest trading partner became the Soviet Union. Geographical proximity would appear to account at least partially for Switzerland's shift to Germany and for Thailand's shift to Japan. Lebanon had traded with the United States as its principal market in 1951, but in 1961 it was an independent node. Its largest trade flow was to Jordan, which was a smaller market. There were no nations for which Lebanon served as a principal market in 1951;

FIGURE 4.6

United States Hierarchy, 1951

UNITED STATES

JAPAN
- China (Taiwan)
- French Somali Coast
- Korea, South
- Paraguay

- Bolivia
- Brazil
- Canada
    British Guiana
- Chile
- Colombia
- Costa Rica
- Cuba
- Ecuador
- El Salvador
- Guatemala
- Haiti
- Honduras
- Lebanon
    Jordan
    Syria
- Liberia
- Mexico
- Netherlands Antilles
    Venezuela
- Nicaragua
- Panama
- Philippines
- Surinam
- Switzerland
- Thailand
- Uruguay

Source: Compiled by the authors.

OVERVIEW OF TRADE HIERARCHIES / 55

therefore, Lebanon had no nations associated with it. Syria and Jordan both had been tied to Lebanon in 1951, but in 1961 they switched to the Republic of China.

The number of nations that were most dependent upon the United States' market continued to grow between 1961 and 1971. For several nations, both large and small, the United States became their largest market in this year. As in the previous decade, most of these additions had been previously linked with the United Kingdom. Unlike the previous decade, however, these were not nations in Latin America; British Honduras was the only territory in this area to switch to the United States. The other nations added to the United States were Spain, Ghana, Iceland, India, and Pakistan. In addition, the Asian nations of Korea and China (Taiwan), previously linked directly to Japan, were now linked to the United States. In Oceania, New Guinea changed from the United Kingdom while the New Hebrides moved from France. Gains far outnumbered losses for the United States between 1961 and 1971, with Turkey, Chile, Indonesia, Somali Coast, and Angola being the only nations directly linked to the United States in 1961 that were not attached in 1971.

The number of nations directly linked to the United States continued to increase between 1971 and 1976. The additions during this period came primarily from Latin America and Africa. The U.S. position in Latin America continued to expand with the addition of Bolivia and Barbados. Further, Argentina entered the U.S. hierarchy, albeit through a third nation (Brazil). The North African nations of Algeria and Libya were now exporting more to the United States than to any other nation. The sub-Saharan nations that switched to the United States between 1971 and 1976 included, once again, several countries that had previously exported most to the United Kingdom—Nigeria, Rwanda, Zambia, and Uganda. Other African additions to the U.S. hierarchy in 1976 were Angola (from Portugal) and People's Republic of the Congo (from Germany). Bangladesh, formed between 1971 and 1976, also became a part of the U.S. hierarchy in 1976. Only a few territories were lost to the hierarchy between 1971 and 1976. British Honduras (now Belize) returned to the United Kingdom. India and Pakistan in Asia and the New Hebrides in Oceania became part of the Japanese hierarchy.

United Kingdom Hierarchy

The evolution of the United Kingdom's hierarchy over the time frame of the analysis can be followed through Figure 4.10 for 1951 and through the United States' hierarchies for 1961, 1971, and 1976 (Figures 4.7-4.9), of which the United Kingdom is a part. Consistent

FIGURE 4.7

United States Hierarchy, 1961*

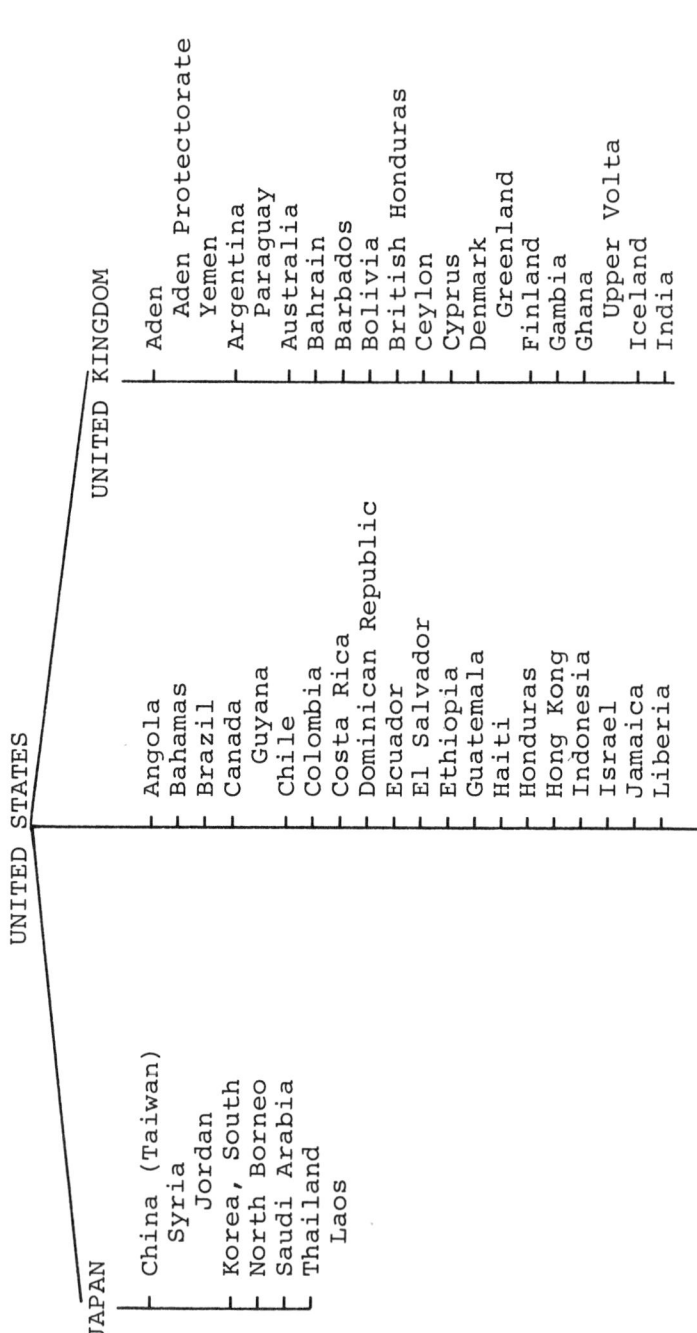

- Mexico
- Netherlands Antilles
- Nicaragua
- Panama
- Peru
- Philippines
- Somali Coast
- Surinam
- Trinidad and Tobago
- Turkey
- Venezuela
- Uganda
- Zanzibar
- Ireland
- Kenya
- Kuwait
- Libya
- Malta
- Mauritius
- New Zealand
- Nigeria
- Norway
- Pakistan
- Portugal
- Mozambique
- Portuguese Guinea
- Rhodesia and Nyasaland
- Sierra Leone
- South Africa
- Spain
- Sudan
- Tanganyika
- Uruguay

*The United States Hierarchy also includes: St. Pierre and Miquelon (tied to Canada); Naru and Trian Barat (tied to Australia); St. Thomas and Prince Islands (tied to Portugal); Maldive Islands (tied to Ceylon); Western Samoa (tied to New Zealand); Ryukyus (tied to Japan); New Guinea, Faeroe Islands, Falkland Islands, Fiji, Leeward Islands, Bermuda, Papua, and Windward Islands (tied to United Kingdom).

Source: Compiled by the authors.

FIGURE 4.8

United States Hierarchy, 1971*

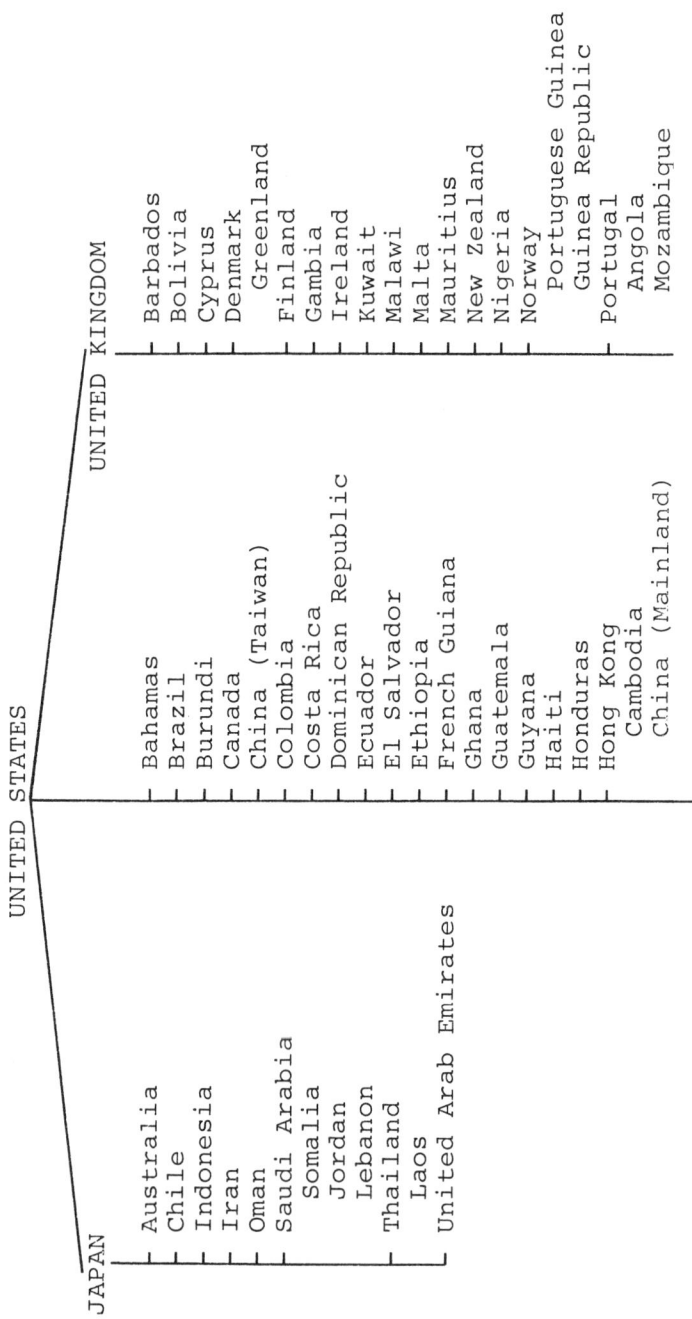

```
Iceland                           Qatar
India                             Sierra Leone
    Nepal                         South Africa
Israel                            Sri Lanka
Jamaica                               Burma
Korea, South                      Sweden
Liberia                           Tanzania
Mexico                            Uganda
Netherlands Antilles                  Kenya
Nicaragua                             Rwanda
Pakistan                          Yemen, P.D. Republic
Panama                                Yemen Arab Republic
Peru                              Zambia
Philippines                           Rhodesia
Spain
    Bahrain
    Equatorial Guinea
Surinam
Trinidad and Tobago
Venezuela
```

*The United States Hierarchy also includes: Papua, Gilbert and Ellice Islands (tied to Australia); British Solomon Islands, Brunei, New Caledonia, and Ryukyus (tied to Japan); Faeroe Islands (tied to Denmark); Naru, Western Samoa (tied to New Zealand); Cape Verde Islands, St. Thomas and Prince Islands (tied to Portugal); Maldive Islands (tied to Sri Lanka); Afars and Issas (tied to Yemen, P.D.R.); Bermuda, Falkland Islands, Fiji, Leeward Islands, Seychelles Islands, and Windward Islands (tied to United Kingdom); St. Pierre and Miquelon (tied to Canada); British Honduras, New Guinea, and New Hebrides (tied to United States).

Source: Compiled by the authors.

FIGURE 4.9

United States Hierarchy, 1976*

```
                           UNITED STATES
                                |
        ┌───────────────────────┼───────────────────────┐
      JAPAN                                        UNITED KINGDOM
        │                       │                       │
   Australia               Algeria                   Belize
   Bahrain                 Angola                    Cyprus
   Chad                    Bangladesh                Denmark
   India                   Barbados                  Greenland
   Nepal                   Bolivia                   Gambia
   Indonesia               Brazil                    Guyana
   Burma                   Argentina                 Ireland
   Iran                    Burundi                   Malawi
   Kuwait                  Canada                    Mauritius
   Malaysia                Yemen (P.D. Republic)     New Zealand
   Oman                    China (Taiwan)            Norway
   Pakistan                Colombia                  Portugal
   Saudi Arabia            Congo, People's           Mozambique
   Somalia                   Republic                Guinea-Bissau
   Lebanon                 Costa Rica                Qatar
   Jordan                  Dominican Republic        Sierra Leone
   Thailand                Ecuador                   South Africa
   Laos                    El Salvador               Sri Lanka
   United Arab Emirates    Ethiopia                  Sweden
                           French Guiana
                           Ghana
                           Guatemala
```

Guinea Republic
Haiti
Honduras
Hong Kong
China (Mainland)
Yemen Arab Republic
Iceland
Israel
Korea, South
Libya
Mexico
Nicaragua
Nigeria
Panama
Peru
Philippines
Rwanda
Surinam
Uganda
Venezuela
Zambia

*The United States Hierarchy also includes: Gilbert and Ellice Islands (tied to Bahrain); Brunei, Papua and New Guinea, and British Solomon Islands (tied to Japan); French Polynesia (tied to Algeria); Seychelles Islands (tied to China, Taiwan); Djibouti (tied to Yemen Arab Republic); Barbados, Jamaica, Netherlands Antilles, St. Pierre and Miquelon, and Trinidad and Tobago (tied to the United States); Faeroe Islands (tied to Denmark); Leeward Islands (tied to Guyana); Western Samoa, Naru, and Tonga (tied to New Zealand); Cape Verde Islands, St. Thomas and Prince Islands (tied to Portugal); Maldive Islands (tied to Sri Lanka); Falkland Islands, Fiji, Gibralter, and Windward Islands (tied to United Kingdom).

Source: Compiled by the authors.

with the diminishing role which the United Kingdom has played in the world over the time period, the hierarchies show a continuing decrease in the number of countries directly linked to the United Kingdom since 1951.

Between 1951 and 1961 many of the European nations that had sent more exports to the United Kingdom than elsewhere had begun exporting more to West Germany. Italy, the Netherlands, and Sweden all fall into this category. Yugoslavia in 1961 was sending the plurality of its exports to Italy rather than the United Kingdom, while Iran had switched to West Germany. While most of the United Kingdom's former possessions that had been attached in 1951 remained so in 1961, there were some exceptions. Burma and Egypt (United Arab Republic) had Mainland China and the Soviet Union, respectively, as their largest export markets in 1961; the small colonies of Jamaica and Trinidad and Tobago had switched to the United States by 1961. In addition to the foregoing, the United Kingdom lost several other nations and territories between 1951 and 1961, representing virtually every region of the world: Israel, Peru, Ethiopia, the Dominican Republic, Indonesia, and Angola had all moved from being within the United Kingdom's hierarchy in 1951 to being directly linked to the United States in 1961. In Southeast Asia, North Borneo shifted to Japan, and Singapore became an independent node at the expense of the United Kingdom. Singapore's largest market was Malaya, an overall smaller market than Singapore itself. Sarawak and Malaya both had Singapore as their major market, and Brunei was linked through Sarawak. All these states were linked to the United Kingdom in 1951. This situation continued in 1971, except that Malaya, Sarawak, and North Borneo had been united to form Malaysia and Brunei had shifted to Japan.

Between 1961 and 1971 the downward trend in the number of countries that relied most heavily upon the British market continued. Once again, as between 1951 and 1961, the nations that left the United Kingdom's hierarchy represented all parts of the globe. In Europe, Spain was exporting more to the United States by 1971 rather than to the United Kingdom. In the Middle East and Africa, Libya was exporting most to Italy, Rhodesia to Zambia, Bahrain to Spain, and the Sudan to the Soviet Union. Two major South Asian nations, India and Pakistan, were now exporting most to the United States. Australia with Papua had transferred into the Japanese hierarchy and Iceland to the United States. In South America, British Honduras was now linked directly to the United States, Argentina to Italy, and Uruguay to Germany. The United Kingdom had been the largest export market for all of these nations in 1961. In contrast to these losses from its hierarchy, the only gains registered by the United Kingdom between 1961 and 1971 were Sweden, Qatar, and a number of other new territories such as Afars and Issas, Angola, Guinea, and Burma linked indirectly through other states in the hierarchy.

FIGURE 4.10

United Kingdom Hierarchy, 1951*

UNITED KINGDOM

- Anglo Egyptian Sudan
- Argentina
- Australia
- British Persian Gulf States
- Ceylon
- Denmark
  - Greenland
- Dominican Republic
- Ethiopia
- Egypt
- Finland
- Gold Coast
- Iceland
- India
  - Afghanistan
  - Burma
  - Pakistan
- Iran
  - Oman
- Ireland
- Israel
- Italy
  - Libya
  - Somalia
- Jamaica
- Kenya

- Malaya-Singapore
  - Indonesia
  - Sarawak
- Mauritius
- Netherlands
  - Belgium-Luxembourg
  - Belgian Congo
  - Dutch New Guinea
- New Zealand
- Nigeria
- Norway
- Nyasaland
- Peru
- Portugal
  - Angola
  - Mozambique
  - Portuguese Guinea
- Rhodesia, North
- Rhodesia, South
- Sierra Leone
- South Africa
- Southwest Africa
- Spain
- Sweden
- Tanganyika
- Trinidad and Tobago
- Uganda
- Yugoslavia

*The United Kingdom Hierarchy also includes: Naru, New Guinea, and Papua (tied to Australia); Maldive Islands (tied to Ceylon); Faeroe Islands (tied to Denmark); North Borneo (tied to Malaya-Singapore); Brunei (tied to Sarawak); St. Thomas and Prince Islands (tied to Portugal); Spanish Morocco and Spanish Guinea (tied to Spain); Fiji, British West Indies, Western Samoa, Falkland Islands, and British Honduras (tied to United Kingdom).

Source: Compiled by the authors.

Additional losses occurred in the United Kingdom's hierarchy between 1971 and 1976. Most of the losses between these years occurred in the Middle East and Africa. Kuwait became a part of the Japanese hierarchy, and the People's Democratic Republic of Yemen was doing the bulk of its exporting to Canada. In Africa, Nigeria and Uganda were most closely associated with the United States in 1976 and Tanzania with West Germany. In addition, two African nations and territories linked to the United Kingdom through third countries in 1971 were tied to other nations in 1976: Kenya became a part of the German hierarchy in 1976 and Rwanda became a part of the U.S. hierarchy. In Europe, Finland became part of the Soviet Union's hierarchy, while Malta became attached to West Germany. The remaining losses of the United Kingdom between 1971 and 1976 occurred in the Western Hemisphere. There Bolivia and Barbados had transferred into the United States' hierarchy, and Bermuda had switched to West Germany. The only gains for the United Kingdom were Belize from the United States and Gibralter from France.

The difference between the United Kingdom's hierarchy in the first year and the last year of the study is dramatic. In 1951, the nations primarily dependent upon the United Kingdom as an export market included much of Europe, Africa, Asia, Oceania, and Latin America. By 1976, the United Kingdom's hierarchy had been reduced to consist primarily of Northern Europe and some scattered former colonies in Africa, Oceania, and South Asia.

Japanese Hierarchy

Japan's hierarchy has shown a trend opposite to that of the United Kingdom. Japan was tied to the United States throughout the period of the study (see Figures 4.6 to 4.9). However, during this time period, an increasing number of nations have become linked to the Japanese market. This trend started rather slowly, with Japan adding only two major nations to its hierarchy between 1951 and 1961, Thailand and Saudi Arabia.

By 1971 several major nations had become tied to the Japanese market. Australia, previously linked to the United Kingdom, was now exporting more to Japan than to any other nation. Chile and Indonesia, formerly tied to the United States, were in the Japanese hierarchy in 1971. Iran had switched from the West German hierarchy in 1961 to the Japanese hierarchy in 1971. The Japanese hierarchy included several other smaller nations in 1971 that had not previously been linked to Japan: the United Arab Emirates, Oman, Brunei, Zambia, New Caledonia, Rhodesia (through Zambia), and Lebanon and Somalia (through Saudi Arabia). The only losses occurring in the Japanese hierarchy between 1961 and 1971 were two Asian nations, the Republic of China (Taiwan) and South Korea, both switching to the United States.

The Japanese hierarchy continued to expand through 1976, and by that year had come to encompass much of Oceania, South and Southeast Asia, and the Middle East. The largest additions to the Japanese hierarchy in 1976 were Pakistan and India, both formerly tied to the United States. The Middle Eastern countries of Kuwait, Bahrain, and Oman also became part of the Japanese hierarchy in 1976. Malaysia had been linked to Singapore in 1971, but in 1976 Japan was that nation's chief market, and Chad moved from France in 1971 to Japan in 1976. The losses incurred by the Japanese hierarchy between 1971 and 1976 tended to be outside of the Middle East and Asia. Chile became part of the West German hierarchy in 1976, and Zambia became linked directly to the United States. The small French overseas territory of New Caledonia was the only territory in Oceania lost from the Japanese hierarchy in 1976.

West German Hierarchy

The West German hierarchy throughout the time frame of the study is depicted in Figures 4.11 to 4.14. Figure 4.11 shows that in

FIGURE 4.11

West German Hierarchy, 1951

```
GERMANY
   ├─ Austria
   │    Trieste, Free Territory of
   ├─ Cyprus
   ├─ Greece
   └─ Turkey
```

Source: Compiled by the authors.

FIGURE 4.12

West German Hierarchy, 1961*

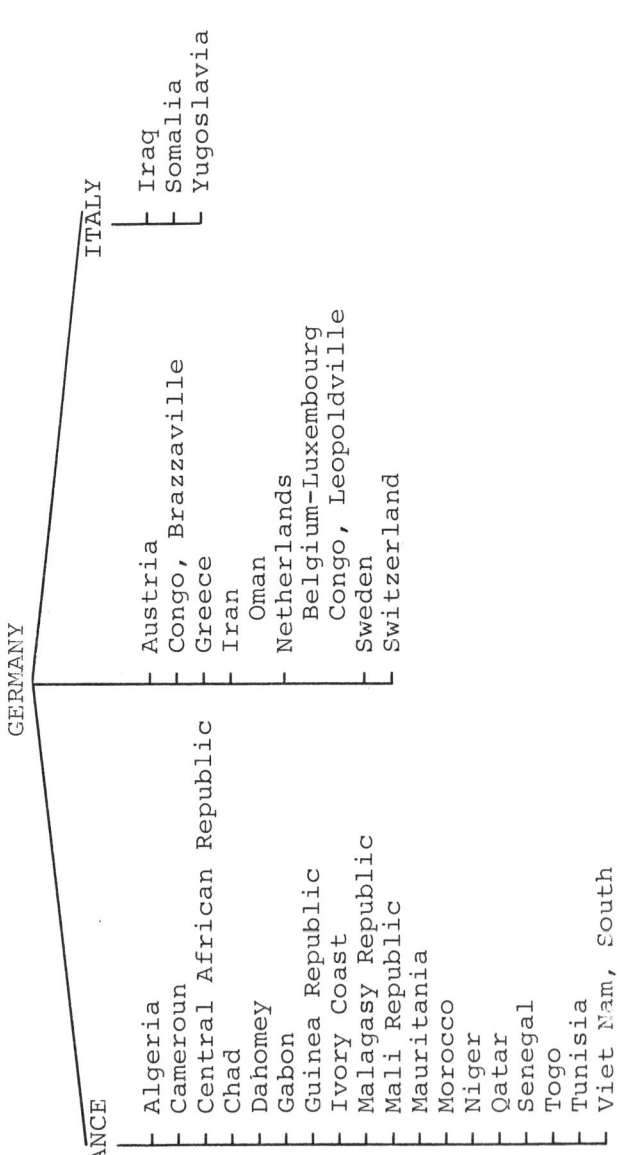

*The West German Hierarchy also includes: New Caledonia, New Hebrides, Guadeloupe, Martinique, and Reunion (tied to France).   Source: Compiled by the authors.

1951 the West German hierarchy was quite small, consisting only of Austria, Greece, Turkey, Trieste, and Cyprus. By 1961, however, the West German hierarchy had expanded to encompass most of Continental Europe. France was perhaps the largest addition to the West German hierarchy in 1961, both because of the economic importance of that nation and because of the addition of the nations and territories linked to France. Other European nations added to the West German hierarchy between 1951 and 1961 included Italy, the Netherlands, Switzerland, Sweden, and Yugoslavia (through Italy). Most of these nations had been previously tied to the United Kingdom, and their entry into the German hierarchy reflects the recovery of the German economy following the war and, in the cases of France, Italy, and the Netherlands, the inauguration of the Common Market. The other nations directly linked to the West German market in 1961 that had not been directly linked in 1951 were Iran and Congo (Brazzaville). All of the remaining additions to the West German hierarchy in 1961 came through third nations, primarily France, and some through the Netherlands and Italy. The losses incurred by the West German hierarchy between 1951 and 1961 consisted of two of the original four nations found in its 1951 hierarchy: Turkey had switched to the United States, and Cyprus had become part of the United Kingdom's hierarchy.

Between 1961 and 1971 the West German hierarchy expanded somewhat, but not greatly, since the losses almost equaled the gains. In Europe, Germany became the largest market for Belgium's exports, that nation having previously been linked to the Netherlands, and only indirectly to Germany. Further, Turkey had returned to the West German hierarchy in 1971, after being linked to the United States in 1961. Conversely, Sweden was not within the West German hierarchy in 1971, nor was Yugoslavia. Outside of Europe, Algeria and Liberia, linked to France in 1961, had become tied to West Germany in 1971, and Uruguay had come into the German hierarchy from the United Kingdom's hierarchy. The only major loss to the outside of Europe was Iran.

Although the West German hierarchy experienced further expansion between 1971 and 1976, once again, the net expansion could not be considered dramatic. The largest nation added to the hierarchy between these years was Chile, previously tied to Japan. Other additions to the 1976 West German hierarchy were Malta, Afghanistan, Kenya, Equatorial Guinea, Tanzania, and Bermuda. The only direct losses to the West German hierarchy between 1971 and 1976 were Algeria and People's Republic of the Congo. Argentina, which had been part of the West German hierarchy in 1971 through its trading ties with Italy, was part of the 1976 U.S. hierarchy through its trade with Brazil.

FIGURE 4.13

West German Hierarchy, 1971*

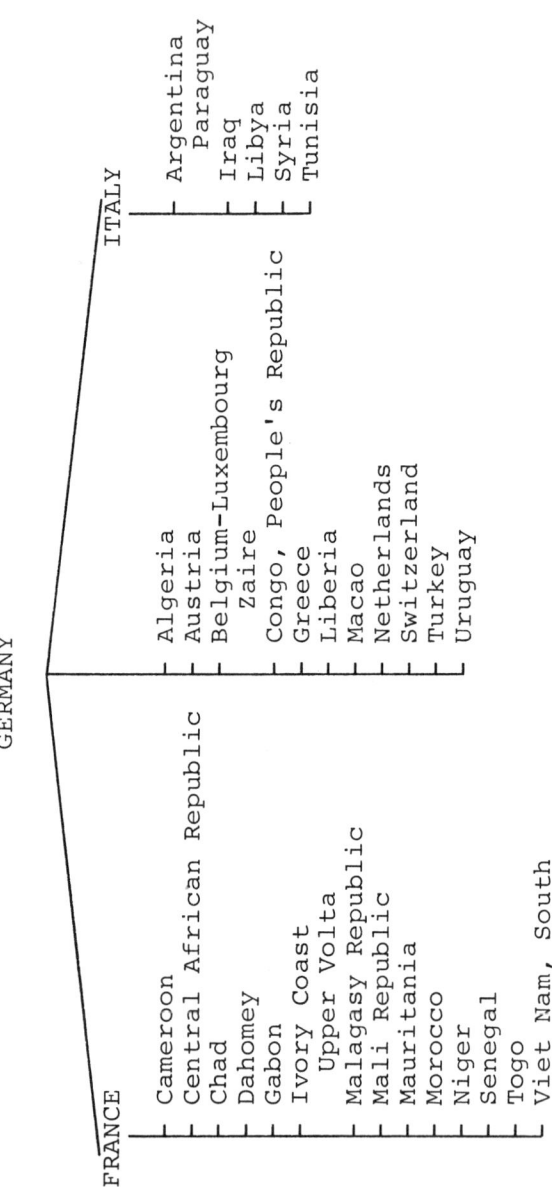

*The West German Hierarchy also includes: Gibralter, Guadeloupe, Martinique, and Reunion (tied to France).
Source: Compiled by the authors.

French Hierarchy

The French hierarchy in 1951 is portrayed in Figure 4.15, and its hierarchies in 1961, 1971, 1976 are shown as part of the West German hierarchy in Figures 4.12 to 4.14. An analysis of the French hierarchy over time shows that, unlike the United Kingdom, France has been able to maintain close trading relationships with its former colonies.

Between 1951 and 1961 the French hierarchy remained almost static. Two Middle Eastern nations that had been a part of the hierarchy in 1951 had transferred to other nations—Iraq went to Italy and Saudi Arabia to Japan. One important African nation, Liberia, had been added to the French hierarchy in 1961. Otherwise, very little change occurred over this decade. The most notable change that occurred between the years was the names of the attached nations. In 1960, French West Africa was divided into Mauritania, Senegal, Mali, Guinea, the Ivory Coast, Niger, and Upper Volta. Separate trade data also was available for Togo which, while never a part of French West Africa, had been associated for trade reporting purposes. In the same year, French Equatorial Africa had been divided into Chad, the Congo-Brazzaville, the Central African Republic, and Gabon. The Cameroons and the Malagasy Republic (Madagascar) had also become independent. Except for the Congo-Brazzaville, these states were still tied to French markets in 1961.

A few of France's former colonies had developed larger trading relations with other nations between 1961 and 1971, although, for the most part, the former colonies remained attached to France. Algeria had become attached to Germany during the time period, and Guinea to Norway. In addition, Tunisia was exporting more to Italy in 1971. There were also no significant additions to the French hierarchy between 1961 and 1971.

Between 1971 and 1976 the French hierarchy again managed to remain approximately the same size. One former colony, Chad, had switched to the Japanese hierarchy, as had Oman. Gibralter had shifted to the United Kingdom. However, these losses were more than compensated for by the additions to the French hierarchy of two major nations, Iraq and Spain. In addition, the French hierarchy in 1976 contained the small territories of New Caledonia and the New Hebrides. In this year the nations attached to France were with two exceptions former colonies or overseas departments. Among the former sub-Saharan African colonies, only Guinea, the Congo-Brazzaville, and Chad had major markets other than France. The remaining twelve states remained in France's hierarchy. Upper Volta had shifted to Germany in 1961 but returned in 1971. As a result, the continuity in France's hierarchy has been great among these states. Adebayo Adedji

FIGURE 4.14

West German Hierarchy, 1976*

```
                         GERMANY
┌─────────────────────────────┐
│ FRANCE                      │
│   ┬ Benin                   ┬ Afghanistan
│   ├ Cameroon                ├ Austria
│   ├ Central African         ├ Belgium-Luxembourg
│     Empire                    Zaire
│   ├ Gabon                   ├ Chile
│   ├ Iraq                    ├ Equatorial Guinea
│   ├ Ivory Coast             ├ Greece
│   ├ Malagasy Republic       ├ Kenya
│   ├ Mali Republic           ├ Italy
│   ├ Mauritania                Syria
│   ├ Morocco                   Sudan
│   ├ Niger                     Tunisia
│   ├ Senegal                 ├ Liberia
│   ├ Spain                   ├ Macao
│   ├ Togo                    ├ Malta
│   └ Upper Volta             ├ Netherlands
└─────────────────────────────┘ Paraguay
                              ├ Switzerland
                              ├ Tanzania
                              ├ Turkey
                              └ Uruguay
```

*The West German Hierarchy also includes: Guadeloupe, Martinique, New Caledonia, New Hebrides, Reunion, and Comoros Islands (tied to France); Timor (tied to Austria); and Bermuda (tied to Germany).

Source: Compiled by the authors.

(1970, pp. 225-6) and Frederick Arkhurst (1970, p. 381) both noted that in the colonial period France sought to integrate the economies of the colonies with that of the metropole. "This system resulted in a degree of political and economic identification with the metropolitan country that was unique" (Arkhurst, p. 381). It has been noted that Britain did not dominate the trade of its colonies to the extent that France did (O'Conner 1971, p. 180). This factor may explain the United Kingdom's decreasing importance as an export market for many of its former African territories. The identification with France has been furthered by the admission of the former French colonies (as well as the Belgian and Italian ones) into the EEC as associate members. African trade identification with Europe may increase even further since the former British African territories, as well as those in the Pacific and Caribbean have also been admitted to associate status with the entrance of the United Kingdom into the EEC.

FIGURE 4.15

French Hierarchy, 1951

FRANCE

- Algeria
- Cameroun
- French Equatorial Africa
- French Morocco
- French West Africa (including Togo)
- French West Indies
- Indochina
- Iraq
- Madagascar
- Saudi Arabia
    - Aden
        - Aden Protectorate
        - British Somaliland
- Tunisia

Source: Compiled by the authors.

Soviet Union Hierarchy

For purposes of completeness, the Soviet Union's hierarchies over time are also analyzed here, although the confidence in the trade data of the communist-bloc nations is not as great as for most of the other nations included in the study. Due to the rather static nature of the Soviet hierarchy over time, Figure 4.16 represents the 1951 hierarchy and the additions to and deletions from the hierarchy that occurred between each of the years of the study. In 1951 the Soviet hierarchy contained only the communist nations of Eastern Europe and Mainland China. Between 1951 and 1961 the Soviet hierarchy had maintained its hegemony over Eastern Europe and China, and had added the new communist nation of Cuba. In addition, the Soviet hierarchy in 1961 contained the United Arab Republic and the contiguous nation of Afghanistan.

Few changes also occurred in the Soviet hierarchy between 1961 and 1971. With the Sino-Soviet split, Mainland China was no longer doing most of its exporting to the Soviet Union. Two nations, however, were added to the Soviet hierarchy between these years, Yugoslavia and Sudan. Little movement was again seen in the Soviet hierarchy between 1971 and 1976. Between these years Finland had joined the Soviet hierarchy, Sudan had transferred to Italy, and Afghanistan had switched to West Germany.

CONCLUSIONS

While the analysis of the world maps of the hierarchies provided an initial overview of the evolution of international trade structure, much about the nature of that evolution was not revealed. The subsequent analysis of the six major trade hierarchies has indicated additional underlying patterns associated with the nature of international trade relationships since World War II. In 1951 trade relations were highly fragmented, appearing to follow traditional core-periphery relationships. Over time, many of these traditional relationships began to break down. The "break-up" of the United Kingdom's trade empire best illustrates this phenomenon, while France has managed to retain many of its early trade ties. Concurrently, the United States, Germany, and Japan continued to expand their trade ties to other nations, absorbing much of what had been the previous periphery nations of the United Kingdom and, to a lesser extent, France.

The United States has remained the major export market for much of the world, despite the international economic problems this nation has been experiencing. In fact, the number of nations attached to the United States has continued to expand during the 1970s, the

FIGURE 4.16

U.S.S.R. Hierarchy, 1951-1976

U.S.S.R. HIERARCHY, 1951

- Albania
- Bulgaria
- China (Mainland)
  - Hong Kong
  - Macao
- Czechoslovakia
- East Germany
- Hungary
- Poland
- Rumania

U.S.S.R. HIERARCHY, 1951-1961

Gains	Losses
Afghanistan	Hong Kong
Burma	Macao*
Cuba	
United Arab Republic	

U.S.S.R. HIERARCHY, 1961-1971

Gains	Losses
Sudan	China (Mainland)
Yugoslavia	Burma

U.S.S.R. HIERARCHY, 1971-1976

Gains	Losses
Finland	Afghanistan
	Sudan

*Data were not available for Macao in 1961. In 1971 and 1976 it was not part of the Soviet Union's hierarchy.

Source: Compiled by the authors.

period during which the dollar has been experiencing the greatest difficulties.

The evolution of the structure of world trade that is indicated by the hierarchies is definitely in the direction of geographic determinants. If one were to analyze the hierarchies of Germany, the United States, the Soviet Union, and Japan in 1976, there is a clear pattern of geographic proximity dominating trade relations. The United States is the dominant market in the Western Hemisphere. West Germany is the dominant market in Western Europe with the exception of the United Kingdom; and although the United Kingdom is still tied to the United States, that nation's entry into the EEC probably makes its transfer to the West German hierarchy inevitable. The United Kingdom's trade with Common Market nations has increased dramatically since 1971, thus providing some support for this projection. In 1971 exports to EEC nations accounted for 27.4 percent of total British exports; by 1976 that figure had risen to 35.5 percent (International Monetary Fund 1977).

While West Germany dominates Western Europe, the Soviet Union has maintained its hierarchy in Eastern Europe. The Middle East from Saudi Arabia west, South and Southeast Asia, and Oceania are dominated by Japan. Although it may be difficult at this time to argue that Japan is in any way dominant over its oil suppliers in the Middle East, most of the remainder of the Japanese hierarchy appears to be strongly attached to the Japanese market. Only Africa is substantially divided among the major hierarchies, showing no clear directions. Each major hierarchy has its own attached nations in Africa, but, with the exception of France, these attachments have tended to be unstable since 1961.

The structure of international trade, therefore, appears to be evolving more according to geography than politics. Political elements are certainly involved in many trading relationships, but the overriding tendency seems to be toward close economic relations with the most proximate superpower. In the next chapter, the relations between the dominant nations and their hierarchies will be explored in greater depth through an examination of the actual levels of dependence that exist between them.

5

DEPENDENCY PATTERNS AMONG NATIONS

The presentation of the hierarchies and the changes that have occurred in the composition of the hierarchies provides a general indication of the changes in the patterns of international trade since World War II. It is difficult, however, on the basis of this material to draw implications concerning political associations or influence that the dominant nations may have with the nations in their hierarchies. The fact that a nation does the greatest amount of its exporting to a certain country does not necessarily lead to the conclusion that the dominant nation is in a position to exert political influence. Wide variation exists in the degree to which nations are dependent upon their largest export markets. Some nations have trade that is widely dispersed across several nations, and the largest market receives only a small proportion of their total exports. Conversely, other nations send the majority of their exports to one country and have little trade with other countries. Political influence is more likely to arise in the latter instance than in the former.

A second source of variation that has implications for political influence through trade concerns the extent to which a nation's economy relies upon trade. In some cases only a small segment of a nation's economy may be trade related, while in others the national economy may be highly dependent upon trade. Regardless of the proportion of its total trade done with its largest trading partner, a nation whose economy does not depend upon external trade relations is not in a position to be politically influenced through such relations. On the other hand, even if a nation does not depend heavily upon any single trading partner, it may be in a position to be influenced by its largest trading partner if its economy is closely tied to its trade.

76 / THE UNITED STATES AND WORLD TRADE

The present chapter considers the issue of political dependence through trade by examining the level of trading ties that exist in the hierarchies presented in Chapter 4. This chapter will also provide some quantitative measures of the extensiveness of each of the hierarchies, and it will explore the general issue of whether the nations of the world are becoming more integrated in terms of their trade relationships with other countries. All of the preceding topics are associated with the political influence that can be exerted through international trade. The findings of the study generally indicate that trade ties with dominant nations have weakened between 1951 and 1976 with respect to the proportion of exports sent to the largest trading partner. Conversely, the expansion that has occurred over the time period in the amount of international trade has left many nations' economies equally or more dependent upon their largest export markets.

The chapter first analyzes the five major hierarchies with respect to the proportion of each attached nation's exports that are sent to the dominant nation. The same type of analysis is then performed with regard to the proportion of the attached nations' economies involved in exports to the dominant nations. The last section of the chapter discusses whether the extent of nations' tied with their largest export markets has changed perceptibly over the period of the study.

PROPORTIONATE TRADE WITH DOMINANT NATIONS

The analysis of trade proportions takes the form of first identifying those nations that are directly linked to the dominant nations in the hierarchies. The dominant nations included in this analysis are the United States, West Germany, France, the United Kingdom, and Japan. The latter three nations are not positioned at the top of a hierarchy, but each has had a number of directly linked nations throughout the period of analysis. Nations that are linked to one of the five dominant nations through a third country are not included in this analysis since the proportionate trade such nations have with the dominant nation would not reflect the extent of their trading ties to their largest export markets. The Soviet Union's hierarchy is not incorporated into this section due to the problems of obtaining reliable data. Trade statistics for the Soviet Union and Eastern European countries present some special difficulties. Their trade with the Western countries usually is tabulated with reference to Western currencies, since Eastern European currencies are not readily convertible on the international market. Trade between the communist countries, on the other hand, is either reported in local currencies or the "trade ruble." Neither the local currencies nor the trade ruble have any meaningful exchange rates. They are totally artificial and, as a result, have created some problems for the governments involved in determining appropriate values for trade items (Holzman, 1976, pp. 24-33; Herman 1969).

A number of the smaller territories included in the hierarchies also are not included in the analysis. These areas are the ones for which trade data were derived from the partner reports. As a result, while major flows were identified, meaningful total figures for the trade of these areas are lacking, and proportionate levels could not be derived with any accuracy.

The percentage of total exports represented by exports to the dominant nations was then calculated for each of the attached countries. These calculations were made for each of the four time points in the study: 1951, 1961, 1971, and 1976. On the basis of these percentages, the nations in each hierarchy during each of the years were categorized as belonging to one of three groups according to their level of dependence upon the largest market. A high level of dependence is said to exist if the nation exports 40 percent or more of its total exports to the dominant nation. A medium level of dependence is indicated by an export percentage to the dominant nation of between 20 percent and 39 percent. A low level of dependence exists if the level of exports is less than 20 percent. The selection of these cutoffs is arbitrary, but it was felt that the percentages for each category provide useful guidelines for the analysis of the data.

The hierarchies associated with each of the dominant nations over the time period are examined individually, beginning with the United States. At the end of the discussion of each hierarchy, the nations that have been linked to the dominant nation since at least 1961 are identified. The percentage of exports to the dominant nation since 1961 is then analyzed for these countries in order to assess the general direction of trade ties within each hierarchy.

United States

Table 5.1 presents the nations linked to the United States according to the strength of the trade ties they had with that country during each of the years of the study. The proportionate trade data show a wide variation both between and within the years in the strength of the dependence that the nations in the hierarchy had with the United States.

In 1951 the U.S. hierarchy consisted primarily of other Western Hemisphere nations, and it was smaller than at any time during the study. The proportionate trade data, however, indicate that in this year the strength of the trading relationships that the United States had with the countries in its hierarchy were the greatest. Of the 22 nations linked directly to the United States, 17 are in the high depend-

TABLE 5.1

UNITED STATES: Export Percentages from Attached Nations

	1951		1961		1971		1976	
High Dependence	Guatemala	87.8	Panama	93.9	Bahamas	83.1	Haiti	75.3
	El Salvador	86.1	Bahamas	86.8	Dominican Republic	74.4	Dominican Republic	69.5
	Panama	81.9	Surinam	74.6	Canada	66.0	Trinidad–Tobago	69.2
	Colombia	81.4	Honduras	63.8	Haiti	65.0	Canada	64.7
	Costa Rica	76.9	Dominican Republic	62.3	Burundi	62.2	Mexico	55.7
	Honduras	72.9	Ecuador	61.1	Mexico	60.7	Honduras	54.0
	Mexico	70.5	Mexico	60.8	Netherlands Antilles	58.8	French Guiana	53.8
	Bolivia	65.6	Colombia	59.8	Honduras	56.3	Netherlands Antilles	52.8
	Philippines	63.1	Costa Rica	58.3	Korea, South	49.8	Angola	48.7
	Ecuador	60.0	Canada	54.6	Panama	49.0	Congo, People's Republic	44.3
	Haiti	59.5	Guatemala	53.3	Trinidad–Tobago	45.2	Ecuador	44.0
	Canada	59.1	Haiti	53.2	Jamaica	44.6	Nigeria	43.4
	Nicaragua	55.5	Philippines	53.2	Ethiopia	43.9	Burundi	43.3
	Cuba	54.5	Nicaragua	47.2	China (Taiwan)	43.4	Jamaica	43.2
	Chile	51.3	Brazil	40.1	New Guinea	42.7	Algeria	42.5
	Brazil	49.0			Costa Rica	40.7	Rwanda	41.1
	Uruguay	43.4			Ecuador	40.7		
					Surinam	40.6		
					Philippines	40.4		

78

Thailand	29.3	Ethiopia	39.8	Colombia	37.7	Venezuela	39.7
Lebanon	23.3	Venezuela	39.0	Venezuela	37.7	Costa Rica	39.5
Netherlands Antilles	23.0	Chile	36.5	Iceland	36.7	Panama	38.7
		Peru	35.9	Nicaragua	35.2	China (Taiwan)	37.5
		Jamaica	35.7	Hong Kong	35.0	El Salvador	36.6
		El Salvador	33.7	British Honduras	32.3	Philippines	36.0
		Netherlands Antilles	32.3	Japan	31.6	Colombia	33.6
		Japan	25.3	Guatemala	30.7	Surinam	33.5
				Peru	28.7	Uganda	33.4
Medium Dependence		Trinidad-Tobago	24.5	Brazil	26.2	Guatemala	33.0
		Indonesia	23.8	Guyana	25.9	Korea, South	32.3
				Ghana	24.3	Nicaragua	31.2
				El Salvador	22.8	Barbados	30.9
						Hong Kong	29.1
						Iceland	28.9
						Ethiopia	27.9
						Guinea Republic	27.3
						Bolivia	26.6
						Libya	26.6
						Peru	24.6
						Japan	23.7
						Zambia	22.9
		Angola	19.4	Israel	19.4	Brazil	18.2
Japan	14.0	Turkey	18.8	India	16.6	Israel	18.1
Low Dependence		Hong Kong	17.0	Spain	15.4	Ghana	17.2
Switzerland	12.7	Israel	16.0	United Kingdom	11.9	Bangladesh	16.1
		United Kingdom	7.8	Pakistan	10.1	United Kingdom	9.6

Source: Compiled by the authors.

ence category; all but one of these 17 nations are in the Western Hemisphere. These data demonstrate the high degree of dominance which the United States maintained over the external economic relations of North and South American nations. The nations in the low dependence category are two of the most economically advanced countries in the hierarchy, Japan and Switzerland. This inverse relationship between the level of economic development and the level of trade with the largest trading partner is found throughout all of the hierarchies. Such a relationship should be expected since the more advanced nations tend to have a greater number of trading partners, resulting in relatively less trade with their largest markets than is the case with developing nations.

The data in Table 5.1 show that some changes took place in the distribution of proportionate trade between the United States and its hierarchy from 1951 to 1961. The United States maintained its hegemony over the Western Hemisphere during this period, although the degree of dependence had lessened somewhat. Most of the nations that had been in the high dependence category in 1951 remained there in 1961, but in many cases their levels of dependence were not as great as they had been in 1951. The expansion that occurred in the U.S. hierarchy between 1951 and 1961 was not characterized by the addition of nations that had a high level of dependence on the U.S. market. Three relatively small nations that were "new" to the U.S. hierarchy in 1961 had a high level of dependence, the Bahamas, Surinam, and the Dominican Republic. The other nations added to the U.S. hierarchy between 1951 and 1961 were all in the medium and low dependence categories. The combined effect of the reduction of the level of exports to the U.S. among nations in the high dependence category and the addition of nations to the U.S. hierarchy that were not highly dependent on the U.S. market was to reduce the mean proportion of exports among nations in the hierarchy from 55.5 percent in 1951 to 44.3 percent in 1961.*

In 1971 several nations remained highly dependent upon the U.S. market, but several quantitative and qualitative changes had occurred since 1961. The nations in the high dependence category still were located primarily in the Western Hemisphere, but they mostly repre-

---

*Mean proportion of exports is calculated by simply summing the export percentages of all attached countries and dividing by the number of countries. Such a mean is therefore unweighted and highly aggregate. It is employed in the analysis as a general indicator of the level of attachment that the nations in a hierarchy have to the dominant nation, but its aggregate nature should be recognized.

sented the smallest nations in this region. The larger South American nations of Brazil and Colombia had dropped into the medium dependence group. The high dependence category in 1971 also included more nations from outside the Western Hemisphere; South Korea, Ethiopia, China (Taiwan), and Burundi had all become highly dependent upon the U.S. market. However, the mean level of proportionate ties to the U.S. market dropped slightly between 1961 and 1971, from 44.3 percent to 40.1 percent.

The character of the dependence ties between the United States and the nations in its hierarchy continued to change through 1976. While the number of nations directly linked to the United States grew between 1971 and 1976, the mean proportion of exports to the United States from these nations fell from 40.1 percent to 37.6 percent. Several of the nations that had previously been highly dependent upon the U.S. market had dropped into the medium dependence category: Costa Rica, Panama, Surinam, China (Taiwan), and the Philippines. Brazil had moved into the low dependence category. The high dependence category was developing a different composition, with more than one-third of the nations falling into this group being countries from Africa: Nigeria, Angola, People's Republic of the Congo, Burundi, Algeria, and Rwanda.

The reduction in the dependence of the nations in the U.S. hierarchy upon the U.S. market is probably greater than the figures indicate. As noted, in 1976 a large percentage of the high dependence nations were located in Africa, and it is doubtful that trade relations between those nations and the United States are stabilized to the point that it could be expected that they will all remain in the U.S. hierarchy. Between 1951 and 1976 the African nations in general have shown less stability in their trade relations than have nations in any other region of the world. Meanwhile, the nations that have consistently resided in the U.S. hierarchy tend to be reducing their dependence upon the U.S. market. Table 5.2 identifies the nations that have been linked to the United States since at least 1961 and presents the proportionate exports of each nation to the United States during each of the years of the study. The table shows that most of the nations that have been linked to the United States since 1961 have become decreasingly dependent upon the U.S. market. This is particularly true for the nations in the Western Hemisphere, long considered to be "periphery" nations to the United States. Very few nations have substantially increased their dependence on the United States, and those that have tend to be among the smallest countries in the hierarchy, such as Trinidad-Tobago, Jamaica, and Haiti. This trend is not without exceptions: Canada has increased its dependence upon the U.S. market; Venezuela has remained relatively constant; Japan has varied, but not in a clearly identifiable direction. For most of the nations, how-

TABLE 5.2

UNITED STATES HIERARCHY: Historical Export Percentages

Country	1951	1961	1971	1976
North America				
Canada	59.1	54.6	66.0	64.7
Mexico	70.5	60.8	61.0	55.7
South America, Central America, and Other Western Hemisphere Countries				
Brazil	49.0	40.1	26.2	18.2
Colombia	81.4	59.8	37.7	33.6
Costa Rica	76.9	58.3	40.7	39.5
Dominican Republic	—	62.3	74.4	69.5
Ecuador	60.0	61.1	40.7	44.0
El Salvador	86.1	33.7	22.8	36.6
Guatemala	87.8	53.3	30.7	33.0
Haiti	59.5	53.2	65.0	75.3
Honduras	72.9	63.8	56.3	54.0
Jamaica	—	35.7	44.6	43.2
Netherlands Antilles	23.0	32.3	58.8	52.8
Nicaragua	55.5	47.2	35.2	31.2
Panama	81.9	93.9	49.0	38.7
Peru	—	35.9	28.7	24.6
Surinam	—	74.6	40.6	33.5
Trinidad and Tobago	—	24.5	45.2	69.2
Venezuela	—	39.0	37.7	39.7
Middle East				
Israel	—	16.0	19.4	18.1
Asia				
Hong Kong	—	17.0	35.0	29.1
Japan	14.0	25.3	31.6	23.7
Philippines	63.1	53.2	40.4	36.0
Africa				
Ethiopia	—	39.8	43.9	27.9

Source: Compiled by the authors.

DEPENDENCY PATTERNS AMONG NATIONS / 83

ever, the trend is one of decreased dependence upon the U.S. market.

United Kingdom

Throughout the period of the study, the United Kingdom has not had the level of ties with its hierarchy that has been the case for the United States. Table 5.3 shows that even in 1951, when the United Kingdom had its own hierarchy, only a minority of the directly linked nations had a high level of dependence on the U.K. market. Ten of the nations and territories were in the high dependence category in 1951. Approximately one-third of the nations in the U.K. hierarchy were in the low dependence category, including most of the European nations that were linked to the United Kingdom in 1951. A possible explanation of the relatively low level of dependence exhibited by the nations within the U.K. hierarchy, including the United Kingdom's colonies at the time, relates to the wide geographic area covered by the hierarchy. The hierarchy covered every part of the world. Thus, given the propensity noted in Chapter 4 for nations to trade with proximate nations, the geographically dispersed nature of the countries linked to the United Kingdom meant that these countries might also have significant trade relations with neighboring states. In addition, some of the empire (east Africa, for example) were not part of the imperial preference system established in the 1930s in an effort to cope with the problems of the Great Depression (O'Conner, 1971, pp. 179-80). The United States, on the other hand, was characterized by a high level of dependence from the countries in its hierarchy at least partially because it was the only proximate major market in the Western Hemisphere.

The distribution of export proportions among the attached nations in the U.K. hierarchy did not show substantial change between 1951 and 1976. The mean proportionate exports to the United Kingdom from the directly-linked nations in the hierarchy is 36.2 percent in 1951, 35.0 percent in 1961, 31.2 percent in 1971, and 29.2 percent in 1976. The overall levels of attachment thus have decreased at a slower rate than those for the United States. It might have been expected that the level of attachment would have decreased at a faster rate, since the United Kingdom had lost considerable stature in the international economic community during the time period.

The constantly decreasing number of countries attached to the United Kingdom throughout the four years of the study causes some difficulties in analyzing the dependency trends. It should be noted, however, that by 1976 the data in Table 5.3 indicate most of the nations highly dependent upon the U.K. market are very small. Ireland

TABLE 5.3

UNITED KINGDOM: Export Percentages from Attached Nations

	1951		1961		1971		1976	
High Dependence	Sierra Leone	88.7	Mauritius	81.8	Ireland	65.9	Mauritius	68.0
	Ireland	83.9	Sierra Leone	79.0	Sierra Leone	62.3	Ireland	48.7
	Nigeria	76.4	Ireland	74.4	Mauritius	52.1	Sierra Leone	43.9
	Sudan	66.5	British Honduras	55.8	Bolivia	45.8	Fiji	40.0
	Mauritius	61.0	Gambia	51.7	Malawi	44.4		
	Jamaica	59.4	Fiji	51.5	Cyprus	41.3		
	Northern Rhodesia	58.0	Barbados	50.8	Malta	40.4		
	New Zealand	57.4	New Zealand	50.8				
	South Africa	56.6	Bolivia	49.2				
	Dominican Republic	50.2	Rhodesia and Nyasaland	46.4				
	Gold Coast	41.4	Nigeria	44.1				
	Tanganyika	41.2						
Medium Dependence	Southern Rhodesia	38.7	Cyprus	36.6	Gambia	38.9	Belize	39.7
	Denmark	38.2	Libya	35.9	Barbados	33.8	Malawi	32.3
	British Persian Gulf States	33.3	Tanganyika	34.8	Qatar	31.9	Gambia	29.8
			South Africa	32.9	New Zealand	31.8	Norway	29.4
			Kuwait	32.7	Fiji	28.9	Cyprus	27.3

Australia	32.7	Ceylon		South Africa	26.8	Portugal	22.7
Israel	32.4	(Sri Lanka)	29.2	Portugal	22.6	Guyana	22.5
Ceylon		Ghana	28.8	Uganda	21.8	Qatar	20.9
(Sri Lanka)	30.8	Malta	26.1	Nigeria	21.6		
Kenya	30.0	Denmark	24.8	Tanzania	21.3		
Uganda	30.0	India	24.6				
Trinidad–Tobago	27.7	Uruguay	24.2				
Finland	27.3	Iceland	24.1				
India	25.3	Kenya	22.4				
Peru	23.9	Finland	21.6				
Iceland	23.3	Norway	20.7				
Malaya–Singapore	20.0						
Norway	19.8	Australia	19.7	Finland	19.0	New Zealand	18.1
Argentina	19.7	Bahrain	19.6	Denmark	18.9	Denmark	17.1
Portugal	19.6	Sudan	19.2	Norway	18.8	South Africa	14.6
Egypt	19.2	Argentina	18.0	Kuwait	17.8	Sweden	11.3
Sweden	18.9	Spain	16.9	Ceylon		Ceylon	
Yugoslavia	18.4	Pakistan	14.5	(Sri Lanka)	17.1	(Sri Lanka)	10.8
Iran	17.3	Portugal	13.5	Sweden	13.5		
Netherlands	15.6	Aden (Yemen)	12.0	Yemen, P.D.R.	11.7		
Spain	15.6						
Italy	13.5						
Ethiopia	9.1						

Low
Dependence

Source: Compiled by the authors.

is by far the largest nation within the group of high dependence countries in 1976.

Table 5.4 shows the proportion of exports to the U.K. market from the countries that have been linked to the United Kingdom since 1961. A pattern of diminishing dependence upon the U.K. market is apparent in this table, particularly among the larger nations that have been in the hierarchy throughout the period. Denmark, Ireland, South Africa, and New Zealand, while still more dependent upon the U.K. market than any other, have become decreasingly attached throughout the time period. This same pattern exists for the smaller nations of

TABLE 5.4

UNITED KINGDOM HIERARCHY: Historical Export Percentages

Country	1951	1961	1971	1976
Europe				
Denmark	38.2	24.8	18.9	17.1
Ireland	83.9	74.4	65.9	48.7
Norway	19.8	20.7	18.8	29.4
Portugal	19.6	13.5	22.6	18.3
Middle East				
Cyprus	—	36.6	41.3	27.3
Africa				
Gambia	—	51.7	38.9	29.8
Mauritius	61.0	81.1	52.1	68.0
Sierra Leone	88.7	79.0	62.3	43.9
South Africa	56.6	32.9	26.8	14.6
Asia				
Ceylon (Sri Lanka)	30.8	29.2	17.1	10.8
Other Countries				
Fiji	68.9	51.5	28.9	40.0
New Zealand	57.4	50.8	31.8	18.1

Source: Compiled by the authors.

Sri Lanka and Sierra Leone. Many of the remaining nations in the table show considerable variation in the percentage of exports they have sent to the United Kingdom. These data provide further evidence of the decline of the United Kingdom's role in the world. Its hierarchy is becoming smaller, and at the same time the links that remain in the hierarchy are becoming weaker.

Japan

Japan has not had a significant associated hierarchy throughout the 25 years covered by the study. It has only been since 1971 that a substantial number of nations have been linked directly to Japan. Even within this relatively brief time period, however, certain trends can be seen in the dependency relationships that appear to be forming within the Japanese hierarchy (see Table 5.5).

Many of the nations linked to Japan in 1971 and particularly in 1976 were oil producing nations. Thus, it is probably not realistic to refer to those nations as being dependent upon the Japanese market during this period of an extreme sellers' market for petroleum. The discussion of the dependency relationships within the Japanese hierarchy will therefore focus upon the nations that are not members of OPEC.

The very fact that the Japanese hierarchy has experienced considerable growth since 1961 implies an overall growth in dependence upon the Japanese market. The principal economic nations attached to Japan in 1976 are Australia, India, Pakistan, Indonesia, and Thailand. Of these five nations, only Indonesia would be considered highly dependent upon the Japanese market, and a large percentage of these exports probably consisted of petroleum. Australia and Thailand, however, have become increasingly dependent upon the Japanese market since becoming attached to Japan, although both are grouped in the medium dependence category in 1976. Thailand sent only 13.7 percent of its exports to Japan in 1961, but by 1971 that figure had reached 24.8 percent and remained almost the same in 1976. Australia was not even in the Japanese hierarchy in 1961, but in 1971 was shipping 27.8 percent of its exports to Japan. In 1976 Australia had increased its dependence upon the Japanese market to 33.7 percent. India and Pakistan are shown in the low dependence category in 1976, and it is too early to accurately predict the prospects for their future dependence upon the Japanese market. However, if the regional concentrations of trading activities continue to evolve, then India and Pakistan may become increasingly dependent upon Japanese markets for their exports.

TABLE 5.5

JAPAN: Export Percentages from Attached Nations

	1951		1961		1971		1976	
High Dependence	China (Taiwan)	66.6	Ryukyus	87.4	Brunei	96.2	Brunei	79.4
	Korea, South	59.3	Korea, South	50.9	Ryukyus	85.1	Oman	43.3
					New Caledonia	47.0	Indonesia	41.7
					United Arab Emirates	44.1		
					Indonesia	43.8		
Medium Dependence			Paraguay	20.9	China (Taiwan)	28.9	Iran	33.7
					Oman	36.4		
					Australia	33.6	Papua and New Guinea	32.6
					Thailand	27.8	United Arab Emirates	27.6
					Zambia	24.8	Thailand	25.7
						20.5	Kuwait	23.6
							Malaysia	21.1
Low Dependence					Saudi Arabia	14.3	Chile	19.1	Iran	19.8
					Thailand	13.7	Saudi Arabia	17.1	Saudi Arabia	19.6
									Bahrain	18.8
									Chad	16.8
									India	12.3
									Pakistan	8.3

Source: Compiled by the authors.

DEPENDENCY PATTERNS AMONG NATIONS / 89

West Germany

The nations in the West German hierarchy have never exhibited a high level of dependency on the German market. Over the four years of the study, Table 5.6 shows that not one nation is placed in the high dependency category. The nations in the West German hierarchy have shown a rather even split between the medium and low dependency categories.

One explanation for the relatively low level of dependence that the attached nations have upon the German market is that these nations tend to be located in Europe, and they tend to be relatively economically advanced. The European location places these nations in close proximity to several other large national markets for exports. Thus, the exports of European nations are more likely to be divided among a number of countries. The relative level of economic advancement would also imply lower dependence upon the dominant market, since, as noted above, there tends to be an inverse relationship between economic development and the level of dependence upon the largest trading partner.

It was not until 1976 that the nations attached directly to West Germany contained more countries from outside of Europe than inside. In this year, the West German hierarchy consisted of nations from Africa, South America, and Asia, as well as the traditional attachments from Europe. Most of the nations that joined the hierarchy more recently are in the low dependence category in 1976. It is therefore too early to predict whether the addition of these nations represents a stable pattern of growth of Germany's economic influence.

Table 5.7 shows the dependency levels of the nations directly linked to West Germany since 1961. The figures in the table indicate very little variation in the levels of dependence upon the German market among these nations. Only the Netherlands shows a notable increase in dependence since 1961. The other nations tend to vary around a central point or show slight decreases in their dependence on the German market. It appears, therefore, that despite the expansion that has consistently characterized the West German hierarchy, the level of potential influence that Germany has over its attached nations is not as great as that of the United States throughout the period. In addition, the figures do not suggest that Germany's potential influence over its hierarchy is going to increase in the future.

France

It was noted in Chapter 4 that France had been able to maintain strong trading relationships with its former empire to a considerably

TABLE 5.6

WEST GERMANY: Export Percentages from Attached Nations

	1951		1961		1971		1976	
	Turkey	26.6	Congo, Brazzaville	30.7	Netherlands	33.7	Netherlands	31.0
	Cyprus	26.2	Austria	27.5	Algeria	26.0	Malta	24.5
			Iran	23.7	Belgium	25.3	Liberia	24.4
			Netherlands	23.1	Congo, People's Republic	23.7	Austria	23.4
Medium Dependence					Austria	22.9	Belgium	23.2
					Italy	22.7	Macao	22.7
					Liberia	22.3	Greece	21.6
					France	21.1		
					Greece	20.2		
	Greece	19.9	Greece	18.9	Turkey	19.4	Turkey	19.2
	Austria	15.1	Italy	17.9	Macao	16.8	Italy	19.0
			Switzerland	17.9	Switzerland	15.2	Afghanistan	18.4
			Sweden	15.7	Uruguay	11.7	France	16.9
Low Dependence			France	15.2			Switzerland	15.6
							Tanzania	13.8
							Chile	13.7
							Uruguay	13.0
							Kenya	12.7

Source: Compiled by the authors.

TABLE 5.7

WEST GERMAN HIERARCHY: Historical Export Percentages

Country	1951	1961	1971	1976
Europe				
Austria	15.1	27.5	22.9	23.4
France	—	15.2	21.1	16.9
Greece	19.9	18.9	20.2	21.6
Italy	—	17.9	22.7	19.0
Netherlands	—	23.1	33.7	31.0
Switzerland	—	17.9	15.2	15.6

Source: Compiled by the authors.

greater extent than the United Kingdom. While some of the nations arising out of the old French empire became attached to other hierarchies, the majority retained France as their major export market. The data presented in Table 5.8, however, suggest that despite the continuation of primary attachment to the French market, most of these nations have been continually decreasing their level of dependence on the French market.

By 1961 most of the French empire had obtained independence, particularly the colonies in Africa. Table 5.8 shows that in 1961 most of these former colonies were highly dependent upon the French market for their exports. Of the 22 nations and territories directly attached to France in 1961, 17 are in the high dependence category, and none are in the low dependence category. The figures for 1971 portray a significant change in the dependence of the nations in the hierarchy on the French market. Only slightly more than half of the 17 directly linked nations are in the high dependence group in 1971, and the mean level of dependence on the French market dropped from 64.4 percent in 1961 to 47.2 percent in 1971; a substantial reduction, but it still indicates a relatively high level of dependence on the French market among the attached nations.

The level of dependence on the French market dropped substantially further from 1971 to 1976. In 1976 only seven of the 20 attached nations could be considered highly dependent on France, and the mean level of dependency went to 41.0 percent. The reduction of French influence in its former colonies is even greater than indicated by these

TABLE 5.8

FRANCE: Export Percentages from Attached Nations

	1951		1961		1971		1976
	Madagascar	73.2	Martinique	100.0	Martinique	94.9	Guadeloupe	84.9
	French Equatorial		Mauritania	100.0	Reunion	83.1	Niger	82.7
	Africa	73.2	Guadeloupe	99.0	Guadeloupe	75.6	Reunion	75.8
	French West		Niger	95.6	Niger	69.8	Martinique	70.4
	Africa	72.1	Reunion	92.5	Gabon	54.1	New Hebrides	69.7
	Algeria	68.3	Algeria	81.9	Central African		Senegal	54.5
	Cameroun	61.8	Central African		Republic	51.9	New Caledonia	50.9
	Tunisia	45.2	Republic	77.5	Senegal	51.9		
			Senegal	76.2	Vietnam, South	43.9		
			Chad	74.9	Dahomey (Benin)	42.1		
High			Dahomey (Benin)	72.7				
Dependence			Mali Republic	59.2				
			Cameroun	59.0				
			Gabon	55.8				
			Tunisia	54.9				
			Malagasy					
			Republic	54.4				
			Ivory Coast	51.7				
			Togo	49.5				

	French Morocco	39.9	Morocco	36.8	Central African Empire	36.8
	Indo-China	37.9	Vietnam, South	36.1	Mali Republic	34.7
	Iraq	26.5	Liberia	36.1	Togo	34.3
			Qatar	31.9	Mali Republic	34.2
			Guinea Republic	20.3	Malagasy Republic	33.4
					Ivory Coast	31.5
					Togo	27.1
					Cameroun	21.5
					Mauritania	
Medium Dependence			Morocco		Central African Empire	38.2
			Oman		Togo	36.9
			Malagasy Republic		Mali Republic	32.3
			Ivory Coast		Malagasy Republic	28.8
			Togo		Ivory Coast	25.2
			Cameroun		Cameroun	24.8
			Mauritania		Morocco	24.0
					Mauritania	22.8
					Gabon	22.5
					Upper Volta	22.4
					Benin	21.8
Low Dependence	Saudi Arabia	19.2	Chad	16.6	Iraq	17.5
					Spain	14.5

Source: Compiled by the authors.

TABLE 5.9

FRENCH HIERARCHY: Historical Export Percentages

Country	1951	1961	1971	1976
South America, Central America, and Other Western Hemisphere Countries				
Guadeloupe	—	99.0	75.6	85.0
Martinique	—	100.0	94.9	70.4
Africa				
French Equatorial Africa	73.2			
Central African Republic		77.5	51.9	38.2
Gabon		55.8	54.1	22.5
French West Africa	72.1			
Dahomey (Benin)		72.7	42.1	21.8
Ivory Coast		51.7	33.4	25.2
Mali Republic		59.2	34.7	32.3
Mauritania		100.0	21.5	22.8
Niger		95.6	69.8	82.6
Senegal		76.2	51.9	54.5
Other Africa				
Cameroun	61.8	59.0	27.1	24.8
Malagasy Republic	73.2	54.4	34.2	28.8
Morocco	39.9	36.8	36.8	24.0
Reunion	—	92.5	83.1	75.8
Togo	—	49.5	31.5	36.9

Source: Compiled by the authors.

figures. The highly dependent nations tend to be very small economic entities, many of them small island nations or territories.

The diminution of French influence over its former colonies is portrayed more clearly in Table 5.9. This table shows the percent of exports sent to France by all nations that have been directly linked to France since 1961. It can be seen that most of the nations are characterized by diminishing levels of dependence on the French market for their exports. The decreases have been constant since 1961, and there are only a few exceptions to this observation. Therefore, even though France has remained the primary market for the exports of much of its former empire, the strength of these ties tends to be constantly decreasing. It is probably safe to predict that this erosion in French influence will continue into the future with respect to its old empire.

Summary

Most of the hierarchies have been characterized by a decreasing level of dependence between the dominant and subordinate countries with respect to the proportion of subordinate nations' exports going to the dominant country. This has particularly been the case for the hierarchies that have been an outgrowth of the periphery-core relationships of the 1950s. The United States, the United Kingdom, and France are all accounting for smaller proportions of their attached nations' exports, and it could be projected that this trend will continue. West Germany and Japan represent exceptions to this observation, each in a different manner. The nations linked to Germany tend to be among the more advanced nations of the world, and thus have never been highly dependent upon their largest export market. Japan's hierarchy did not really exist to any great extent until 1971, which makes it difficult to plot trends. On the basis of limited information, however, it appears that Japan may be expanding its influence over its attached countries, and that this is occurring especially within Southeast Asia and Oceania.

DEPENDENCY OF NATIONAL ECONOMY ON DOMINANT NATIONS

The discussion in Chapter 2 noted that dependency theorists often consider the proportion of a nation's economy represented by exports to the core nation to be an indicator of the level of dependency that exists between the countries. The greater the reliance of a nation's economy upon the core nation, the greater the dependency. The direct relationship between the economy and level of dependency is probably not linear, since at relatively low levels it is difficult to posit the existence of economic dependence. However, after a certain point is reached in the proportion of a nation's economy that is represented by exports to a dominant nation, the level of dependence may increase at an increasing rate. Alternatively, the nonlinear relationship between dependency and the level of the economy represented by trade could be explained by Richardson and Kegley's (1977) idea that a threshold level of trade ties exists that is more important in determining dependency than the absolute level of trade ties.

The exact point at which a nation's economy becomes highly dependent upon its exports to one other nation is difficult to estimate. Richardson (1976) placed the export percentage of GNP indicative of a high level of dependence at 5 percent. His figure was based on Singer's (1972) suggestion that if a nation's total trade (exports and imports) with one other nation represents 10 percent or more of its GNP, the nation is economically dependent upon its trading partner. The present study employs cutoff points that are based on the work of Richardson and Singer, with some modification made to provide a clearer presentation of the data.

The measure of economic dependence used in the present study is the percentage of a nation's Gross Domestic Product (GDP) represented by exports to the dominant nation in the hierarchy. As in the analysis of the proportion of trade to the dominant nation, the analysis of the GDP figures will only include nations that are directly tied to one of the five dominant nations, the United States, West Germany, the United Kingdom, France, and Japan. All nations that are tied to one of these five countries through third nations are excluded from the analysis.

Gross Domestic Product is employed as the measure of the national economy primarily on the basis of availability. This is the most available indicator of gross economic size that appears in national account data, and thus permits the most extensive analysis of dependency ties. The primary data sources used to obtain GDP figures were the International Monetary Fund's <u>International Financial Statistics</u> and the United Nations' <u>Statistical Yearbook</u>. It should be noted that, in general, GDP figures are not as reliable as the trade figures employed in the previous analyses. Their reliability is highly dependent upon the statistical data gathering facilities of the individual countries, and considerable variability exists in this respect. Due to the variable reliability, the figures that are provided in these analyses should be viewed in more of a general, rather than a specific, context, and small differences should not be viewed as significant. A second problem related to the use of national account statistics such as GDP is that they are not as universally available as trade statistics. Thus, some nations had to be omitted from these analyses because GDP data were not available, or only available in certain years.

The formal analysis of the proportion of GDP was performed in essentially the same manner as the analysis for proportion of trade presented in the first part of this chapter. The percentage of GDP represented by exports to the dominant nation was calculated for each of the attached nations in 1951, 1961, 1971, and 1976. The derived percentages were then used to place each nation in each year of the study into one of three categories based on the level of dependence on the dominant nation. A <u>high</u> level of dependence was considered to exist if the nation's exports to the dominant country equalled or exceeded 10 percent of its GDP. The 10 percent figure as an indicator of high dependence is higher than suggested by Richardson, but is more consistent with the derived data. A medium level of dependence is indicated by a proportion of GDP represented by exports to the dominant nation that is between 5 and 10 percent. Finally, a low level of dependence is said to exist if the export proportion of GDP to the dominant nation is less than 5 percent. The hierarchies associated with each of the five dominant nations are examined over the time period of the study, and the trends in the level of dependence of the attached nations in each hierarchy are discussed.

United States

The previous analysis of the proportion of exports showed that the nations in the U.S. hierarchy are tending to become relatively less dependent upon the U.S. markets for their exports (see Tables 5.1 and 5.2). The proportionate GDP data presented in Table 5.10 for the United States, however, suggest that any conclusion concerning a diminution of dependence upon the U.S. market will have to be heavily qualified, if not retracted. Table 5.10 shows that in 1951 there was the tendency for nations in the U.S. hierarchy to exhibit a medium level of dependence upon the U.S. market with respect to their economies. In most of the cases, the medium dependent nations in terms of GDP were nations that had shipped over 40 percent of their exports to the United States in 1951. Relatively few nations were in the high dependence GDP category in 1951, and all of these nations are in the Western Hemisphere. The low dependence category also contained very few nations (for which GDP data were available), and two of the three nations in this category were economically advanced nations located outside of the Western Hemisphere, Japan and Switzerland.

The 1961 data in Table 5.10 include several more nations than are shown in 1951. The additional nations are due to the growth in the U.S. hierarchy during that time period, as well as to the increased availability of national account data for 1961. With the exception of Hong Kong, all of the countries that were at the high or medium dependence level in 1961 are located in the Western Hemisphere. Most of the low dependence countries are located outside of the Western Hemisphere. The overall trend between 1951 and 1961 appears to be toward less dependence upon the United States among the attached nations, although the majority of the nations were still in the high or medium category in 1961. The mean proportion of GDP represented by the nation's exports to the United States dropped from 8.0 percent in 1951 to 7.2 percent in 1961.

TABLE 5.10

UNITED STATES: Exports as a Percentage of GDP from Attached Nations

	1951		1961		1971		1976	
High Dependence	Costa Rica	18.7	Surinam	29.3	Hong Kong	30.5	Honduras	18.4
	Dominican Republic	12.3	Trinidad and Tobago	14.4	Surinam	22.1	Republic of China (Taiwan)	17.7
	Haiti	11.4	Dominican Republic	12.8	Honduras	16.1	Surinam	15.2[2]
	Canada	10.7	Venezuela	11.7	Guyana	14.5	Canada	13.3
	Honduras	10.0	Hong Kong	11.5	China (Taiwan)	13.9	Dominican Republic	12.7
			Honduras	10.9	Canada	12.8	Venezuela	12.5[1]
					Jamaica	10.9	El Salvador	12.4
					Dominican Republic	10.0	Ecuador	10.9
Medium Dependence	Guatemala	9.7	Costa Rica	9.4	Venezuela	9.8	Costa Rica	9.9
	Colombia	9.1	Jamaica	8.8	Costa Rica	9.0	Korea, South	9.8
	Nicaragua	8.9	Canada	8.5	Iceland	9.0	Zambia	9.3
	Thailand	7.6	Nicaragua	8.0	Nicaragua	7.3	Nicaragua	9.3
	Mexico	7.2	Peru	7.5	Haiti	6.7	Barbados	9.1[1]
	Philippines	6.8	El Salvador	7.0	Philippines	5.9	Jamaica	8.6
	Ecuador	6.7	Ecuador	6.5	Korea, South	5.8	Iceland	7.9[1]
	Chile	5.4	Haiti	6.4			Bolivia	7.6[1]
	Brazil	5.3	Colombia	5.6			Ghana	6.9[2]

		Guatemala	5.5			Haiti	6.5[1]
						Guatemala	6.4
						Panama	5.5
						Philippines	5.2
Panama	3.5	Philippines	4.8	Ecuador	4.8	Colombia	3.5[1]
Switzerland	1.6	Panama	4.4	El Salvador	4.8	Israel	3.5
Japan	1.3	Chile	4.1	Panama	4.8	Peru	2.8
		Mexico	3.8	Guatemala	4.4	Ethiopia	2.4[2]
		Ethiopia	3.1	Ghana	3.8	Mexico	2.4
		Indonesia	2.8	Peru	3.8	Japan	2.3[1]
		Brazil	2.7	Colombia	3.4	United Kingdom	2.0
Low		Japan	2.1	Japan	3.4	Brazil	1.1[1]
Dependence		Israel	1.3	Ethiopia	2.9		
		United Kingdom	1.1	Israel	2.9		
		Turkey	1.1	Mexico	2.5		
				United Kingdom	1.9		
				Brazil	1.7		
				Spain	1.2		
				India	0.7		
				Pakistan	0.6		

[1] Based on 1975 trade and GDP figures.
[2] Based on 1974 trade and GDP figures.
Source: Compiled by the authors.

The 1971 data indicate the addition of several nations to the low dependency category. Many of these additions were countries that had previously exhibited a medium level of dependence, such as Ecuador, El Salvador, Guatemala, Peru, and Colombia. Other nations new to the low dependency category were not in the U. S. hierarchy in 1961, such as Spain, India, and Pakistan. Conversely, in 1971 some nations had increased their reliance on the United States, such as Canada and Honduras. The most notable difference between the 1961 and 1971 figures is the relatively large number of nations from outside the Western Hemisphere that appear in the high and medium dependence categories, particularly nations from the Far East. In 1951 and 1961, the nations in these categories were almost exclusively from the Western Hemisphere. The general picture that emerges from a comparison of the 1961 and 1971 figures is a mixed one. While there were several more nations in the low dependence category in 1971, there were also more in the high dependence category. The average level of dependence among the attached nations remained virtually unchanged from 1961 to 1971, going from 7.2 percent to 7.5 percent.

The 1976 data in Table 5.10 indicate a change from 1971, although the change is not in the anticipated direction. Contrary to the proportion of trade data for 1976, the GDP data shows a general growth in the level of dependence on the U. S. market. The average level of dependence grew from 7.5 percent to 8.1 percent. Many of the nations that had been in the low dependence category in 1971 were in the medium or high dependence categories in 1976: Ecuador, El Salvador, Panama, Guatemala, and Ghana. In addition, some of the previously low dependence nations, such as Spain, India, and Pakistan, were no longer attached to the United States in 1976.

The data for the United States have thus suggested a slightly U-shaped pattern in the level of dependence of attached nations on the U. S. market, as measured by the proportion of GDP represented by exports to the United States. The level of dependence was relatively high (8.0 percent average) in 1951, dropped to 7.2 percent in 1961, and then increased in 1971 and again in 1976. While average percentages of this type can be misleading, since they combine data from a diverse set of nations, the U-shaped relationship tends to be supported by examining the data from individual countries in the U. S. hierarchy. Table 5.11 presents the percentage of GDP represented by exports to the United States for all nations that had been attached to the United States since at least 1961. The table shows that of the 15 countries attached to the United States for which GDP data were available in 1951, ten had a decrease of greater than 0.5 percent from 1951 to 1961, two remained within ± 0.5 percent, and three nations showed an increase of greater than 0.5 percent. From 1961 to 1971, however, the direction of the country figures is less clear. Of the 23 nations

TABLE 5.11

UNITED STATES HIERARCHY: Historical GDP Percentages

Country	1951	1961	1971	1976
North America				
Canada	10.7	8.5	12.8	13.3
Mexico	7.2	3.8	2.5	2.4
Europe				
United Kingdom	2.2	1.1	1.9	2.0
South America, Central America, and Other Western Hemisphere Countries				
Brazil	5.3	2.7	1.7	1.1^1
Colombia	9.1	5.6	3.4	3.5^1
Costa Rica	18.7	9.4	9.0	9.9
Dominican Republic	12.3	12.8	10.0	12.7
Ecuador	6.7	6.5	4.8	10.9
El Salvador	N/A	7.0	4.8	12.4
Guatemala	9.7	5.5	4.4	6.4
Haiti	11.4	6.4	6.7	6.5^1
Honduras	10.0	10.9	16.1	18.4
Jamaica	—	8.8	10.9	8.6
Nicaragua	8.9	8.0	7.3	9.3
Panama	3.5	4.4	4.8	5.5
Peru	—	7.5	3.8	2.8
Surinam	—	29.3	22.1	15.2^2
Venezuela	—	11.7	9.8	12.5^1
Africa				
Ethiopia	—	3.1	2.9	2.4^2
Middle East				
Israel	—	1.3	2.9	3.5
Asia				
Japan	1.3	2.1	3.4	2.3^1
Korea, South	—	0.8	5.8	9.8
Philippines	6.8	4.8	5.9	5.2

[1] Based on 1975 trade and GDP figures.
[2] Based on 1974 trade and GDP figures.
Source: Compiled by the authors.

included in these two years, eight increased the proportion of GDP by greater than 0.5 percent, eleven nations decreased the percentage by more than 0.5 percent, and four nations remained relatively constant. From 1971 to 1976, however, there was a trend toward an increase in economic dependence upon the U.S. market. Eleven of the 23 nations showed increases, six nations remained relatively constant, and six nations decreased their dependence.

The most striking feature of the percentage of GDP data within the U.S. hierarchy is the level of dependence that most Western Hemisphere nations have on the U.S. economy. Perhaps the most surprising aspect of the data is that the level of dependence that Western Hemisphere nations have on the United States appears to be increasing rather than decreasing. It is true that many of the larger Latin American nations have substantially reduced their levels of dependence upon the United States. Mexico, Brazil, Colombia, and Peru are no longer in the high or medium dependence categories. However, two of the most affluent Western Hemisphere nations appear to be increasing their dependence on the United States, Canada and Venezuela. Further, many of the smaller Latin American republics, such as the Central American countries, have shown substantial increases in their level of dependence on the United States.

Comment on the apparent contradiction between the percentage of trade dependency data and the percentage of GDP dependency data will be withheld until the end of this section. The contradiction that appeared in the U.S. hierarchy data is also found within some of the other hierarchies. Thus, a general discussion will be made following the presentation of the individual hierarchies.

United Kingdom

The percentage of GDP represented by exports to the United Kingdom from nations linked directly to that country during the years of the study is presented in Table 5.12. With the exception of 1951, the number of nations shown in each year reflects the dwindling number of countries for which the United Kingdom is the largest export market. Although the United Kingdom had the greatest number of attached nations in 1951, the paucity of GDP data in that year limited the number of countries that could be shown.

The data available for 1951 indicate a relatively high level of dependence of the attached nations upon the U.K. market. While the nations in the high dependence category tend to be small, several economically advanced nations from Europe and Oceania are included in the medium dependence category. This situation is substantially different in 1961. Few nations that could be considered economically advanced are in the medium or high dependence category in 1961. Many of the advanced nations tied to the United Kingdom in 1951 had become tied to West Germany by 1961. Of those that remained attached to the U.K. market, many had reduced their dependence significantly. Denmark's exports to the United Kingdom represented 9.5 percent of its GDP in 1951, but only 5.8 percent in 1961; New Zealand dropped from 19.5 percent in 1951 to 10.5 percent in 1961. Most of the nations in the medium and high dependence categories in 1961 were from the Third World. Even with the addition of several Third World nations in 1961, many of which had been British colonies, the average GDP of all attached countries dropped from 1951 to 1961, from 8.9 percent to 8.1 percent.

The trend toward fewer and smaller nations in the U.K. hierarchy continued through 1971. In this year the high and medium dependence categories consisted of primarily small Third World nations. Most of the relatively advanced nations that remained attached to the United Kingdom are in the low dependence category in 1971. The average dependency percentage among the nations linked directly to the United Kingdom, however, remained fairly constant at 8.0 percent in 1971. These trends continue in 1976, with one noticeable exception. The number and size of the countries attached to the United Kingdom appear to decline, but the level of dependence that the remaining nations have on the United Kingdom tends to increase. The mean percentage of GDP represented by exports to the United Kingdom rises to 11.3 percent; when Mauritius, seemingly an outlier in the 1976 data, is removed from this computation the mean is 9.1 percent, greater than the 8.0 percent mean in 1971. Thus, the level of dependence appears to be increasing in the most recent year of the study, similar to the findings for the United States.

The pattern of dependency levels within the U.K. hierarchy is more clearly portrayed in Table 5.13. This table presents the percentage of GDP represented by exports to the United Kingdom from the nations which had been directly linked to that nation during at least three of the years of the study. If a difference of greater than ± 0.5 percent is considered to be an increase or decrease in the level of dependency, the following results are found. Of the nine countries for which data were available in both 1951 and 1961, six showed a decrease from 1951 to 1961, two increased, while one remained relatively unchanged. From 1961 to 1971, four to twelve nations decreased their dependence on the United Kingdom, five increased, and three remained constant. From 1971 to 1976, four of ten nations show an increase, four a decrease, and two stay the same.

TABLE 5.12

UNITED KINGDOM: Exports as a Percentage of GDP from Attached Nations

	1951		1961		1971		1976	
	Mauritius	22.1	Mauritius	30.7	Ireland	18.9	Mauritius	40.5[1]
	New Zealand	19.5	Kuwait	25.2	Mauritius	16.9	Ireland	21.9
	Trinidad and Tobago	17.9	Aden (Yemen PDR)	20.6	Gambia	14.7	Guyana	21.7[1]
High	Ireland	17.5	Ireland	19.4	Sierra Leone	13.4	Gambia	11.0
Dependence	Nigeria	15.2	Barbados	16.1	Kuwait	11.1	Sierra Leone	11.9[1]
	Dominican Republic	12.3	Gambia	12.9				
	Ceylon	12.1						
	Jamaica	11.4						
	Denmark	9.5	New Zealand	10.5	Bolivia	8.8	Malawi	9.6
	Australia	7.5	Sierra Leone	9.2	Barbados	8.7	Cyprus	9.2
	Finland	6.9	Bolivia	9.1	Fiji	8.2	Fiji	8.6
Medium	South Africa	5.7	Iceland	7.5	Malawi	8.0	Norway	7.4
Dependence	Netherlands	5.4	Ceylon	7.3	Malta	7.8		
			Ghana	6.5	Cyprus	7.6		
			Nigeria	6.4	Nigeria	7.4		
			Cyprus	5.9	New Zealand	5.9		
			Denmark	5.8	Yemen P.D.R.	5.6		
			South Africa	5.6				

	Sweden	4.8	Finland	4.1	Denmark	4.0
	Norway	4.7	Kenya	4.1	Finland	4.0
	Peru	4.6	Norway	3.9	Uganda	3.9
	Portugal	3.7	Australia	2.9	Norway	3.8
	Israel	2.5	Sudan	2.8	Portugal	3.5
Low	Argentina	1.8	Uruguay	2.7	South Africa	3.0
Dependence	Italy	1.3	Malta	2.5	Sweden	2.8
	Spain	0.8	Portugal	1.7		
			Argentina	1.2		
			India	1.0		
			Spain	1.0		
			Pakistan	0.7		

Denmark	New Zealand	4.0
	South Africa	3.6[1]
	Portugal	3.4
	Sweden	2.9[1]
		2.7

[1] Based on 1975 trade and GDP figures.
Source: Compiled by authors.

TABLE 5.13

UNITED KINGDOM HIERARCHY: Historical GDP Percentages

Country	1951	1961	1971	1976
Europe				
Denmark	9.5	5.8	4.0	4.0
Finland	6.9	4.1	4.0	—
Ireland	17.5	19.4	18.9	21.9
Norway	4.7	3.9	3.8	7.4
Portugal	3.7	1.7	3.5	2.9[1]
Africa				
Gambia	N/A	12.9	14.7	11.0
Mauritius	22.1	30.7	16.9	40.5[1]
Nigeria	15.2	6.4	7.4	—
Sierra Leone	N/A	9.2	13.4	11.9[1]
South Africa	5.7	5.6	3.0	3.4
Middle East				
Cyprus	—	5.9	7.6	9.2
Other Countries				
New Zealand	19.5	10.5	5.9	3.6[1]

[1] Based on 1975 trade and GDP figures.
Source: Compiled by the authors.

Japan

Analysis of dependency patterns within the Japanese hierarchy is difficult due to the relative recency of that hierarchy's existence. Table 5.14 shows the percentage of GDP represented by exports to Japan among the nations in the hierarchy. It can be seen that there is a general trend toward increasing dependency throughout the four years of the study. However, such a conclusion has to be heavily qualified. Most of the nations that appear in the high and medium dependency categories are oil exporters. As mentioned previously, it is difficult to justify strong conclusions concerning the "dependency" of oil exporters on their markets at this time, although this situation could

TABLE 5.14

JAPAN: Exports as a Percentage of GDP from Attached Nations

	1951		1961		1971		1976	
High Dependence			Saudi Arabia	6.7	Saudi Arabia	13.4	Kuwait	21.0[1]
							Saudi Arabia	16.2
							Indonesia	9.6
Medium Dependence					Iran	8.8	Iran	6.1
					Zambia	8.4	Australia	5.4
					Indonesia	5.4		
Low Dependence	China, Taiwan	3.1	China, Taiwan	3.2	Australia	3.9	Thailand	4.8
	Paraguay	2.5	Thailand	2.3	Thailand	2.9	Pakistan	0.7
	Korea, South	2.5	Korea, South	0.8	Chile	1.9	India	0.6[2]

[1]Based on 1975 trade and GDP figures.
[2]Based on 1974 trade and GDP figures.
Source: Compiled by the authors.

change in the future. At the present the situation could be described as one of mutual dependence, at most. Among the few non oil exporting nations for which GDP was available, the trend appears to be in the direction of greater dependence. Australia and Thailand are perhaps the best examples of such nations, since both have shown increases in their dependence upon the Japanese market. More definitive statements about the dependency patterns within the Japanese hierarchy will require the passage of more time.

West Germany

The data in Table 5.15 portray the dependency patterns in terms of GDP percentage for the German hierarchy. The nations that have been attached to Germany over the four years of the study have tended to have a relatively low dependency upon the German market for their exports. In 1951 and 1961 none of the countries in the West German hierarchy were in the high dependency category, very few were in the medium dependency category, while most were in the low dependency category. The average level of dependence in 1951 and 1961 was 3.2 percent and 4.3 percent, respectively. Part of the reason for these low levels of dependency undoubtedly lies in the economic recovery that West Germany was undergoing at the time. Another part of the reason probably lies in the relatively high level of economic development of most of the nations in the German hierarchy and the fact that such nations tend to divide their trade among a number of other nations.

From 1961 to 1971 a perceptible increase occurred in the general level of dependency among the nations within the German hierarchy. The average percentage of GDP represented by exports to West Germany rose from 4.3 percent in 1961 to 5.6 percent in 1971. The Benelux countries and Liberia had become highly dependent upon the West German market. From 1971 to 1976, however, the West German hierarchy remained relatively steady. While some new countries had entered the hierarchy between these two years, the mean level of dependence remained constant at 5.6 percent. Of the nations that had been in the German hierarchy in both 1971 and 1976, none had shifted from one dependency category to another.

The relatively static nature of the German hierarchy is further illustrated in Table 5.16 which portrays the percent of GDP that was shipped to Germany by all nations that have been in the hierarchy since at least 1961. With the exception of the Netherlands, there is little variance in the figures for any of the individual nations since 1961. Thus, the German hierarchy represents a different pattern than those of the United States and the United Kingdom in terms of the dependency patterns of the attached nations.

TABLE 5.15

WEST GERMANY: Exports as a Percentage of GDP from Attached Nations

	1951		1961		1971		1976	
High Dependence					Netherlands	17.5	Netherlands	13.9
					Liberia	11.4	Belgium	10.6[1]
					Belgium	11.2	Liberia	10.2[1]
Medium Dependence	Cyprus	8.1	Iran	9.9			Malta	9.1[1]
			Netherlands	8.1				
Low Dependence	Austria	2.1	Austria	4.7	Austria	4.4	Austria	4.9
	Turkey	1.9	Congo, Brazzaville		Algeria	4.1	Chile	4.8[1]
	Greece	0.8		4.7	Switzerland	3.6	Italy	4.1
			Switzerland	3.8	Italy	3.4	Switzerland	4.0
			Sweden	3.0	France	2.7	Kenya	3.0
			Italy	2.0	Greece	1.2	France	2.8
			France	1.6	Turkey	1.1	Greece	2.5
			Greece	1.1	Uruguay	0.8	Uruguay	2.2[1]
							Turkey	1.0

[1]Based on 1975 trade and GDP figures.
Source: Compiled by the authors.

TABLE 5.16

WEST GERMAN HIERARCHY: Historical GDP Percentages

Country	1951	1961	1971	1976
Europe				
Austria	2.1	4.7	4.4	4.9
France	—	1.6	2.7	2.8
Greece	.8	1.1	1.2	2.5
Italy	—	2.0	3.4	4.1
Netherlands	—	8.1	17.5	13.9
Switzerland	—	3.8	3.6	4.0

Source: Compiled by the authors.

France

The French hierarchy is difficult to analyze over the time period due to the lack of data. In 1951 most of the nations currently in the French hierarchy were parts of French West Africa or French Equatorial Africa, and the GDP data for these areas could not be obtained. In addition, GDP information for many of these countries could not be obtained for the most recent year of the study. Therefore, many of the nations in the French hierarchy have only two years of GDP information, 1961 and 1971.

The GDP data that could be obtained for the nations in the French hierarchy are presented in Table 5.17. Within the confines of the data limitations, the table suggests the existence of the U-shaped pattern of dependency over time among the nations in the French hierarchy. In 1961 eight of the 20 nations listed were in the high dependence category, with most of the remaining nations in the medium dependence category. The mean GDP percentage among the nations in 1961 was 11.5. In 1971 there was a marked decrease in the number of countries in the high dependence category. The medium dependence group in 1971 contained many nations that had been in the high dependence category in 1961. The mean level of dependence had increased to 9.5 percent, although this mean is based on data that are less complete than in 1971. The validity of the increased mean level of dependence in 1976 is further brought into question when analyzing the GDP level of

TABLE 5.17

FRANCE: Exports as a Percentage of GDP from Attached Nations

	1951		1961		1971		1976	
High Dependence	Algeria	17.2	Martinique	36.6	Gabon	23.2	Gabon	18.9[2]
			Guadeloupe	26.7	Guadeloupe	13.2	Senegal	15.7
			Gabon	20.3	Mauritania	10.5	Iraq	11.1[1]
			Reunion	20.0	Reunion	10.5		
			Senegal	15.0	Martinique	10.1		
			Liberia	14.5				
			Ivory Coast	14.2				
			Algeria	11.2				
Medium Dependence	Iraq	5.1	Tunisia	9.8	Ivory Coast	9.6	Togo	8.6[1]
			Cameroun	9.1	Dahomey	9.2	Cameroun	8.5[2]
			Togo	8.0	Senegal	8.2	Ivory Coast	8.3[1]
			Chad	7.6	Central African Republic	8.1		
			Morocco	7.0	Niger	7.3		
			Niger	6.9	Togo	5.9		
			Central African Republic	6.7	Cameroun	5.1		
			Dahomey	6.7				
Low Dependence			Guinea Republic	4.9	Morocco	4.9	Morocco	3.8
			Mali Republic	2.1	Mali Republic	3.0	Spain	1.2
			Mauritania	1.1	Chad	1.9		
			Vietnam, South	0.6	Vietnam, South	.05		

[1]Based on 1975 trade and GDP figures.
[2]Based on 1974 trade and GDP figures.

Source: Compiled by the authors.

112 / THE UNITED STATES AND WORLD TRADE

the nations for which data exist in both 1971 and 1976. Of the six nations for which direct comparisons between 1971 and 1976 can be made (Cameroun, Gabon, Ivory Coast, Morocco, Senegal, and Togo), only three increased their dependence on France, while three decreased their dependence. Thus, it is difficult to draw any conclusions about the level of GDP-related dependence within the French hierarchy.

DEPENDENCY AND INTERDEPENDENCY IN INTERNATIONAL TRADE

At the outset of the chapter it was speculated that trade patterns since 1951 would reflect a trend toward decreasing dependence upon individual core nations and greater overall integration of the nations of the world into the international economic system. Such a trend would suggest that nations are becoming less dependent upon one other nation in their international economic interaction. It would also suggest the existence of greater interdependence within the international economic community. The data that have been examined in this chapter do not permit such conclusions to be drawn without major qualification. While there has been a tendency toward a wider geographic distribution of nations' trade, it cannot be concluded that nations are becoming less economically dependent upon their largest trading partners.

The preceding analyses of trade with nations' largest trading partners focused on the nations within the individual hierarchies. The following analyses will be concerned with trade ties with the largest trading partner on global and regional levels. First, the percentage of exports shipped to the largest trading partner will be analyzed for all of the nations in the study over time. Second, the proportions of these nations' GDPs represented by exports to the largest market will be examined over time.

Proportionate Trade: A Global View

A diminution of proportionate trade with the largest trading partner would suggest that nations are geographically diversifying the structure of their trading relationships. It would further suggest that nations are becoming more integrated into the world economic system. The analyses of the individual hierarchies indicated that such a phenomenon is occurring among the nations that are linked directly to the United States, the United Kingdom, and France. These three dominant nations are perhaps the most significant core nations, representing the traditional colonial or neocolonial system. However, since

TABLE 5.18

Regional Export Percentages to Largest Markets

Area	1951	1961	1971	1976
North America	48.9	44.3	50.2	47.1
Europe	22.1	21.5	23.5	21.5
South America, Central America, and Other Western Hemisphere Countries	55.7	51.8	43.4	40.0
Middle East	38.3	20.5	26.0	26.0
Africa	56.5	53.8	37.9	34.4
Asia	42.4	34.8	35.3	29.6
Oceania Countries	63.7	49.9	43.4	40.8
"World" Average	46.8	39.5	37.1	34.2

Source: Compiled by the authors.

many of the nations of the world are not linked directly to one of these three dominant nations, it is not possible to generalize from these cases to the world as a whole.

Table 5.18 presents the average percentage of exports among the nations of each major region of the world to their largest export markets, in addition to the world averages in each year. The percentage of exports figures for each of the individual countries is presented in Appendix B at the end of the book. The world average shown in Table 5.18 indicates that overall nations are exporting proportionately less to their largest trading partners. The average percentage decreases rather consistently from each year of the study to the next. Over the quarter of a century represented by the years of the study, proportionate exports to the largest market dropped from 46.8 percent to 34.2 percent.

The regional figures shown in Table 5.18 indicate that the overall decrease in proportionate trade was not shared by all of the regions of the world. European nations remained almost constant throughout the four years. North American nations varied in the proportion of exports to the largest market, but do not indicate any consistent pattern. The regions that best reflect the pattern of diminishing export proportions to the largest market are Asia, South America, and Africa.

In the latter two areas, the average proportion of exports to the largest market was over 55 percent in 1951 and 40 percent or less in 1976, while Asian nations dropped from 42.4 percent in 1951 to 29.6 percent in 1976. Significantly, it is in these three areas that most of the so-called "periphery" nations of colonial and neocolonial periods are located.

When taken as a whole, the regional data seem to lead to the general conclusion that nations are becoming less dependent on their largest markets from the standpoint of their proportionate exports to these markets. It seems particularly appropriate to conclude that many periphery nations appear to be lessening their relative reliance upon traditional core countries. However, this conclusion must be qualified. Many of the periphery countries located in Asia have not decreased their proportionate exports to their largest markets. Likewise, the smaller economically advanced nations located in Europe, shown to be dependent upon the larger industrialized states, have not tended to decrease their relative reliance upon their largest markets. The periphery nations that have shown a tendency to reduce their relative dependence on their largest markets are those that had been characterized by very high (greater than 50 percent) export concentrations in the past.

Proportionate GDP: A Global View

While the proportionate export figures seem to support the general contention that reliance upon nations' largest international markets is diminishing, such is not the case with regard to global and regional figures concerning the dependence of nations' economies on their largest export markets. The analyses of the United States hierarchy, and to a lesser extent the United Kingdom and French hierarchies, indicated a slight U-shaped pattern with respect to the dependence of the linked nations' economies on their largest export markets. The regional and world figures represented in Table 5.19 also suggest a pattern of increasing dependence upon the largest export market, although it does not take the U-shaped form indicated in the hierarchy analyses.

The average world percentages of GDP represented by exports to the largest market indicate a rather constant level of dependence through 1971 and an upswing in 1976. The only regions to follow the U-shaped pattern, however, are Africa and North America, and the data from Africa must be qualified by the fact that only a small number of territories are included in 1951. The other regions of the world showed different tendencies. South America and the Middle East both showed an increase in GDP dependence from 1951 to 1961, a decrease

TABLE 5.19

Regional Exports to Largest Markets as a Percentage of GDP

Area	1951	1961	1971	1976
North America	6.2	4.3	5.4	5.7
Europe	4.2	4.3	5.3	5.5
South America, Central America, and other Western Hemisphere Countries	9.2	10.5	8.4	10.8
Middle East	4.8	7.4	6.2	8.5
Africa	15.1	9.7	7.6	9.3
Asia	5.9	3.6	7.2	6.7
Oceania	13.5	6.7	6.0	5.7
"World" Average	7.3	7.6	7.1	8.2

Source: Compiled by the authors.

from 1961 to 1971, and an increase from 1971 to 1976. Europe had a slow but steady increase throughout the years of the study, while Asia portrayed an erratic pattern of GDP dependence. Despite the different patterns within the areas of the world, all of the regions but Asia and Oceania showed an increase in average GDP dependence from 1971 to 1976. (GDP figures for the individual nations are presented in Appendix C.)

An increase in the percentage of GDP represented by exports to largest export markets suggests a general increase in the level of dependence upon dominant nations. That this is occurring at the same time that proportionate exports to dominant countries is either decreasing or remaining relatively static represents an apparent paradox with regard to the data. This paradox is particularly relevant to periphery nations in South America and Africa that, on the one hand, have substantially reduced their exports to their respective core nations, yet, on the other hand have increased their GDP dependence upon those same nations.

The explanation of this paradox seems to lie in growth that has occurred in international trade since 1971 relative to the growth which has occurred within national economies. Table 5.20 shows the growth that has taken place in exports for the world and for the individual regions of the world. It can be seen that world exports almost tripled

TABLE 5.20

Increases in World Trade: 1971-1976
(in millions of U.S. dollars)

Area	1971	1976	% increase
World	315,311	895,865	284
Industrial Countries	218,138	591,430	271
OPEC Countries	11,012	63,613	578
Other Developing Countries	51,005	141,587	278
Europe	161,793	437,032	270
Western Hemisphere[1,2]	17,181	50,944	297
Asia[2]	20,868	55,839	268
Africa[2]	7,979	19,400	243

[1] Excludes U.S. and Canada
[2] Excludes OPEC countries
Source: Direction of Trade, Annual 1970-1976 (Washington, D.C.: International Monetary Fund, 1977), pp. 2-4.

from 1971 to 1976. While some variation exists in the export growth of the individual regions, all have recorded substantial increases. The smallest rate of growth occurred among the African nations, but even here 1976 exports were 2.43 times greater than 1971 exports. Reliable figures could not be obtained on the growth of world GDP from 1971 to 1976, but it seems safe to state that it did not approach the growth which occurred in world exports. To illustrate, export and GDP data from Nicaragua will be examined.

In 1971 Nicaragua shipped 35.2 percent of its exports to the United States, and this figure dropped to 31.2 percent in 1976. However, from 1971 to 1976 the proportion of Nicaragua's GDP represented by its exports to the United States rose from 7.3 percent to 9.3 percent. Over the same period of time, Nicaragua's total exports had grown from $187.14 million (U.S.) to $544.83 million, a gain of 291 percent. The growth of Nicaragua's GDP during this time was from $826.6 million to $1764.5 million, a gain of 213 percent. Thus, export growth far outpaced the growth that occurred in the national economy.

While it is impossible to generalize on the basis of data from one country, it seems likely that the paradox noted above can be at least partially explained by differential growth rates in trade and national economies. Under these conditions nations may be increasing the dependence of their national economies on their largest export markets while at the same time decreasing the proportionate exports that are sent to those markets. Given that this phenomenon seems to be occurring in at least some cases, and given that in other cases nations have been increasing both proportionate exports to their largest markets and the proportion of GDP represented by those exports, it cannot be concluded that there has been a general diminution in international dependency patterns.

6

INTERNATIONAL HIERARCHIES: CONCLUSIONS AND IMPLICATION

There are a number of general conclusions on international trade, as well as the position of the United States in the international economic system, that can be drawn from the analyses in the previous chapters. First, it is possible to comment on the hierarchies that were derived and to evaluate the overall utility of the methodology used. Comments on the potential implications of some of the observed trends can also be made. Secondly, although the previous analyses did not directly deal with all aspects of dependency theory, some comments can be made in this area and on the possibilities of political compliance resulting from economic ties. Finally, the role of the European Economic Community in the international economic system in the past and the future will be briefly discussed since the economic impact of this grouping is of considerable importance.

INTERNATIONAL HIERARCHIES

The Methodology

The methodology introduced in Chapter 3 proved useful in delineating hierarchies and world trade patterns. The linking process provided a means of determining the relative influence both directly and indirectly held by the major industrial nations. The trading relationships of individual nations and territories—large or small, rich or poor—were also placed within a larger and more comprehensive framework than previous analyses of international trade patterns. A consideration of only the ties to the largest market without the inclusion of the various levels of the hierarchy would have understated the importance of West Germany and the United States, since France, Japan, and the United Kingdom provided links to many other territories in various years. Trade ties to other nations such as Italy, the Netherlands, Portugal, or even Australia and Saudi Arabia, while few in number individually, did have a cumulative impact. In addition, the methodology utilized did pinpoint important economic relationships, such as the linkage of the People's Republic of China to the United States via Hong Kong, that may have been unexpected due to existing political estrangements.

The Major Hierarchies

The hierarchies that were derived clearly indicated the continuing importance of the United States in the international economy. The position of the United States in various years was a central one for many states, either directly or through third nations. While changes have occurred, some of which were of major magnitude, the United States continued as a major hierarchical node for the exports of many nations. It should be noted that it would be misleading simply to judge the position of the United States through the years, or that of any other nodal country, solely on the number of nations in some segments of the hierarchy in a given year, since data were available for many additional territories in the later years.

One major change and a number of trends can be observed for the United States hierarchy over time. A major occurrence was the entrance of the United Kingdom to the U. S. hierarchy between 1951 and 1961. If the United Kingdom should shift to West Germany as a result of its entrance into the EEC, such an event would also be major. As was noted in Chapter 4, there has been an increasingly regional makeup for those states exporting directly to the United States as a major market. Western Hemisphere territories clearly predominant, and countries from other continents have shifted away in many cases. On the whole, the makeup of those states with direct ties to the United States appears to have been relatively stable, although there were changes in some of the links between the United Kingdom and Japan and other countries.

The West German hierarchy over time was less constant, reflecting the economic resurgence of that state. As in the case of the United States, there was the major addition of France and its associated territories between 1951 and 1961. For the various years of the analyses, there was a relatively slow but steady increase in the number of directly linked countries after 1961. There were also some indications of geographic concentration in Europe and Africa.

The three hierarchies derived in the various years for France, the United Kingdom, and Japan displayed quite different patterns. The French hierarchy changed very little over time. The number of attached territories, taking into account the aggregated statistics of 1951, remained relatively constant, and the composition of this group was slow to change. The hierarchy for the United Kingdom has shown a clear decline over time. Many of the territories remaining in the 1976 hierarchy were small, former colonial areas. Most of the larger exporters that remained in the U.K. hierarchy may eventually shift as a result of the United Kingdom's entrance into the Common Market. Norway, Sweden, and Portugal had been members of EFTA, while New Zealand benefited from Commonwealth preferences. Without these respective advantages, which were lost with the United Kingdom's entrance into the EEC, the British market may be less attractive. Since Ireland and Denmark also joined the EEC and since the United Kingdom has been their major traditional market, these nations may continue to rely upon the United Kingdom as the major destination of their exports.

The Japanese hierarchy has shown a trend of consistent expansion. This pattern corresponds to the expansion of the German hierarchy and reflects a similar economic resurgence. There is an obvious geographic orientation towards Asia and Oceania that was present in all the time periods used. The future of the Japanese hierarchy may become problematical to the United States. It is possible Japan will become less reliant on the United States as a market and become an independent node. This tendency might be exacerbated by efforts to limit some Japanese exports to the United States. If the Japanese hierarchy, whether as an independent node or as part of the U.S. hierarchy, continues to grow, the key question will be from which other nations it will draw its new members.

As mentioned in Chapter 2, a number of works specified perceived hierarchical relationships among the major western states. Gantzel (1973) argued that Western Europe was dominated by the United States, and could even be considered a "subsidiary" of the United States (p. 207). He also felt that the EEC had to be seen from the perspective of "an instrument of exploitation vis-a-vis the Third World (with the USA naturally participating)" (p. 206). Hveem (1973, p. 331) also felt that the United States dominated Western Europe. The hierarchies that were derived, however, do not provide strong support for these views. France and Germany are not dominated by the United States, and they are obviously important in their own right. If any nation is in a key position to dominate Western Europe, it is Germany—through France and, to a lesser extent, Italy, Belgium, and the Netherlands. The United States has been economically important in Europe through the United Kingdom, but that state appears to be rapidly diminishing in importance in the international trading system. Also, it appears likely that the United Kingdom will become linked to West Germany in the near future.

Hveem and Gantzel had differing views in regard to the position of Japan in an hierarchical international system. Hveem (p. 331) thought that Japan would be less dominated by the United States than Europe in the hierarchy among center nations. In fact, the opposite would appear to be true since Japan has been within the trade hierarchy of the United States for all of the study years. Gantzel (p. 208) used Japan as an example of indirect United States dominance. He felt that Japan was an intermediate link between the United States and Southeast Asia. The results for 1971 and 1976 in particular would support this view, although Japan's area of influence extends beyond Southeast Asia.

The last major hierarchy was that of the Soviet Union. This hierarchy had a very stable core for the various years with a shifting group of additional states, reflecting in part the changing patterns of international political ties. Eastern Europe, with the partial exception of Yugoslavia, remained within the economic orbit of the Soviet Union. Data were unavailable for North Korea, North Vietnam (and then an unified Vietnam), and Mongolia. Given that Mongolia has sided with the Soviet Union in the ongoing dispute with China, its trade is probably concentrated with the Soviet Union. The relationship of the other two states in terms of largest export market is more doubtful. The other states included in the Soviet hierarchy at various times were more varied. Some of the countries, such as Afghanistan and Finland, border on the Soviet Union and shifted into and out of the hierarchy in various years. Geographic proximity may be at least a partial explanation for these intermittent ties. Other, more distant states, such as the Sudan, Eygpt, and Cuba entered or left the hierarchy apparently in response to international political conditions. The reattachment of Yugoslavia to Soviet markets also could have reflected better political relations that came about after the Sino-Soviet split.

Decreasing Number of Hierarchical Nodes

The decrease in the number of major hierarchies from 1951 to 1961 was mentioned earlier. While this change reflected an increasingly integrated international trading system, it also reflected a more open one. Stephen D. Krasner (1976) argued that the international trading system would be more open when there was a hegemonic power present in the system. The United States was clearly the hegemonic power politically after World War II as far as the Western world was concerned. Using tariff levels as an indication of openness, Krasner found that the period from 1945 to 1970 was one of "great openness" with decreasing regional concentration except in the case of Eastern Europe (pp. 331-2). The present analyses would support this finding, although this longer time period makes direct comparisons difficult. Thus, it is not clear whether a hegemonic state is instrumental in this process as Krasner concluded (p. 343). In 1976, the United States was exerting less influence than in 1951 or 1961 in political terms. The decreasing export concentrations and irregularly lower GDP ratios also indicate lessening economic impacts. Yet, the system still remained open as evidenced by the various hierarchies. If Japan were to become an independent market node, however, support for Krasner's theory might be provided in that a less open system would parallel a system with a declining hegemonic political actor.

The Soviet grouping was not included in Krasner's analysis of the international economic system. This trade bloc, while apparently becoming somewhat more open, remains a relatively separate group. Whether or not the United States reestablishes hegemonic influence and succeeds in maintaining an open system will probably have little effect on economic decisions in Moscow. It is not clear to what extent the Soviet Union will permit increasing economic ties to Western Europe or the United States to be created in the future.

DEPENDENCY THEORY

Exports and Development

The preceding analyses did not address all aspects of the dependency theory that were discussed earlier. The analyses in Chapter 5 would indicate that some aspects of dependency may be decreasing. The relative levels of market concentrations for exports for most countries in the world trading system have been on the decline. In fact, it has only been among the more industrialized areas of the world, North America and Europe, that export concentrations showed any increases from the first years of the analysis. Export concentrations for Latin America, the Middle East, Africa, Asia, and Oceania, on the other hand, steadily decreased. Thus, while the figures from these areas of the world are still higher than those for Europe (though not North America), they are on the decline. Either efforts at lessened dependence or natural trends have led to greater diversification of markets.

The position of the United States in regard to the dependency situation appears to be different from that of the other industrialized states in some respects. North American export concentration is high, reflecting in part the large volumes of trade between the United States and Canada. As the hierarchies indicated, the territories most consistently linked with the United States market were in Latin America. Other than North America, Latin America had the highest level of export concentration in these years. While this level has decreased, the decline has not been as rapid as in the other Third World areas. In 1951, for example, Africa and Oceania had higher levels of export concentration than Latin America, but not in 1971 or 1976. To the extent that the export concentration level is associated with dependency, the United States may therefore be more involved in this type of economic relationship than the European nations or Japan.

Export dependence expressed relative to overall GDP also indicated that Latin America's position vis-a-vis its major trading partner was a more dependent one. The findings have indicated that Latin America has ranked consistently high in terms of the proportion of GDP that is represented by exports to the largest market. Again, since the United States is the major market for most of the Latin American states, this nation may be more heavily involved in ties that could be termed dependent than the Western European nations or Japan.

As we noted in Chapter 5, world trade totals in all probability have increased much faster than total GDP in the years between 1971 and 1976. Dependency theorists might conclude from this comparison that the increased trade has not really been of aid in the development of the Third World nations. Of course, the proof would require comparisons of GDP growth rates for various countries and areas of the world. Differential rates might (there being many confounding factors) indicate a disadvantage for Third World countries in general. Per capita GNP growth rates for the period between 1963 and 1974 collected and published by the World Bank (1975), however, would indicate otherwise. The growth rate for the United States was about average for the Western Hemisphere. The countries of the Western Hemisphere on the whole, moreover, generally had lower rates than other areas of the world. Not only were growth rates usually higher in Europe, but they were generally higher in Asia and Africa as well. That portion of the world most closely tied in terms of trade to the United States, as well as the United States itself, does not seem to have fared well in a comparative sense. Thus, the economic ties that exist between these countries may be hindering development in both directions, or the linked states may suffer from ties to a major market that has been experiencing economic problems and relatively lower growth rates. In a sense, the United States may be exporting its economic difficulties, but rather than to the world at large, more specifically to its Western Hemisphere trading partners.

Hierarchical Shifts

The differential composition of the hierarchies over time may reflect some aspects of changing levels of dependency. Countries on the periphery have generally remained dependent, at least in that they were not market nodes in the hierarchies. It is not possible to state whether those states that shifted from one major market node to another are less dependent than those that remained tied to the same market. Of the countries that have tended to change their major markets, three general groups seem to be present—some of the African states, petroleum producers, and some of the larger periphery states.

The shifts among the new African states were noted. These states are, for the most part, neither oil producers nor large in terms of total GNP. Associate status with the EEC for the former French and Belgian colonies might explain their continued ties with their former colonial metropoles. The shifts among the former British territories and a few others might reflect an ongoing search for the best export ties, a process not yet complete.

Iran typifies a shifting oil producer. In 1951, the United Kingdom was its chief market. In 1961, it had shifted to West Germany. In 1951, the United Kingdom was its chief market. In 1961, it had shifted to West Germany. In 1971 and 1976, it was Japan that was its largest market. Libya, Iraq, Oman, Bahrain, and Algeria have also tended to shift in terms of their largest export ties. These shifts in terms of largest market could reflect a position of increasing economic independence. Such an argument would be particularly likely for petroleum producers; however, the argument that petroleum producers are not dependent could be made even if the export market had not changed during the four years in question.

Some of the larger Third World states have also shifted to different major markets from one study year to the next. For example, while Brazil has consistently had the United States as the largest market for its exports, Chile and Argentina tend to shift. Argentina joined the U. S. hierarchy only in 1976, and then through a third nation. In the earlier years it was first linked to the United Kingdom and then to Italy. Chile started in the U. S. hierarchy, then shifted to Japan, and then to Germany. In the case of Chile, Moran (1974) in a study of the copper industry in that country found that shifting markets did not greatly lessen Chilean export dependence. After nationalization of the multinational copper firms, government control of exports led to an effort to find new markets. Such markets were in fact found, but overall dependence decreased little, if at all. In Asia, India, Pakistan, and Indonesia (also an oil producer) exhibited similar patterns of shifting to different major markets from study year to study year.

The above shifts do not necessarily indicate a lessening of dependence. Such economic flexibility may reflect a position more characteristic of interdependence than dependence. If such is indeed the case, it might be reasonable to expect larger states to be more likely to be able to exert influence on their trading patterns than smaller territories. Among the non-oil producers, it has noticeably been some of the larger exporters that have displayed such flexibility. Of course, it is also possible that some states that had the flexibility to change major markets chose not to do so. A choice not to shift markets could be just as great an indicator of interdependence or independence as constant shifts.

Political Compliance: Unanswered Questions

The relationship of trade ties and political compliance have not been directly considered in the various analyses. The derived hierarchies, however, did indicate that more than one country might seek appropriate political behavior from linked states. While United Nations (UN) roll call votes are only one aspect of political compliance (since symbolic deviation might be permitted in some cases), an analysis of trade ties of nations in the French hierarchy in 1961 could explain some UN votes more effectively than trade ties to the United States. For example, most of the former French African territories in the period from 1960 to 1962 did not vote in favor of various UN resolutions calling for immediate independence for Algeria. They also did not support other resolutions critical of French policy in that territory. These former colonial territories, as newly independent states, could have reasonably been expected to support such resolutions. The strong trade ties between these states and France have been hypothesized as explaining the votes in the UN on the Algerian resolutions (Rubin and Weinstein 1974, p. 96; Esseks 1971, p. 1068). The derived trade hierarchies clearly provide support for this view. In other cases, the trade hierarchies might indicate which states might be expected to "agree" with the stand of a major state.

While the exact relationships between dependency and the trade hierarchies are not clear, the hierarchies at least provide indications of the most salient ties in the international economic system. Linkages through third countries provide some problems for determining dependency or pressure for political compliance. A nodal country may find it difficult to use economic pressure against a country indirectly linked to it. It might, however, be able to bring economic or political pressure to bear on the intermediary third country to attempt to exert such pressure in economic terms. Thus, the United States might attempt to influence Thailand by pressuring Japan to use its position as Thailand's major market. Political compliance might also result more indirectly. The nodal country might exert pressure on its suppliers to follow a particular policy. Once bound to a policy, these suppliers in turn might pressure their suppliers to conform with the expected policy, since more support for the policy might be deemed useful by the intermediary state.

THE ROLE OF THE EEC

If the EEC had been included in the derivation of the hierarchies as a single economic unit (either as the Six or the Nine), then only two major hierarchies would have been present in the last three study years. The Common Market would have been the principal nodal market for virtually all the territories in the world except the Eastern European countries. Such an overall hierarchical trading system would have reflected a well-integrated pattern of trade, but it would have been one with a principal node composed of an only partially integrated actor. While the EEC as a whole constitutes a major economic fact for world trade, its direct political impact is not nearly as large. Individual countries, however, such as France and West Germany, can be important politically as well as economically. No doubt their political influence is enhanced by their economic strength.

The EEC may grow to be even more important in terms of economic impact, even when considered as a loose grouping of eight individual economic units (Belgium-Luxembourg being in effect only one such unit). It would seem that sooner or later the United Kingdom will join the West German hierarchy in some form. The number of associate members of the EEC is also increasing. In addition to the former Belgian, French, and Italian colonies, associate status has been offered to the former British colonies in Africa, the Caribbean, and the Pacific (excluding Australia and New Zealand). Such status could bring these areas into the German hierarchy independent of their ties to the United Kingdom. Austria, Greece, Turkey, and Israel have either requested or been granted such a status as well. Increasing democratization in Portugal and Spain may make these countries more acceptable for either associate membership or full membership. In 1976, Spain had already shifted to France as its largest market.

If the Common Market's impact through the German hierarchy (or Germany's impact through the Common Market) comes to include many of the above countries, the world trade system may become more segmented geographically than is presently the case. The United States may remain a nodal market for most of the Western Hemisphere, and this hierarchy as a whole may have lessening portions of world trade. It has been noted that the associate status for an increasing number of countries may limit the exports of the Latin American states which will not have this preferential status (Ingram 1966, p. 130; Mandel 1970, p. 81; Pertot 1972, p. 140). Krause (1973) noted that there could be an impact on the United States in an indirect fashion. If the Latin American states have to curtail their exports, then American exports may also suffer (p. 113). The geographic segmentation would be greater if Japan becomes a nodal market for parts of Oceania and Asia— including many of those states not eligible for an associate status with the EEC. Regardless of trends in the EEC, it is not likely that the Soviet hierarchy will greatly change; thus, another geographic segment of the world trading system will remain. While the longitudinal analyses conducted earlier do not definitely point to this trend towards segmentation, the increasing geographic concentration of United States influence in the Western Hemisphere is just one indication of the strong possibility of its future occurrence.

The Common Market may offer some positive collaboration for Krasner's theory of the international trading system. The EEC may be becoming a hegemonic economic power, though it clearly is not such a political actor. The United States still occupies that position, but the increasing economic power of the EEC (and Japan) could reflect the decreasing political influence of the United States and reduce its ability to maintain an open system.

SUMMARY

While some of the above issues have not been resolved by the analyses undertaken in this part of the present study, the preceding chapters do provide a basis for future work in the various areas. The possibility that dependency relationships might be different in different hierarchies or world areas is a subject that could benefit from further research. The resolutions of this question as well as other unanswered research questions are involved ones and beyond the scope of this study. Still, some useful background for this further work has been provided.

With regard to the specific findings of the present study, similar analyses in future years may provide additional indications of the impacts of such economic and political trends as increasing integration among the Common Market countries, greater East-West trade, or the continuance of detente. The derived hierarchies already have identified economic shifts resulting from such political factors as the shift of Egypt to the USSR or the change of China's trade from an orientation to the Soviet Union to one toward the West. Future hierarchies might well reflect similar political impacts. Thus, Egypt might turn toward Western markets, or Mozambique, Ethiopia, and Angola may shift to the Soviet bloc. Such changes can be better understood in regard to overall world trade patterns, both at a specific time in the present and those of the past.

PART II

THE TECHNOLOGY-INTENSIVE EXPORT POSITION OF THE UNITED STATES

7

THE ROLE OF TECHNOLOGY IN EXPORT TRADE

The previous chapters have indicated that trade and trade ties are important in the international system. Exports are especially important in trade since, barring foreign aid or subsidies, they are the chief source of income for the purchase of imports. Since the United States is the largest national market in the world economy, its ability to pay for its imports is critical in many respects. Thus, its trade balances are a factor of great significance in the international trading system. The role of the dollar as an international currency heightens this significance.

Among the major industrialized countries, such as those that had large numbers of nations directly attached to them in the hierarchies derived in Chapter 4, trade balances are important to national policies. In the case of the United States, there has been increasing concern over the recent negative trade balances that have been occurring. One important component of the export goods of the industrialized countries has been those products requiring relatively large levels of technology inputs. Such technology-intensive trade is important for the industrialized countries if for no other reason than such trade has been increasing faster than nontechnology-intensive trade (Kelly 1977, p. 5).

THE POSITION OF THE UNITED STATES IN TECHNOLOGY-INTENSIVE TRADE

Among exports of manufactures, which are not synonymous with high technology-intensive products in all cases, the relative share of the United States has declined. While U. S. exports of manufactures increased over 100 percent from 1960 to 1970, similar exports for France, West Germany, the Low Countries, Canada, Italy, and Japan increased by much larger amounts. Of the major industrial nations, only the United Kingdom showed a smaller increase for this period (Peterson 1971b, pp. 8-9). The recent decline in the American share of the world exports of manufactures is even more pronounced since this decline is a reversal of a 150-year trend (Lipsey 1972, p. 21).

The importance of technology-intensive products among American exports can be seen in the light of the decline of exports in other sectors. In fact, the overall deterioration in the trade balance of the United States would have been even greater had it not been for the export surpluses generated by industries that were technology intensive (Lowinger 1975, p. 221). Another indication of the importance of these types of products for the export trade of the United States is that capital goods have had a positive balance for the United States in every year during the period from 1925 to 1970 (Branson and Junz 1971, p. 289). The export surplus of technology-intensive products for the United States, however, may be changing. Jack Baranson (1976-77) has warned that the United States might be losing its technological edge. Peter G. Peterson (1971b, pp. 18-21) noted generally deteriorating balances with other industrial countries in technology-intensive products from 1960 to 1970. Robert E. Lipsey (1972, p. 23) observed the same trends, but he was less concerned since the U.S. imports of technology-intensive goods started at such a low level, especially when compared to the level of exports for such goods.

Whatever the trends and their causes, technology-intensive items loom as an important component of American exports. Regina K. Kelly (1977, pp. 14, 17) found that trade in high technology products was much more important for the competitive performance of the United States than for other industrialized countries. Technological innovation has also been viewed as a primary means by which American products can remain competitive (Quinn 1966, p. 127). With more countries becoming competitive in terms of nontechnology-intensive products, it is increasingly likely that American export competition will be even more dependent on technology-intensive products (Peterson 1971b, p. 16).

LEONTIEF'S PARADOX AND THE SEARCH FOR ANSWERS

The impact of technology on the export pattern of a given country has been recognized as important only relatively recently, especially in comparison with some of the concepts discussed in Chapter 2. The impetus for the consideration of technology factors in the analysis of trade developed out of a surprising finding of Wassily Leontief (1956) in his application of data from the 1948 input-output tables to American foreign trade. Prior to this work, a two-factor theory of trade, the Heckscher-Ohlin model, had been generally accepted. The two factors in the model were labor and capital. In essence, this model assumed that a given country would, for the most part, export goods requiring more of the particular factor that was most abundant in the state. The conventional wisdom about the United States was that since the country had an abundance of capital, its exports would be more capital intensive than its imports, which would tend to be labor intensive. Leontief's findings presented a paradox. U.S. exports were relatively labor intensive while those imports competitive with domestic production were more capital intensive. This unexpected discovery resulted in a search for suitable explanations. In the process, this search generated much of the literature either directly or indirectly concerned with the role of technology intensity in trade.

The various attempts to explain Leontief's paradox can be divided into three basic groups. First, there are studies that considered the role of technology inputs directly. Second, some attention has been directed to the idea of human skill or capital intensity. Third, other factors have appeared in the literature that may have a peripheral impact on the role of technology. These factors have been suggested as possible explanations for Leontief's findings. The following sections will consider these three areas, with the emphasis on the role of technology. A fourth area of concern in the previous literature overlaps with the first three. Many of the empirical studies have been country specific or comparative in terms of testing for the impact of technology in different countries. The findings of these studies for the major industrial countries will be summarized since these countries will be the main focus of analysis for the later chapters.

TECHNOLOGY FACTORS IN TRADE

One of the results of Leontief's findings was an emphasis on the possible impacts of technological factors on trade flows. The emphasis on new factors was strengthened by empirical findings confirming the paradox, both for other countries and other time periods (Baldwin 1971, p. 133; Keesing 1967, p. 255; Wilkenson 1968, p. 87). While a large portion of the subsequent work dealt with conditions in the United States, the importance of technology in international trade patterns is obvious for other countries as well. The enquiries into the role of technology can be considered in two general categories. First, there have been the studies that have concentrated on the role of technology inputs. Second, there are a number of works that have looked at the product life cycle as a potential explanatory factor for trade patterns.

Technology Inputs and Trade

The importance of technology inputs into trade has been recognized in the literature. Technology factors have been considered to be important in the expansion of world trade (Chipman 1970, p. 95; Kelly 1977, p. 2). The many studies that have considered technology inputs also provide evidence of an increased awareness of its importance. It should be noted that the technology impact is most likely to be the greatest in the export mix of only some countries. With existing advantages in terms of labor, capital, technology, natural resources or land, a country is most likely to make a choice between concentration in either technology-intensive exports or nontechnology-intensive exports. In regard to imports, on the other hand, there is a greater likelihood of a mix of both types of products (Leamer 1974, p. 369). Such an import mix would probably not include the exact items that are exported, but most countries will need both technology and nontechnology items regardless of the major products for which export advantages exist.

A number of different studies have attempted to test for the impact of technology on the export mix of different industrialized countries. These studies, the results of which will be mentioned below, usually have used surrogate measures for the actual technology inputs, since it is difficult to get accurate and useful information on the level of technology involved in any given product. Also, since industries have been aggregated, and thus products, in most studies, some uniform measure was necessary. The two most common measures have been research and development (R&D) expenditures and the percentage of the labor force in the industry or industries that is composed of scientists and technicians. This second measure is related to the human capital or skill concept that will be discussed in another section, but it also reflects some of the technology inputs into the products of different industrial categories.

The level of R&D expenditures as a measure of technology inputs for various products has proven to be an important variable in many studies. In terms of general productivity, such expenditure levels have been found to be important in explaining the growth and expansion of different industries, while limited expenditures have been associated with declining productivity (Kendrick 1973, p. 143; Tuebal 1976, p. 395). Similar results have been present in studies concerned with export performance. For example, various industries or industry groups that have been used in different studies that have had higher levels of R&D expenditures have also had a greater percentage of their total production devoted to foreign trade (Gruber et al. 1967, p. 22; Keesing 1968, p. 185; Gruber and Vernon 1970, p. 241). The higher concentration in export markets of the production from these industries would indicate either greater competitiveness of technology-intensive products or a greater need for such products among foreign consumers. In a sense, in either case technology inputs are important. Results from other studies have indicated that the level of R&D expenditure has been highly correlated in a positive direction with the presence of technology-intensive items in the export mix (Wilkenson 1968, p. 157; Gruber and Vernon 1970, p. 254; Baldwin 1971, p. 136; Branson 1971, p. 758; Branson and Junz 1971, p. 332; Kelly 1977, p. 8). In some cases, R&D intensity has been stressed as the single most important explanatory variable for understanding the export performance of various industries or industry groups (Stryker 1968, p. 170; Lowinger 1975, pp. 229, 232). In general, the level of R&D expenditures has been associated with export competitiveness for various industries, indicating that technology inputs are extremely important.

The second measure of technology inputs has been the proportion of skilled personnel in the workforce of various industries. The presence of skilled personnel, such as scientists and technicians, has been used as a twofold measure of technology. On the one hand, their presence in relatively large numbers indicates the probable existence of technologically intensive products or production processes. Secondly, such high levels are also likely to reflect high R&D levels for the industries. If a large number of skilled personnel are employed, then it is probable that some are employed in research and development activities. In a number of works, high levels of such skilled personnel have been associated with export competitiveness (Keesing 1967, p. 39; Wilkenson 1968, p. 144; Gruber and Vernon 1970, pp. 236, 241; Baldwin 1971, p. 136; Lowinger 1975, p. 224), thus confirming the importance of technology inputs.

A few studies have found technology to be less directly important in explaining export performance. Homi Katrak (1973, p. 347) found R&D to be less relevant than a number of other factors. Branson (1971, p. 757), even though he found some evidence for technological inputs, also found other factors to be more important. These studies did not discount the impact of technology intensiveness, but they indicated that its impact may be overstated or operating indirectly. In general, however, the previous literature has identified direct technology inputs as an important factor in international trade competitiveness.

The importance of technology in export fields has been highlighted in another form. The governments of several Western European countries and Japan have an official policy of encouraging national firms to acquire recent technological advances, particularly from the United States (Baranson 1976-77, p. 188). Japan's rise to trading prominence and her ability to compete internationally has been ascribed in part to such technological borrowing (Ozawa 1968, p. 201).

The importance of technology is also indicated in the case of patents. Patent control provides a competitive edge to any industry. Such patent holdings, however, can be viewed in different ways. Baranson (1976-77) looked upon the increasing percentage of patents granted in the United States to foreign nationals as an indication of decreasing technological advantage for the United States. Of course, this increased registration could be viewed as increased control by American firms of technological innovation worldwide, to the detriment of other industrialized nations. Galtung (1971), in fact, in his structural theory of imperialism and dependency considered patent control to be one aspect of a continued maintenance of dependent relations. He considered the increased foreign patent registration in the United States to be one part of dependency relationships.

The importance of technology inputs seems much less important for imports than for exports. Those American industries that are competitive with foreign imports had a much lower level of R&D expenditures than those industries engaged in export production (Baldwin 1971, p. 136). It may be the case that industries low in R&D invite competition in domestic markets from imports. If comparative advantage is derived from technology inputs and an industry is not a technology-intensive one, it may be unable to compete with foreign producers deriving a comparative advantage from some other factor.

On the whole, technology intensiveness has been seen as providing a comparative advantage in international trade to those countries able to utilize it. The ability to provide new products or commodities with high inputs of technology has been postulated as an ongoing means of generating demand for exports (Jones 1970, pp. 84-5; Branson and Junz 1971, pp. 303-4). In the case of the United States, a number of studies have noted that continued competitiveness of American products in world markets will have to rely on R&D intensity and associated high technology levels (Keesing 1967, p. 44; Quinn 1966, p. 127; Grove 1969, p. 21; Young 1974, p. 87; Lowinger 1975, pp. 227-9).

Product Life Cycle

The concept of the product life cycle is closely related to the technology aspects of trade. For example, there is, naturally enough, a correlation between R&D expenditures and the introduction of new products (Branson and Junz 1971, p. 332). The idea of the product life cycle is particularly relevant to technology-intensive exports and thus most directly applies to the exports of the industrialized countries such as the United States. While most of the discussion of this aspect of technology has focused on the United States, it is equally relevant to Japan, most Western European nations, and other advanced countries. William Gruber et al. (1967) and Gruber and Raymond Vernon (1970) noted that all products, and technology-intensive products in particular, go through a product life cycle, and this cycle can have an effect on trade, including exports.

When a product first appears, an initial advantage accrues to the company that first introduces the product to the market. The initial advantage of the new innovation or process is protected by secrecy or patents, but eventually this temporary position of advantage may be dissipated, and producers in other countries can begin to effectively compete for the markets for this product, including the market in the country where it first appeared (Gruber et al. 1967, p. 21). Notwithstanding patents or even secrecy, there can be an additional advantage from being the first to introduce a technologically involved product. With a sufficiently long lead time for production the initial producer has yet another advantage.

Once a product is introduced in the world market, it eventually becomes possible for duplication to occur in other countries. Standardization, one step in the product life cycle, will occur in many cases, and once this happens, other producers will set up production for the home markets (Lowinger 1975, pp. 224-5). Trade, that is, exports in a particular good, might be possible only until other nations successfully imitate the product (Posner 1961, p. 323; Ozawa 1968, p. 191). Thus, the exports of the original innovating country, barring an expanding market of some magnitude, will be hurt since some demand will be supplied from the new domestic sources for the former foreign markets. The level of exports may decrease for another reason. With standardization the new producers in foreign countries may even begin to export. Thus, an original monopoly position will become one where the relative share of the export markets of the original producer is bound to decline (Lowinger 1975, pp. 224-5; Wilkenson 1968, p. 114; Adler 1970, p. 315).

Belgium provides an example of a country that has undertaken to produce only standardized products for the export market since it cannot compete internationally for most specialized products (Balassa 1969, p. 203; Hufbauer 1970, p. 177). Smaller countries like Belgium also lack the buffer of a large domestic market in many cases. Even the presence of the EEC does not alleviate this problem since many products that are not standardized can have national characteristics. It should also be noted that not all new products will necessarily increase exports. The new product may displace an old one in which the innovative country had a large share. The new product may also not sell in foreign markets, and other producers of the old product will gain an increased market share (Katrak 1973, p. 341).

The initial technology gap that occurs in regard to a particular product need not disappear entirely after a period of time. The original innovation in a given area can provide an important lead for the introduction of related products. Potential foreign competitors also may either be unwilling or unable to close the initial gap (Posner 1961, p. 339). Thus, the exports of a country may show a constant shift to new products, and these new products will maintain an international competitive edge for the producing country. For a country with a high technology export mix, it would be reasonable to expect a change in the mix of products with those further along in the product life cycle being replaced by those just starting the cycle. As exports of one good decrease, newer ones will appear to take their place (Adler 1970, p. 315; Ozawa 1968, pp. 204-5).

The product life cycle and the shifting export mix point up one problem in dealing with technology-intensive products. Eventually, as a product becomes standardized, the technology input in the production process will become more limited. Ideally, particular products would be removed from a list of technology-intensive products and new ones would be added (Lipsey 1972, p. 23). Of course, the new products might be similar to the old and replacements for them. Thus, they would be in the same category of products in most cases. Any aggregation of technology-intensive categories would thus group the old and new together. Automobiles, for example, are relatively complicated machines, but the technology involved has largely been standardized. The U.S. share of world exports of automobiles constantly increased until 1958, after which time it has declined. This decline, however, may not reflect a disadvantage in terms of technology intensity (Branson and Junz 1971, p. 289; Peterson 1971b, p. 27). The product life cycle approach anticipates this occurrence, and the decrease in exports would not be considered a decline in American technology-intensive competiveness.

There are some additional facets in the product life cycle concept that should be noted. It has been suggested that the direct investment of United States companies abroad represents a part of the cycle. Such investments could be viewed as the last step in a cycle that started with the original production (Gruber et al. 1967, p. 30). B.W. Wilkenson (1968, p. 117) found that transfers of operations abroad can result after standardization has taken place. After the technology advantage has largely been lost, wage rates may become more important. Companies may seek to locate in areas with lower wages to cut production costs (Wilkenson 1968, p. 117; Lowinger 1975, pp. 224-5). Relocation to foreign locations may be perceived by a company as a means of protecting its position in a particular foreign market by locating a production facility in that state (Gruber et al. 1967, p. 21). Another factor leading to direct foreign investment and the loss of the

THE ROLE OF TECHNOLOGY IN EXPORT TRADE / 139

technology advantage to other countries may be related to the development of advanced models of the basic product. Technological changes may bring about obsolescence, and additional income can be generated in the short term by direct foreign investment with associated patent fees and licensing arrangements (Ozawa 1968, p. 204).

Baranson (1976-77) considered this last step of the product life cycle as dangerous to the continued export position of the United States. He argued that direct foreign investment resulted in the establishment of direct competition for the exports of the United States (p. 184). The product life cycle becomes important in any attempt to determine the validity of this argument. Direct foreign investment in one case may be natural, as would the decline in competitiveness of American export goods. Such declines may not be avoidable. Baranson did, however, note another problem—the answer to which is less clear. Direct investment and technology transfer can result not only in the immediate loss of export competitiveness, but in future losses as well. The transfer of technology may permit foreign companies to develop the means to challenge the United States in the future by drawing upon knowledge transferred, both in terms of information and the training of indigenous personnel (p. 184). While no hypothesis on this subject will be tested in the present work, if technology-intensive exports from the United States are on the wane, licensing and direct investment abroad may be one relevant causal factor.

The various ideas about the product life cycle are an important addition to the concepts of the role of technology in trade and the export mix of various countries. This cycle would explain many of the occurrences in international trade. It also provides an explanation as to what the role of many of the industrialized countries can be in international trade. In addition, it provides a sound reason for avoiding overreaction to every loss of position in the export markets by American products, or the products of any other industrialized country for that matter. In fact, it would be an unreasonable expectation under the assumptions of the product life cycle for one country to maintain the same relative share of the world market for a particular technology-intensive product.

HUMAN CAPITAL OF SKILL INTENSITY

Thomas C. Lowinger (1975, p. 225) noted that in the final stage of the product life cycle the cost of unskilled labor could become the most important factor in the choice of manufacturing location. This observation points out another explanation that has been put forward as an answer for the paradox that Leontief found. Leontief (1956, p. 399) himself felt that the skill levels of the American labor force were higher than equivalent groups in other countries. Thus, the labor intensity of exports was explained since in terms of skill, American labor was the most abundant factor available to be used in international competition for markets. As the above comments on the proportional levels of scientists and technicians employed in the labor force have indicated, a definite relationship exists between skill levels and technology intensity. With this relationship in mind, some of the findings of the previous empirical studies on the role of skilled labor or human capital will be discussed.

Relative education levels of the work force, both across industries in a single nation and for industries across nations, have proven to be important for competitiveness. John W. Kendrick (1973, p. 143) found that overall productivity levels were positively associated with high worker levels of education. The relative level of exports among total production has also been found to be correlated with higher average educational levels among the work force (Quinn 1966, p. 120; Fareed 1972, p. 636). Peterson (1971a, p. 25) observed that Japan had a major advantage in international trade since its educational system graduated more engineers and technicians than did that of the United States. The opposite has been argued for Europe. Limited support for higher education in Europe has resulted in a shortage of trained scientists, technicians, and managers. It is also possible that this shortage is aggravated by the relatively low social status granted to individuals in these occupations (Quinn 1966, p. 120).

The general level of skilled labor available to an industry or industry group has also been connected to export productivity. The level of skilled labor has usually been determined by categorization of the labor force. Either dichotomous variables, such as skilled or unskilled, or finer breakdowns, have been used to measure the impact of the skill factor. Skilled labor factors have often been found to be associated with international comparative advantage (Harkness and Kyle 1975, pp. 154, 161; Keesing 1966, p. 256; Gruber and Vernon 1970, p. 236; Branson and Junz 1971, p. 323; Katrak 1973, p. 347; Carlsson and Ohlsson 1976, p. 166; Branson 1971, p. 759). A number of studies that used finer breakdowns of the labor force discovered that comparative advantage in industries was closely associated not only with scientists and technicians but also with specialized manual skills such as those held by electricians, machinists, and tool and die makers (Keesing 1966, p. 254; Baldwin 1971, p. 136).

The relationship between skilled labor and exports has not carried over into import competitive industries. Those American industries that have been competing against imports from abroad had a much lower occupational index of skill than did those industries involved in exporting to foreign markets (Waehrer 1968, p. 33; Keesing 1966, p. 258). Imports to the United States have been less skill intensive than such products would be were they produced domestically (Keesing 1967, p. 42). Thus, the American trade balance clearly has reflected an "export" of skill to other parts of the world while "importing" less skilled labor.

Skilled labor has been directly connected with the intensity of technology inputs as measured by R&D expenditures beyond the relationship between technology intensity and the relative level of technicians and scientists employed. William H. Branson and Helen B. Junz (1971, p. 232) found a high positive correlation between R&D and a human capital measure. Lowinger (1975, p. 227) observed that skill intensity was related to technology and the appearance of new products, resulting in comparative advantage. Wilkenson (1968, p. 108) noted that "education-training levels are crude measures of significance of technical advance," and that his related findings about skill levels supported theories of technology-intensive comparative advantage. Skill intensity has also been considered important for technology in that the existing skilled personnel can train additional skilled personnel, both for the present and for the future (Keesing 1966, p. 253).

Human capital or skill intensity apparently has been one factor responsible for Leontief's paradox. This factor can also be important for the gaining of comparative advantage in the export sector. More importantly for the present study, this skill factor has been associated with technology-intensive products in the export sector, thus further emphasizing the importance of this type of export product for the United States.

OTHER FACTORS

A number of other factors have been pinpointed as being of some importance to various industrialized countries in regard to competition in the international markets. Some of these factors have been found to be important in connection with American exports, and some are related to technology intensity. Some of the findings in the literature will be briefly described below.

Scale Economies

Economies of scale have been of some importance for the general productivity of many American industries (Kendrick 1973, p. 143). Such scale factors have also proven to be important for export competitiveness, particularly for countries like the United States which have large domestic markets that encourage economies of scale in production (Gruber et al. 1967, p. 28; Stryker 1968, p. 170; Branson and Junz 1971, p. 325; Katrak 1973, p. 347). The advantages of scale economies to the export sector, however, have not been supported by all studies. Branson (1971, p. 759) found scale economies to be minimal, the opposite of some of his earlier findings. Similarly, Robert E. Baldwin (1971, p. 143) found that scale economies did not "account for the U.S. trade pattern in a statistically significant manner." N. V. Posner (1961, p. 329) noted that not all goods traded internationally are mass produced; thus, they are not amendable to potential profits from scale economies. He included machine tools, a product with technology inputs, in this category.

The somewhat conflicting empirical findings discussed above may well reflect the presence of a distinct relationship between scale economies and some of the other factors already discussed. Scale economies, in fact, may be present in conjunction with other factors and in combination lead to a comparative advantage for exports. Morris Teubal (1976, p. 401), for example, found that the level of R&D expenditures was a function of firm size. Donald B. Keesing (1967, p. 45, 1968, p. 185) noted that if all other things were equal, R&D was more attractive if scale economies were present. Others have also discovered that R&D levels and scale economies were related (Branson and Junz 1971, p. 332; Gruber and Vernon 1970, p. 250). In addition, Edward E. Leamer (1974, pp. 371-2) noted that scale economies might also have a link with the product life cycle. Standardization is more likely if scale economies are present. Given the relationship between R&D, technology intensity, and comparative advantage, it would appear that scale economies may be a significant factor, although not necessarily an independent one.

Natural Resource Industries

The presence of natural resource industries in a country can sometimes present a confounding factor in determining technology impacts on export competitiveness. In those industrialized countries containing major natural resource stocks relative to population levels, export competitiveness has been related to these resources rather than to technology intensiveness (Carlsson and Ohlsson 1976, pp. 166, 173; Wilkenson 1968, p. 106). Jon Harkness and John F. Kyle (1975, p. 161) found that when resource and nonresource industries were separated, capital intensity was more relevant to U.S. comparative advantage among the non natural resource industries. Baldwin (1971, p. 142), on the other hand, found that capital intensity was associated with certain resource industries in the United States. Thus, while the ultimate impact of resource based industries cannot be determined, particularly for the United States in the export field, their overall impacts will tend to be limited in any analysis of technology-intensive exports since natural resource products will normally be technology intensive only if a great deal of processing has been involved to their transformation from the raw state.

Open and Hidden Tariffs

Another factor in international comparative advantage is tariff structures. Foreign tariffs have effectively limited some of the advantages that would have accrued to the United States as a result of technology intensity since some foreign governments have sought to protect their own technology-intensive industries (Lowinger 1975, p. 234). Other governmental policies, such as subsidies, import quotas, and differential exchange rates, may also bias imports in a given country away from technology-intensive products. When Japan signed the General Agreement on Trade and Tariffs (GATT), the Western European signatories and the United States retained the right, in essence, to discriminate against Japanese products. Such discrimination clearly has occurred in the past (Peterson 1971b, p. 27). Discrimination in tariffs and other policies necessitates a certain amount of caution in analyzing international trade in technology-intensive products or interpreting the results of any such analysis.

Nature of Markets

Some aspects of markets and the marketing characteristics of firms have been mentioned as being of some importance in export trade. F. Michael Adler (1970, p. 313) noted that an appropriate customer market must exist for manufactured goods. He also noted that "the more developed the export market, the better should be the market share competitiveness of United States manufactures" (p. 316). The importance of standardization was noted in the product life cycle as being of importance for the entry of new countries into export competition. The presence of marketing skills among U.S. firms has also been postulated as an inherent advantage in export competition (Gruber et al. 1967, p. 30; Grove 1969, p. 21). This marketing expertise may also be related to skill factors. Baldwin (1971, p. 138) found that export industries in the United States have larger numbers of managers and administration executives than nonexport industries. While such marketing factors may be of some salience in gaining markets or keeping existing shares, it does not appear to be likely that their effects are as important as other factors already discussed.

A further marketing-related factor that may explain a portion of any losses that have occurred in U. S. export markets is the lack of aggressiveness that characterizes the export operations of many U. S. companies (Rostow 1978). Many U. S. companies do not actively seek out export opportunities, particularly small and medium sized companies. For such companies markets inside the United States are adequate, and a lack of experience with foreign people and business discourages them from pursuing export operations. Another explanation for this presumed lack of aggressiveness could related to the fact that the U. S. economy has been traditionally only marginally tied to the international economy, with only a small percentage of its GNP devoted to international trade. Such a small reliance would make the development of new export markets lower in priority for the United States, and thus U. S. government support of export operations of U. S. businesses may be considerably less than in other countries.

COUNTRY FINDINGS

The above discussions were basically concerned with general themes, with only passing references to specific countries. Since levels and shares of technology-intensive exports will be compared for five countries over time in the following chapters, a brief summary of specific empirical findings for the five countries and differences among them in regard to both the importance of technology-intensive exports and the sources of comparative advantage will be undertaken. Few comparisons exist across the five countries; thus, many of the observations will be related to single countries.

United States

By far the most work done on technology-intensive products has been directed to the situation in the United States. Most of the findings discussed above related to American industries. In general, R&D surrogates for technology were found to be associated with comparative advantage. Previous empirical findings showed this technology intensity in some cases to be associated with human capital abundance. In a fewer number of cases scale economies were also related to technology intensity. A summary conclusion from these studies would be that technology does indeed grant a comparative advantage. Kelly (1977, p. 9) found, that of the five major countries, the United States had the largest percentage of its exports devoted to technology-intensive products, a finding that would confirm the importance of such products for the United States.

The competitive advantage of the United States does not extend to all products. In 1950, the advantage appeared to be in chemical materials, aircraft, some metal products, capital machinery used in the metal industries, and plastics (Balassa 1964, pp. 110-1). In the late 1960s, a comparative advantage was noted for chemicals and capital goods (Branson and Junz 1971, p. 320). Lewis H. Young (1974, p. 87) noted a similar pattern, but he also included atomic power and computer equipment. More specifically, he observed that the United States has regained a large portion of the electronic calculator market from the Japanese. He regarded this resurgence on the part of U. S. firms as resulting from technological advances in the field (p.87).

United Kingdom

Much less work has been done on the role of technology-intensive products in the trade of the United Kingdom. H. David Willey (1968, pp. 129-30) noted continued losses for English exports in the world market for manufactures. In terms of comparative advantage, the manufactures for which the United Kingdom was most competitive in 1950 were largely nontechnology-intensive (Balassa 1964, p. 111). Gruber et al. (1967, p. 26) in a comparative study of a number of nations felt that the United Kingdom ranked relatively high in terms of industrial innovation and product development, and that the United Kingdom derived its export strength from the same sources as did the United States. In another study, technology-intensive products were found to be important for the United Kingdom, which ranked only behind the United States in terms of the share of technology-intensive products in the total export package. (Kelly 1977, p. 9). Gruber and Vernon (1970, pp. 252-3), however, found only industry concentration related to the level of exports from the United Kingdom. Scale economies and a skilled labor force were found in one case to be important for the competitiveness of the United Kingdom (Katrak 1973, p. 347). Another finding mentioned earlier might indicate some relationship between the situation in the United States and the United Kingdom. Among the major industrialized countries the United States and the United Kingdom have shown the smallest increases in total manufactures exports as noted by Peterson. These relatively low increases might be related to similarities in the industrial structure of the two countries.

European Economic Community

France and West Germany are the two major exporters of technology-intensive products in the EEC. They are also two countries that figured prominently in the hierarchies previously derived. Few detailed studies have been undertaken for these two member states of the EEC. In 1950, the countries that later formed the EEC (the Six) did have an apparent comparative advantage in some products that required technology-intensive inputs (Balassa 1964, p. 111). Gruber et al. (1967) included Germany and France in the comparative study that they undertook. West Germany was also considered to be similar to the United States (and the United Kingdom) in terms of its export make-up in 1962 (p. 26). Kelly (1977, p. 9), on the other hand, found that the share of technology-intensive exports as a percentage of total exports was roughly the same for Germany and France, and both of these countries were below the United States and the United Kingdom. Gruber et al. (p. 24) also found Germany and France to be similar in a number of measures, but they felt that R&D expenditures and government efforts in France in research were largely not devoted to industrial applications.

The impact of the educational systems in Europe was mentioned earlier. In summary, the lack of extended higher education may inhibit the development of competition in international markets of technology-intensive products from these countries. This situation would also explain the governmental policies of encouraging technological borrowing from the United States. This situation might even be part of the explanation for the large number of patents registered by foreign nationals in the United States in recent years. The individuals may well be persons who have migrated to the United States, first for study in universities and then for employment. Of course, the patent situation could also reflect the migration of trained personnel after educations are finished, the so-called "brain drain."

Japan

The importance of technology has been stressed in the case of Japan. In fact, Japanese export expansion after World War II has been attributed to the borrowing of foreign technologies (Ozawa 1968, p. 109). Technology-intensive products, however, have been found to be a relatively small portion of Japan's total exports compared to the exports of the United States, the United Kingdom, France, and Germany (Gruber and Vernon 1970, p. 241; Kelly 1977, p. 9). The one study addressing the source of Japan's comparative advantages in the international markets concluded that such advantages seemed to come instead from raw labor intensity and capital intensity (Gruber and Vernon 1970, p. 254).

SUMMARY

On the whole, the previous literature has clearly identified the fact that technology-intensive export products are important for industrialized countries, particularly the United States. The technology inputs into products seem to have provided distinct comparative advantages, sometimes in conjunction with other factors. In whatever combination, an impact was present. Since the importance of technology is clear, it becomes relevant to consider the export patterns of major industrialized countries and changes in these patterns over time.

There were a number of conflicting results found in the previous literature, both in general and for particular countries. There are a number of possible reasons for the conflicting results. First, the empirical studies usually considered data for single years, and not surprisingly, different studies often used the most recent data then available. These data were invariably not for the same years. Secondly, the industry classifications used in the various studies were at aggregate levels with 15 to 30 industry groups being the norm. Problems can result from any aggregation, and various empirical works used different types of aggregation resulting in categories that were often not directly comparable. Many of the works included caveats in this regard, noting that their findings could in part have resulted from the particular categories chosen (Gruber et al. 1967, p. 33; Gruber and Vernon 1970, p. 260; Katrak 1973, p. 354; Harkness and Kyle 1975, p. 164). Third, in the cases of the studies that undertook multiple country comparisons, relative inputs of labor, capital, and technology per industry for all the countries were based on coefficients from corresponding industries in the United States, a practice that presented certain dangers (Bhagwate 1970, p. 273; Kindleberger 1970, p. 283; Gruber and Vernon 1970, p. 249). These problems have been very real ones, and have clearly had some effects on the results reported, but, perhaps most surprisingly, the general conclusion that technology intensity confers comparative advantage stood out, notwithstanding the different approaches and the different methodologies.

8

ANALYSIS OF TECHNOLOGY-INTENSIVE TRADE

The preceding chapter provided a general overview of the role that technology plays in the trade position of the United States and of the research that has been conducted regarding this position and the changes that have occurred. The present chapter presents a description of the analyses undertaken by the authors to discern the trends associated with patterns of U. S. trade in technology-intensive products. In as comprehensive a manner as possible, the study attempts to accomplish three objectives:

1. To identify the changes that have occurred in the U. S. trade position in high technology products. Such changes will be considered with respect to both exports and imports of these products, and they will be analyzed both prior to and since the 1971 dollar devaluation.

2. To compare the U. S. position in the export of high technology products with the positions of other major trading nations.

3. To identify the changes that have occurred in the U. S. trade position in the export and import of manufactured products that are not considered to be of a high technology nature. The changes in the export position in these products will then be compared with the similar positions of the other major trading nations.

DESCRIPTION OF THE STUDY

Many of the components of the methodology employed in the study are derived from previous studies conducted on the U. S. position in the trade of high technology products by the U. S. Department of Commerce (DOC). For the purposes of their studies, the DOC has developed lists of industries and product categories that could be considered as having a relatively high level of technological input. Two such lists have been developed and used in the DOC studies. The first was based on an unpublished work by Michael Boretsky in which he examined the "new-technology generating inputs" of industries at the two-digit Standard Industrial Classification (SIC) level (Kelly 1976, p. 8). He identified five industries that could be labeled as technology intensive—chemicals, non electrical machinery, electrical machinery, transportation equipment, and instruments. The major problem with the list of industries developed by Boretsky was that it was at too high a level of aggregation. Many of the studies discussed in the preceding chapter noted that the results could have been due to the level of industry aggregation. While the industries as a whole employed higher than average levels of technological inputs in their production processes, many of the individual products manufactured by these industries would not be considered technology intensive. Thus, any trade analyses that incorporated the aggregate export or import figures from these industries would not truly reflect trade in technology-intensive products.

In order to provide a more accurate list of technology-intensive products for trade analyses, the DOC examined the research and development expenditures associated with specific categories of products rather than entire industries. "Research Intensity Indices" were calculated for product categories, primarily at the three-digit SIC level, which were based on research and development expenditures associated with the product category relative to sales. Product categories characterized by research intensity indices greater than the mean research intensity index were considered to be technology intensive. This more disaggregated listing included as technology intensive only 44 percent of the product categories associated with the five industries identified by Boretsky. While this later listing of technology-intensive products is also subject to qualification, it is more accurate than the listing derived from the Boretsky study (Kelly 1976, pp. 9-14; Kelly 1977, pp. 2-4).

Based on this latter list of technology-intensive product categories, the present study employed all of the products that had been generated. In all there are 73 product categories that have been identified as technology intensive. The only difference between the product groups used in the present study and those identified by DOC is that the products employed here are listed according to the Standard International Trade Classification (SITC) system instead of the SIC system. Identification of comparable SIC and SITC product categories has been provided by Kelly (1977), and a complete listing of the technology-intensive product categories and their associated SITC codes can be found in the tables presented in Appendix D, Table D.1.

In order to provide a comparative evaluation of trends of technology-intensive products relative to manufactured products that do not require large inputs of technology, the study also analyzes the trade patterns associated with 83 product categories of the latter type. The product categories selected to be included in the nontechnology-intensive group consist of the product categories that would have been included in the industries identified by Boretsky, but which were found to have a relatively low technology input by the subsequent DOC study. This group of nontechnology-intensive product categories, therefore, cannot be considered exhaustive. However, it does consist of products that are low in technology input relative to the product categories listed as technology intensive. A listing of these nontechnology-intensive product categories and the associated SITC codes is presented in the tables in Appendix D, Table D. 2.

Nations and Trade Data

In order to assess the position of the United States in the trade of technology-intensive products relative to the other major trading nations, it was necessary to gather trade data on the exports and imports of the products employed in the study for all major trading countries. As noted in Chapter 7, most of the earlier studies have concentrated on only U. S. trade in technology-intensive products without regard to the concurrent performance of other nations. Such analyses may not accurately present the position of the United States in the international trade of these products since differential rates of growth may be occurring in the U. S. trade of a product and the trade of other nations in the same product. Thus, while U. S. exports of a particular product may have doubled over a three-year period, the exports of other nations may have tripled during the same period. In such a case the United States' share of exports of that product would have diminished, although the data for only the United States would make it appear that this nation is doing well in exports of that product. Likewise, the U. S. position in the exports of a product could be understated if this nation had experienced only a small growth in the exports of a product, but other nations' exports had remained constant or decreased.

Export and import data were collected from the World Trade Annual for each of the 156 product categories employed in the study for 21 member nations of the Organization for Economic Cooperation and Development (OECD). To provide a longitudinal perspective on the trade in these product categories, export and import data were gathered for 1963, 1972, and 1974. Data were gathered for these partiular years in order to assess the change in the U. S. trade position over the relatively long time period of 1963 to 1974, and to assess the extent of the recovery of the U.S. position since the 1971 dollar devaluation. At the time of the writing, 1974 was the most recent year for which these data were available. The 21 nations for which data were gathered are the United States, Canada, Belgium-Luxembourg, France, West Germany, Italy, the Netherlands, the United Kingdom, Denmark, Norway, Sweden, Austria, Portugal, Switzerland, Iceland, Ireland, Greece, Spain, Finland, Australia, and Japan. Although these nations do not represent 100 percent of the trade in many of the product categories employed in the study, they do represent the overwhelming majority of this trade. Two OECD nations that are part of the study, Israel and Yugoslavia, were excluded because data were not available for them during all of the years of the study.

General Analytical Method

The primary analytical technique that was employed in the study is shift share analysis (Ashby 1964; Huff and Sherr 1967). The shift share approach was used since there are inherent problems in using techniques relying solely either on absolute changes or percentage changes. Alschuler (1976, p. 66) noted the need to measure changes in economic variables in other than absolute terms or percentage ones. Small bases lead to misleading large percentage increases, and absolute change measures may obscure trends among some smaller entities. A shift share analysis avoids these difficulties in large measure. Through a series of computations, this method calculates the relative changes that have occurred in the shares that several participants hold of a particular market over a specified time period. In the case of the present study, the participants are the 21 nations, and the markets are the world markets for exports or imports of the individual products used in the study. The components of shift share analysis as they are applied to the present study are discussed below.

Average Annual Growth Rate

Shift share first computes the growth rate that has occurred in the trade of a product over the time period of the study. In the present study simple average annual growth rates were computed over the periods 1963 to 1974 and 1972 to 1974. The average annual growth rate is computed for each of the individual country's trade in the product and for the total of all countries' trade in the product.

The average annual growth rate for all countries represents the ratio of the difference in the value of total world trade (either exports or imports, but not both) in a particular product during the initial and terminal time period to the total value of trade in the initial time period. This ratio is then divided by the number of years between the initial and terminal time period. Thus, the computational formula for the average annual growth rate for all countries would be:

$$G = \frac{\sum_{i=1}^{m} TR_{i,t} - \sum_{i=1}^{m} TR_{i,t-1}}{\sum_{i=1}^{m} TR_{i,t-1}} \cdot \frac{1}{n} \quad (1)$$

where
- G = average annual growth rate for all countries
- $TR_{i,t}$ = the trade of country i in time t
- $TR_{i,t-1}$ = the trade of country i in time t-1
- m = the number of countries
- n = the number of years between time t and time t-1

The average annual growth rate for each nation for a particular product category represents essentially the same computational formula, with the exception that data from only one nation is used in each calculation:

$$g_i = \frac{TR_{i,t} - TR_{i,t-1}}{TR_{i,t-1}} \cdot \frac{1}{n} \quad (2)$$

where g_i = the average annual growth rate for country i.

Expected Value

An expected value is calculated for each nation's trade. This value is the amount that each country's trade would be in the terminal period if its trade had grown at the same rate as trade for all nations combined. Computationally, the expected value of trade in a product category in the terminal time period is equal to the product of the value of a country's trade in that product category in the initial time period and the average rate of change for all countries. Thus,

$$E(TR_{i,t}) = \frac{\sum_{i=1}^{m} TR_{i,t}}{\sum_{i=1}^{m} TR_{i,t-1}} \cdot TR_{i,t-1} \quad (3)$$

where $E(TR_{i,t})$ = the expected value of trade for country i in time t.

The computation of the expected value permits the calculation of the <u>expected value of change</u> that would have occurred in the amount of a nation's trade between the initial and terminal time periods if that nation's trade had grown at the world rate. The expected change in the amount of a nation's trade represents the difference between the expected value and the value of trade done by the country in the initial time period. Thus,

$$E(\Delta TR_i) = E(TR_{i,t}) - TR_{i,t-1} \qquad (4)$$

where $E(\Delta TR_i)$ = the expected value of change for country i.

Net Shift

The net shift for a particular country is the difference between the country's actual change in trade over the time period and the expected change that would have occurred if the country's trade had grown at the average world rate. This difference for an individual country is denoted as:

$$NS_i = \Delta TR_i - E(\Delta TR_i) \qquad (5)$$

where NS_i = the net shift for country i.

The sum of the net shifts for all of the countries is equal to zero:

$$\sum_{i=1}^{m} NS_i = \sum_{i=1}^{m} \left(\Delta TR_i - E(\Delta TR_i) \right) = 0. \qquad (6)$$

It may seem feasible at this point to compute an index of each nation's change in trade position by computing the ratio of each nation's actual change in trade to its expected change in trade. An index of greater than 1.0 would indicate that the nation's trade had grown at a faster rate than the world average, while a ratio of less than 1.0 would connote the opposite. However, such a ratio, interpreted in the above manner, could be fallacious. This is because $NS_i > 0$ does not necessarily imply that country i's trade increased at a faster rate than the average growth rate for all nations. This would be true only if $E(\Delta TR_i) > 0$. But, if $E(\Delta TR_i) < 0$ and if $E(\Delta TR_i) < \Delta TR_i < 0$, then $NS_i > 0$. In such a case, therefore, the ratio of actual change in trade to expected change in trade would be greater than 1.0,

154 / THE UNITED STATES AND WORLD TRADE

but this ratio would connote that the country's trade did not increase as rapidly as would have been expected.

Percent Net Shift

The final stage in shift share analysis is the computation of the percent net shift figure. This figure permits a meaningful analysis of the shifts that have occurred in nations' trade positions while avoiding the problems encountered through the use of the ratio of actual to expected changes. The calculation of the percent net shift is a multistaged process that builds directly upon the net shift figures computed above.

First, within a single product category, the nations are divided into two groups based upon whether they have positive or negative net shift values. Since the sum of the net shifts for all nations is equal to zero, then:

$$\sum_{i=1}^{m} NS_i = \sum_{i=1}^{p} NS_i^{+} + \sum_{i=1}^{q} NS_i^{-} = 0 \tag{7}$$

where m = total number of nations

p = number of nations with positive net shift

q = number of nations with negative net shift

NS_i^{+} = net shift of the ith nation which had a positive net shift

NS_i^{-} = net shift of the ith nation which had a negative net shift.

Therefore, the absolute value of the positive net shifts is equal to the absolute value of the negative net shifts:

$$\left| \sum_{i=1}^{p} NS_i^{+} \right| = \left| \sum_{i=1}^{q} NS_i^{-} \right| \tag{8}$$

The final calculation involved in computing the percent net shift requires dividing the net shift of each country by the sum of the positive net shifts (or the absolute value of the sum of the negative net shifts, since the two are equal):

$$P_i = \frac{NS_i}{\sum_{i=1}^{p} NS_i^{+}} (100) \tag{9}$$

where P_i = percent net shift of country i.

ANALYSIS OF TECHNOLOGY-INTENSIVE TRADE / 155

Under these conditions, the sum of the percent net shifts for all countries will be zero, the sum of the positive net shifts will be equal to one, and the sum of the negative net shifts will be equal to minus one. Therefore, the percent net shift figure for any given nation will represent the percentage of the gains (if positive) or of the losses (if negative) that that nation experienced relative to the gains or losses of all nations. For example, if a nation had a percent net shift value of 61, it would indicate that, of all nations that experienced increases in market share, that nation accounted for 61 percent of the trade volume associated with those increases.

Change in Market Share

The preceding computations are all part of shift share analysis. In order to supplement the net shift figures, simple changes in market share were also calculated for each of the 21 nations within each of the 156 product categories. The change in market share value represents the difference that exists between an individual nation's market share in the terminal and initial time periods. The computations used to calculate the changes that occurred in nations' market shares involved subtracting the product of a nation's trade in the initial year and the growth rate in trade experienced by all nations between the initial and terminal years from the difference between that nation's trade in the initial and terminal years. The result was then divided by the total trade of all nations in the terminal year. Thus,

$$\Delta MS_i = \frac{(TR_{i,t} - TR_{i,t-1}) - (TR_{i,t-1}) \frac{\sum_{i=1}^{m} TR_{i,t} - \sum_{i=1}^{m} TR_{i,t-1}}{\sum_{i=1}^{m} TR_{i,t-1}}}{\sum_{i=1}^{m} TR_{i,t}} \quad (10)$$

where ΔMS_i = change in market share of country i.

Therefore, if a nation's share of world exports of a specific product was 29 percent in 1963 and 15 percent in 1974, the value derived by the application of the above formula would be $-.14$, or a negative 14 percent.

Shift Share and Market Share

Both percent net shift and change in market share figures are employed extensively in the following analyses of technology-intensive and nontechnology-intensive trade. Each of these figures provides a different perspective on the relative changes that have occurred in the trade of these products. Analysis of the market share figures will indicate whether and to what extent the United States and the other major trading nations have altered their positions in trade related to these products. The net shift figures will indicate the extent of the total gains or total losses that can be attributed to each nation. Thus, if the United States experienced a 2 percent loss in world market share in the export of a particular product, such a situation may not be viewed as important. However, if this 2 percent loss represented 50 percent of the losses experienced by all nations (percent net shift), the situation may be viewed more seriously.

ORGANIZATION

The purpose of the study is to discern the direction of the U.S. position in the trade of technology-intensive products using the information derived by the method presented above. In general, the past findings in this area lead to the expectation that although there may be a decline in the long-term position of the United States in the trade of technology-intensive products, in the years since the devaluation this nation has experienced a more positive trend with respect to trade in these products. Such expectations must be qualified by the fact that most previous studies did not employ the comparative analytical framework used in the present study. Thus, the United States' export resurgence since the devaluation may not represent a gain relative to other nations' exports of these products.

The full presentation of the findings of the study is found in Chapters 9 and 10. Chapter 9 is devoted to a discussion of the U.S. position in technology-intensive trade and compares its trade in this area with its trade in nontechnology-intensive products. Chapter 10 presents comparable findings for the other major trading nations—West Germany, the United Kingdom, France, and Japan. An overview of the analyses presented in these chapters is given below.

The United States and Technology-Intensive Trade

Exports of Technology-Intensive Products

The first section of Chapter 9 will discuss the findings with respect to U.S. exports of technology-intensive products from the standpoint of changes in world market share and net shifts. The time frames for the analyses will be 1963 to 1974 and 1972 to 1974. The former period is used to identify the long-term change that has occurred in the position of the United States in technology-intensive trade, and the latter is used to gauge the impact of the 1971 U. S. devaluation on reversing the direction of the long-term trend. It might be argued that it would have been better to measure these changes in time frames that do not overlap, such as 1963 to 1971 and 1972 to 1974. However, this mode of analysis was rejected for essentially two reasons. First, in order to gauge the long-term trend in U. S. technology-intensive trade it was felt desirable to measure the change over the entire time frame. The need for longitudinal data in analyzing technology impacts has been noted (Gruber and Vernon 1970, p. 235), and the use of these years makes it possible to discern where the United States stood during the most recent year relative to the early 1960s, the time when U. S. technology-intensive trade may have been at its peak relative to other nations. Second, it was felt that for the most part the trends between 1963 and 1971 are implicit in the 1963 to 1974 and 1972 to 1974 data. A decline in market share over the former period that is accompanied by an increase in market share over the latter period would imply that a downward trend existed from 1963 to 1971, but that this trend was reversed between 1972 and 1974.

Exports versus Imports of Technology-Intensive Products

The second stage of the analysis of the U. S. position in technology-intensive trade will be to compare U. S. exports of these products with U. S. imports of the same products. Market shares and net shifts of exports and imports of the same product categories will be undertaken to discover whether the relative changes in the two have remained fairly constant or if they differ in some magnitude. If the U. S. position in the trade of technology-intensive products has, in fact, reversed itself since the devaluation, it should be expected that its import position will have diminished as its export position increased. That is, the U. S. share of the world market for the imports of these products will have declined as its share of the export market increased. However, if such a relationship does not exist between exports and imports, it may suggest that any gains in the export markets may be at least partially offset by gains that occurred in the import markets.

Technology-Intensive Exports versus Nontechnology-Intensive Exports

Throughout both of the preceding stages of the analysis of the U. S. position in technology-intensive products, comparisons will be made between the changes that have occurred in the position of these products and the changes that have occurred in the U. S. position with respect to exports of nontechnology-intensive products. The general magnitude of the changes that have occurred in technology-intensive and nontechnology-intensive exports will be compared. The rationale behind these comparisons is that such an analysis is necessary because if technology-intensive exports are changing at approximately the same rate as nontechnology-intensive exports, then it would not be possible to state that the United States is having a resurgence in trade of the former products. It should be expected, though, that the results will show a faster rate of growth or a slower rate of decline among the technology-intensive products.

Other Major Trading Nations and Technology-Intensive Trade

Chapter 10 will be concerned with the changes that have occurred in the competitive positions of West Germany, France, the United Kingdom, and Japan with regard to technology-intensive and nontechnology-intensive exports. These four countries were chosen for comparison with the United States for two reasons. First, these countries, together with the United States, are the largest exporters among the OECD nations of technology-intensive products. Secondly, they are the nations that had the largest number of attached territories in the hierarchies derived in the earlier chapters. The purpose of these analyses is to determine if these nations have performed better than the United States in these areas, and, if so, to identify the nations that have accounted for the largest portions of lost U. S. world markets. Since the purpose of these analyses is to provide a comparison with the U. S. export position in these products, only exports will be analyzed. It should be expected that Germany and Japan will have increased their shares of the world market in both types of products between 1963 and 1974, but that these gains will not have been as rapid between 1972 and 1974 due to currency revaluation. The United Kingdom should be expected to show a relative decrease in the export of both types of products, while France will probably show the least amount of change of any of the nations.

9

UNITED STATES TECHNOLOGY-INTENSIVE EXPORT POSITION

This chapter focuses directly upon the changes that have occurred in the U. S. trade position with regard to technology-intensive products. It presents the data that reflect upon the direction of these changes and upon the associated magnitudes of these changes. It addresses the question of the changing nature of the U. S. comparative advantage in technology-intensive products. However, in order to provide a thorough analysis of the changes that have occurred with regard to technology-intensive products, it is also necessary to examine the corresponding changes that have characterized nontechnology-intensive products. A comparison of U. S. export performance in both technology-intensive and nontechnology-intensive products permits a relative evaluation of U. S. trade in the former group of products. In addition, the analyses will consider the export performance of U. S. technology-intensive and nontechnology-intensive products relative to U. S. imports of those same products.

The data are presented in descending levels of aggregation. First, the total technology-intensive exports of the United States are examined relative to the total technology-intensive exports of France, West Germany, Japan, and the United Kingdom. The corresponding data are then presented for the nontechnology-intensive exports employed in the study for these five nations. Following this comparison, the U. S. export trends associated with the two sets of products are analyzed at the industry group (one-digit SITC) level of classification; and then these analyses are performed at the two-digit SITC level. At the highest level of disaggregation, primarily the four-digit SITC level, the products are analyzed according to whether the United States' export position increased, declined, or remained relatively constant over the time frames of the study. Finally, U. S. import performance

160 / THE UNITED STATES AND WORLD TRADE

in the products is compared with U.S. export performance in the same products.

The preceding analyses will be performed for two time periods: 1963 to 1974 and 1972 to 1974. The former time period will provide an indication of the overall change that has occurred in the U.S. trade position in technology-intensive products. Since 1963 it should be expected that post-war economic recovery in Europe and Japan has become less of an issue, and these nations have probably been actualizing their true economic potential. The latter time period is also intended to provide some measure of the impact of the dollar devaluation upon the U.S. trade position.

From the previous literature, it should be expected that the United States' market share will have declined between 1963 and 1974 as the dollar became increasingly over-valued and as other advanced nations continued to build their high-technology capacities. It should also be expected that the U.S. market share will have increased between 1972 and 1974, as the dollar devaluation brought down the price of U.S. exports. Such have been the findings of past research (Kelly 1977). The primary issues that are addressed by the present study within this framework are the differences in the magnitudes of changes during these two time periods and the changes that characterize specific industries and product groups. Small increases in the U.S. market share from 1972 to 1974 do not necessarily compensate for large losses from 1963 to 1974. Such findings might indicate a halt in the downward trend, but would not necessarily suggest a reversal of the trend. Likewise, if the gains or losses during either time period are concentrated within certain industries or product categories, it may suggest that the overall trends are really product or industry specific. Conversely, if gains or losses cut across all product groups, the conclusions would be different.

WORLD OVERVIEW

Figure 9.1 depicts the changes that have occurred in total technology-intensive exports between 1963 and 1974 for the United States, France, Germany, the United Kingdom, and Japan. The points on the graph represent the total exports for each of the nations among the product categories that are considered technology intensive. It can be seen on the graph that the United States has increased its technology-intensive exports in all of the four years for which data points are presented. The widest gap between U.S. exports of technology-intensive products and those of the other four nations existed in 1968. Since that time the gap has narrowed, and by 1974 West Germany was exporting almost as much as the United States, although the other nations

FIGURE 9.1

Technology-Intensive Exports
(in billions of U.S. dollars)

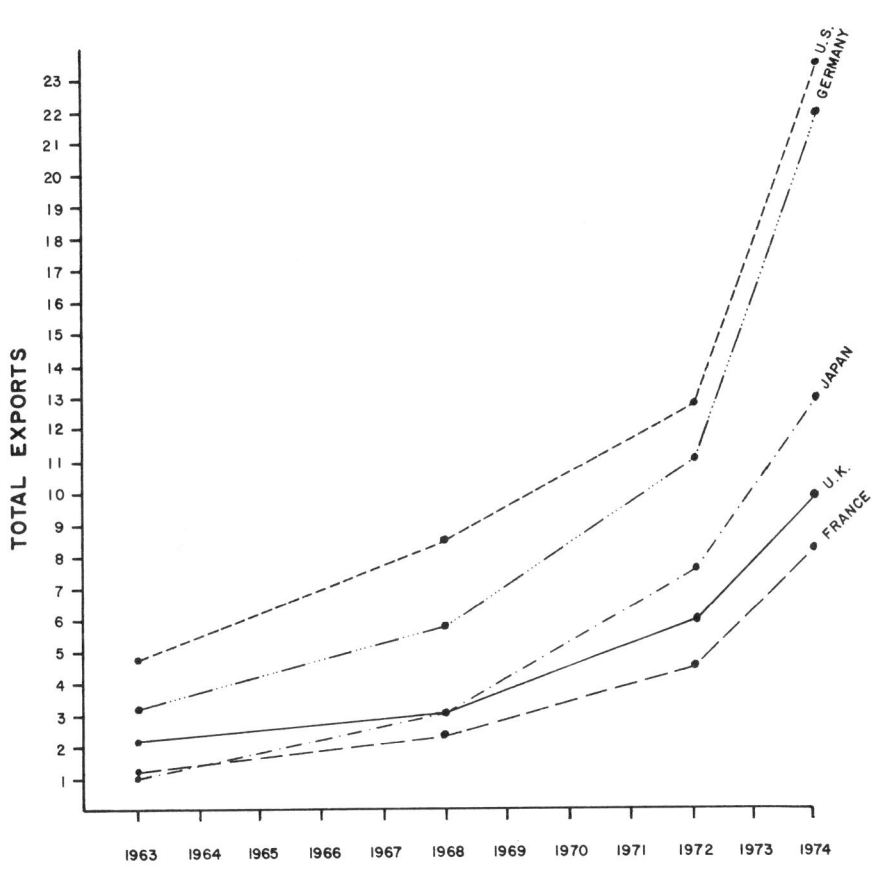

Source: Constructed by the authors.

still lagged far behind the United States in terms of the quantity of technology-intensive exports. A rather dramatic increase occurred in the export of technology-intensive products by the United States between 1972 and 1974 directly following the dollar devaluation. However, the devaluation cannot be the only explanation of the sudden increase in the quantity of exports. While U. S. technology-intensive exports almost doubled over this three year period, so did those of West Germany and France. The United Kingdom and Japan also experienced large increases in their technology-intensive exports, although not as dramatic as the increases registered by the United States, France, and Germany. An additional factor operating during this period that could also provide a partial explanation for the fast growth in the volume of technology-intensive exports is a high level of worldwide inflation caused by the energy crisis.

The changes that occurred between 1963 and 1974 in the exports of the nontechnology-intensive products used in the study are presented in Figure 9.2. This graph indicates that there have been several changes in the positions of the five nations with regard to their rankings among the major trading nations. In 1963 the United States was the largest exporter of these products, closely followed by West Germany. By 1968 West Germany was exporting slightly more of these products than the United States. Thereafter, West Germany continued to export increasingly more than the United States until, in 1974, exports of these nontechnology-intensive products were more than 40 percent greater than those of the United States. Japan in 1963 accounted for the lowest amount of nontechnology-intensive exports among these product categories, but by 1974 that nation was the third largest exporter of these products. In addition, in 1974 Japan closely followed the United States and appears to be in a position to overtake this nation for the position of second largest world exporter of these nontechnology-intensive products. The United Kingdom, on the other hand, experienced the most dramatic loss of position over the time period, dropping from being the third largest exporter in 1963 to being the fifth largest in 1974.

Figure 9.2 indicates that there was also a substantial increase in the exports of these nontechnology-intensive products between 1972 and 1974. The percentage increase for the five nations was approximately 74 percent, almost as large as the five nations' 82 percent increase in the export of the technology-intensive products. Thus, all of the five nations shared in the increase of the nontechnology-intensive exports.

Together, Figures 9.1 and 9.2 indicate that the absolute volume in both categories of products has increased substantially throughout the time period. As expected, there was considerable growth in U. S. exports for both types of products following the 1971 devaluation. Also

FIGURE 9.2

Nontechnology-Intensive Exports
(in billions of U. S. dollars)

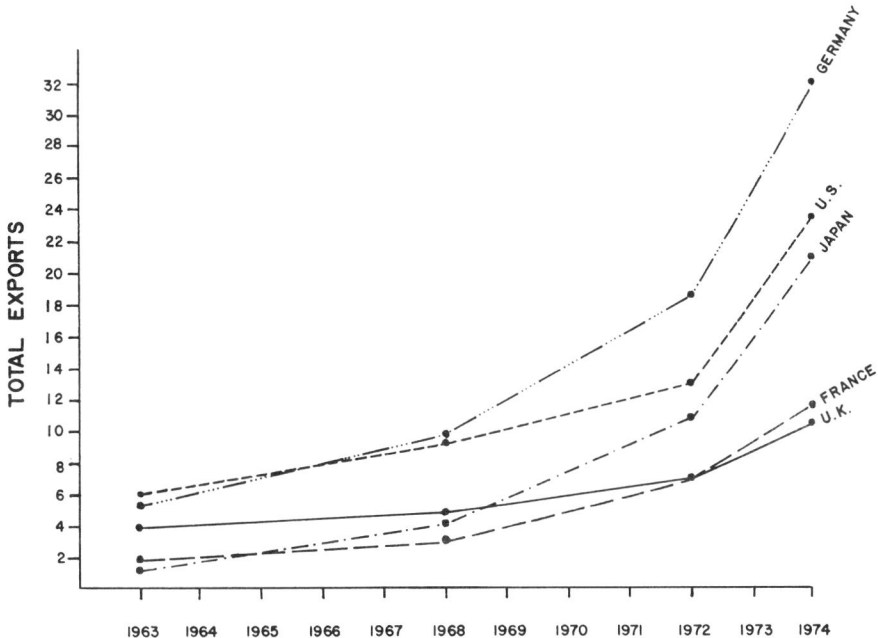

Source: Constructed by the authors.

164 / THE UNITED STATES AND WORLD TRADE

as expected, the growth between 1972 and 1974 was greater for technology-intensive products than for nontechnology-intensive products: the United States experienced an 84 percent growth in its technology-intensive exports between 1972 and 1974, versus a growth of 80 percent in its nontechnology-intensive exports. However, even though these findings are in the anticipated direction, the magnitude of the difference between the two types of products is not as great as might have been expected. The small difference in the magnitudes of change, in fact, suggests that the growth that occurred in both 1972 and 1974 was due more to the price effect caused by the devaluation than to a comparative advantage in the former types of products.

The absolute export figures, however, are not fully indicative of the U.S. position in either type of product. The following sections will analyze the trade figures on a relative basis, first exploring the changes that have occurred in the world market shares of the five major trading nations in technology- and nontechnology-intensive exports, and then discussing the net shifts that have occurred among the five nations.

Market Share Analysis

Figure 9.3 represents a graphic presentation of the changes that have occurred in the market shares of the five leading trading nations with regard to technology-intensive exports. It should be recalled here that the market shares shown in the figure represent the percentage of the total exports of technology-intensive products by the 21 OECD nations employed in the study (see Chapter 8). The United States is depicted in Figure 9.3 as having lost considerable market share in technology-intensive exports between 1963 and 1972, and particularly from 1968 to 1972. From 1972 to 1974, the U.S. market share remained almost unchanged, rising slightly from 21.1 percent in 1972 to 21.3 percent in 1974. Thus, the 84 percent increase in the value of U.S. technology-intensive exports between 1972 and 1974 made only a marginal difference in the share of those exports by this country.

Overall, the data presented in Figure 9.3 suggest that the market shares in technology-intensive exports have been rather static since 1963. The most dramatic change on the figure is associated with Japan, which increased its market share from 5.6 percent in 1963 to 11.8 percent in 1974. The United Kingdom lost market share over the time period, but most of its loss occurred from 1963 to 1968. The three data points on the United Kingdom from 1968 to 1974 varied by only 1 percent. France remained virtually constant throughout the period, varying only between 7.2 percent and 7.5 percent. Germany also showed more variation over the time period than France or the

FIGURE 9.3

Technology-Intensive Export Market Shares
(in percentages)

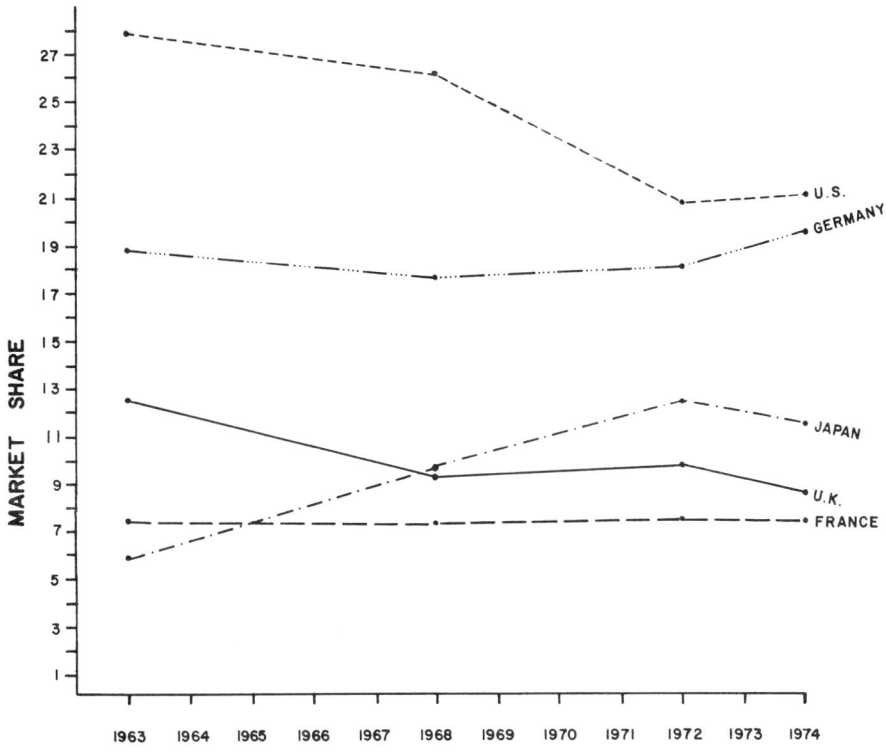

Source: Constructed by the authors.

United Kingdom, going from a low market share of 17.8 percent in 1968 to a 20 percent market share in 1974, but such figures do not indicate a shift of dramatic proportions.

The changes in market shares that followed the 1971 dollar devaluation are also minimal. The largest loss was registered by the United Kingdom (1 percent), and the only other market share loser was Japan (0.9 percent). France remained static, and the United States was characterized by the small increase noted above. Of the five nations, the only one to show a change of greater than 1 percent in market share was Germany, whose share increased from 18.4 percent in 1972 to 20 percent in 1974. These data provide further evidence that the 1971 dollar devaluation did not work to reestablish the U.S. position as an exporter of technology-intensive products. In the short run, at least, it appears that the devaluation only allowed the maintenance of the status quo from the standpoint of the United States. It is interesting to note in this connection that Germany, the only country of the five to experience a noticeable increase in market share from 1972 to 1974, had experienced a substantial revaluation of its currency over the time period.

The market share changes that are associated with the export of nontechnology-intensive products of the five nations from 1963 to 1974 are presented in Figure 9.4. The data represented by the lines in this graph reflect a more dynamic situation than was seen with regard to the technology-intensive products. One reason behind some of the changes indicated on the graph is that the proportion of world exports of these nontechnology-intensive products by the five nations as a group dropped more substantially than was the case for technology-intensive products. In 1963 the five nations accounted for 78.1 percent of the exports of these products, but in 1974 that figure had dropped to 70.1 percent. The comparable figures for technology-intensive exports are 71.5 percent in 1963 and 69.6 percent in 1974. Thus, some of the smaller trading nations among the OECD had begun to increase their market shares in these product categories, notably Canada, Belgium, and Italy.

In 1963, the United States had the largest market share of these nontechnology-intensive exports, followed closely by Germany. Since that time, the United States has fallen considerably behind Germany, even though Germany has registered a slight loss in market share over the time period. Japan, once again, is the nation that changed its position most dramatically from 1963 to 1974. Its market share almost tripled over the period, going from 5.1 percent in 1963 to 15.0 percent in 1974. The United Kingdom was the largest market share loser in nontechnology-intensive exports, dropping from 16.5 percent in 1963 to 7.6 percent in 1974. France showed some fluctuation over the period, but not as much as the other nations, rising slightly from 7.7 percent in 1963 to 8.5 percent in 1974.

FIGURE 9.4

Nontechnology-Intensive Export Market Shares
(in percentages)

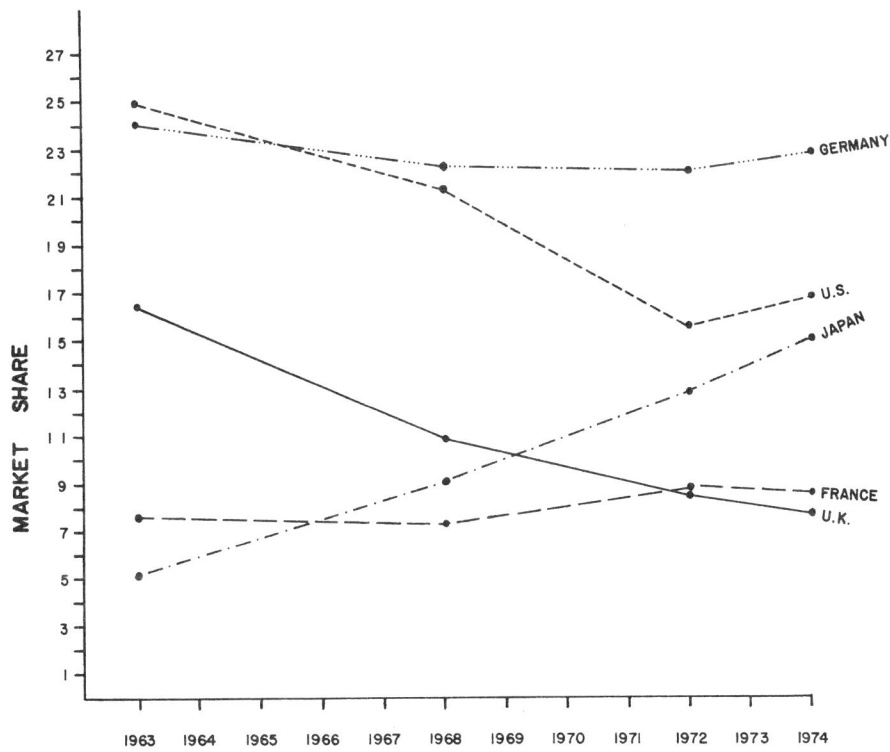

Source: Constructed by the authors.

The changes that occurred in the market share positions of the five nations between 1972 and 1974 for the nontechnology-intensive products provide some contrast to the comparable figures for technology-intensive products. The United States showed somewhat greater improvement in its nontechnology-intensive export position than was the case for technology-intensive exports, increasing its market share by 1.2 percent in the former category versus 0.2 percent in the latter category. In addition, Japan registered a noticeable increase in the market share of nontechnology-intensive products as opposed to the decrease in market share that that nation experienced with regard to technology-intensive products. While Germany increased its market share in both product categories from 1972 to 1974, its increase for nontechnology-intensive products was only half that of its increase for technology-intensive products (0.8 percent versus 1.6 percent). France and the United Kingdom, on the other hand, exhibited approximately the same pattern for both technology- and nontechnology-intensive products, France remaining fairly constant and the United Kingdom losing about 1 percent.

When the market share figures for the technology-intensive and nontechnology-intensive products are viewed together, they provide some interesting deviations from the original expectations of the study. In terms of market share, the United States following the devaluation showed a greater increase in the export of nontechnology-intensive goods than technology-intensive goods. Since it is commonly assumed that the United States has an advantage in the production of the latter types of products, the opposite outcome might have been expected—a reduction in price would have had a larger impact upon the export of those goods in which the United States was competitively superior. It might be argued that technology-intensive products tend to be "unique" goods and, therefore, less sensitive to changes in price. The unique goods argument might explain the situation for the United States, but it is contradicted by figures presented on Japan. Prior to the 1971 dollar devaluation, the Japanese yen was valued 16 percent less relative to the dollar than was the case in 1974. Yet Japan's nontechnology-intensive export share rose substantially between 1972 and 1974, while its technology-intensive export share dropped during that time. Germany's export pattern was somewhat different. That nation continued to gain market share in both categories despite a revaluation of over 30 percent relative to the dollar following the 1971 dollar devaluation.

Net Shift Analysis

The final analysis of the total technology-intensive and nontechnology-intensive exports of the five nations involves the shift share analysis discussed in Chapter 8. The net shift figures produced by the shift share analysis provide an additional dimension by which to understand the changes that have occurred in the United States' trade position from 1963 to 1974. It will be recalled that the net shift figure represents the percent of gains or losses that each nation experiences relative to all of the other nations that have experienced either gains or losses. Such a figure, therefore, provides further information concerning the possible trends that may be occurring in the exports of these product types among the nations in the study.

Table 9.1 presents the net shift figures for the five countries with regard to technology-intensive exports from 1963 to 1974. In order to provide a more comprehensive picture of the changes that occurred between the two years, the table also includes the total technology-intensive exports of each nation in 1974, the market shares of each nation in 1963 and 1974, and the annual growth rate of the technology-intensive exports from each country. The annual growth rate is expressed in terms of the simple percentage increase, not a compounded percentage, and is intended to facilitate comparisons between the countries.

The net shift figure for the United States in Table 9.1 indicates that the United States accounted for most of the total losses experienced by nations that exported technology-intensive products between

TABLE 9.1

1963 to 1974 Technology-Intensive Export Shifts of Major Trading Nations

Country	1974 Exports (thousands of U.S. dollars)	Market Share Percent 1963	1974	Percent Net Shift	Annual Growth Rate (in percent)
United States	23,357,702	27.8	21.3	-53.1	35.3
France	8,238,580	7.2	7.5	2.8	51.6
Germany	21,948,848	18.6	20.0	11.3	53.2
United Kingdom	9,898,227	12.3	9.0	-26.4	33.6
Japan	12,893,201	5.6	11.8	49.7	111.9
21 OECD Nations	109,748,797	100.0	100.0	0	48.8

Source: Compiled by the authors.

1963 and 1974. Of all of the nations in the study that had relative losses in the export of technology-intensive products from 1963 to 1974, the United States accounted for 53.1 percent of those losses. This could be interpreted to mean that most of the gains in relative position of technology-intensive exporters were made at the expense of the United States. In terms of possible trends with respect to technology-intensive exports, this figure indicates that the position of the United States may be more serious than has been depicted by the absolute volume or market share figures.

Of the five major trading nations, the only one to experience a negative net shift besides the United States was the United Kingdom. These two nations account for almost 80 percent of the losses in relative exports of technology-intensive products between 1963 and 1974. At the other extreme is Japan, which accounted for almost 50 percent of the relative gains that occurred in technology-intensive exports over the period. Japan and Germany together accounted for 60 percent of all of the relative gains. France's comparatively small net shift of 2.8 is indicative of that nation's static position with regard to technology-intensive exports, that is, its export growth in this area was slightly greater than the average export growth of all nations for these products.

The growth rate figures in Table 9.1 provide further clarification of the net shift amounts. It can be seen that the growth rates of the United Kingdom and the United States are substantially below those of the other three nations. Japanese exports grew at an annual rate that was more than three times greater than either the United States or the United Kingdom. If U.S. technology-intensive exports had grown at the rate for the combined 21 countries, its total exports of these products would have been in excess of $30 billion.

Table 9.2 presents the net shift figures for the five countries for the 1972 to 1974 time period together with the growth rates and the changes that occurred in each country's market share over the period. The figures presented in the table tend to reinforce the findings from the absolute trade figures and the market share data. From 1972 to 1974, U.S. exports of technology-intensive products grew at a rate that was slightly higher than the combined growth for these exports from 1972 to 1974, 42.2 percent versus the combined rate of 41.0 percent. The United Kingdom continued to have a declining market share during this period, while Germany posted the largest single gain for the period. Japan's exports of technology-intensive products suffered a significant setback from 1972 to 1974, slipping almost 1 percent in market share and accounting for one quarter of all losses during the period.

The 1972 to 1974 net shift figures confirm the technology-intensive trade tendencies that were noted through observing the market

TABLE 9.2

1972 to 1974 Technology-Intensive Export Shifts of Major Trading Nations

Country	1972-1974 Change in Market Share	Percent Net Shift	Annual Growth Rate (in percent)
United States	.18	4.9	42.2
France	.06	1.6	42.2
Germany	1.63	45.5	49.6
United Kingdom	-.96	-26.7	32.7
Japan	-.91	-25.3	35.0
21 OECD Nations	—	0	41.0

Source: Compiled by the authors.

share figures in Figure 9.3. The United States did not stage any type of dramatic comeback in technology-intensive exports following the dollar devaluation. At best it could be said that the downward trend in these exports was temporarily halted. These findings also support the statements concerning the indeterminant price sensitivity of technology-intensive exports. Both Japan and Germany experienced substantial revaluations prior to 1972, yet these two nations' technology-intensive exports responded in opposite ways to the price increases. Germany experienced the largest net gain, while Japan had one of the largest net losses.

Table 9.3 provides the 1963 to 1974 net shift figures for nontechnology-intensive products. It can be seen that even though the U.S. growth rate for nontechnology-intensive products was lower than the corresponding rate for technology-intensive products, the negative net shift figure for the former exports was not as large. This phenomenon can be partially attributed to the fact that world growth in nontechnology-intensive exports was not as great as it was for technology-intensive exports: 43.3 percent versus 48.8 percent. However, the primary factor involved in the net shift differential for the United States was the steep decline of the United Kingdom as an exporter of nontechnology-intensive exports. As a result of the United Kingdom's large relative decline as an exporter of these products, that nation absorbed the plurality of the net shift losses for the period.

TABLE 9.3

1963 to 1974 Nontechnology-Intensive Export Shifts of Major Trading Nations

Country	1974 Exports (thousands of U.S. dollars)	Market Share Percent		Percent Net Shift	Annual Growth Rate (in percent)
		1963	1974		
United States	23,559,009	24.8	16.8	-42.8	26.6
France	11,829,016	7.7	8.5	4.2	48.7
Germany	32,058,103	24.0	22.9	-5.9	41.0
United Kingdom	10,615,801	16.5	7.6	-47.9	15.1
Japan	20,958,362	5.1	15.0	53.5	146.1
21 OECD Nations	139,969,890	100.0	100.0	0	43.3

Source: Compiled by the authors.

Table 9.3 also indicates that even Germany suffered a small negative net shift in nontechnology-intensive exports from 1963 to 1974. In fact, the United States, the United Kingdom, and Germany combined accounted for more than 96 percent of the relative losses incurred among the 21 OECD nations used in the study. The table shows that the primary nation to gain over the period was, once again, Japan, which accounted for more than half of the relative gains. France also gained, but only slightly. The remainder of the net shift gains were divided among the smaller OECD nations mentioned above, with Canada experiencing the largest positive net shift of over 17 percent.

The 1972-1974 net shift figures for nontechnology-intensive exports are presented in Table 9.4. These data also tend to reinforce the market share findings, since they indicate the United States staged a more pronounced comeback in nontechnology-intensive exports following the 1971 devaluation than it did in technology-intensive exports. The simple growth rate for all nations during the period was 33.8 percent, yet U.S. exports grew at 40.8 percent, and the United States recaptured 1.2 percent of the market share that it had lost up to that time. Germany also regained most of the market share that it had lost in nontechnology-intensive exports from 1963 to 1972. However, the most notable increase identified through the shift share analysis was experienced by Japan. That nation accounted for 45.3 percent of the net shift gains which were registered from 1972 to 1974.

When the 1972 to 1974 net shift figures for the United States, Germany, and Japan are combined, it is found that these nations accounted for 88.2 percent of the shift share gains recorded by the 21 OECD nations. In contrast to the total 1963 to 1974 period, therefore, the latter three years were characterized by a reassertion of the dominant nations of the United States and Germany in nontechnology-intensive exports, together with the continued assertion of Japan in this area. While the United Kingdom and France recorded negative net shifts, their combined net shift figure was only -32.0. The remaining countries which recorded negative net shifts consisted primarily of the the European Common Market nations of Italy, Belgium, and the Netherlands, which had a combined net shift of -34.6, and Canada with -32.6.

TABLE 9.4

1972 to 1974 Nontechnology-Intensive Export Shifts of Major Trading Nations

Country	1972-1974 Change in Market Share	Percent Net Shift	Annual Growth Rate (in percent)
United States	1.2	26.2	40.8
France	-0.3	-7.1	31.1
Germany	0.8	16.7	37.2
United Kingdom	-1.2	-24.9	23.2
Japan	2.1	45.3	47.9
21 OECD Nations	—	0.0	33.8

Source: Compiled by the authors.

Summary

The preceding findings support the conclusion that, if the United States ever did possess an export advantage in technology-intensive products, it appears to be losing this advantage. Such a conclusion would have to be accompanied by all of the necessary qualifications, primarily relating to the nature of the product categories which have been identified as technology-intensive, and the fact that those product categories may contain specific products that are not, in fact, technology-intensive. Also, it is possible that the product life cycle argument discussed in Chapter 7 may be relevant to these temporal trends. Such a conclusion would be reached regardless of the operation of a price effect with respect to technology-intensive exports. If a price effect indeed operates for such goods, then the sudden reduction in the price of U.S. exports following the dollar devaluation did nothing more than keep this nation from losing further ground after 1971. On the basis of such findings, it is difficult to infer that a general "turnaround" occurred in U.S. exports of technology-intensive goods after the devaluation. Likewise, if one takes the more theoretically acceptable approach to the analysis of technology-intensive products and assumes that their uniqueness makes them less responsive to price changes, the conclusion remains the same. The continued decline in U.S. market share from 1963 to 1972, and the leveling off that occurred thereafter, cannot but lead one to conclude that the U.S. position is deteriorating, at least in an overall sense.

The preceding conclusion, however, must be viewed as preliminary due to the aggregate nature of the technology-intensive data from which it was derived. It is possible that the sums of all technology-intensive exports which were used in the preceding analyses mask some industry- and product-specific variations in the U.S. export position. If the U.S. decline can be attributed to a limited number of industries or product categories, then the overall deterioration in its position may not be viewed quite so seriously. Such a situation may reflect a tendency toward increased international specialization among high-technology nations. The following analyses explore the U.S. trade position within an industry and product category context in order to provide further clarification to the analyses of the total technology-intensive and nontechnology-intensive trade figures.

INDUSTRY-SPECIFIC EXPORT POSITIONS

The products from which the technology-intensive and nontechnology-intensive export data were derived represent four major industrial groupings according to the SITC classification system: chemicals, basic manufactures, machines and transport equipment, and miscellaneous manufactured goods. Data for each one of these industry groups were analyzed separately using the shift share analysis discussed in Chapter 8. Once again, both technology-intensive exports and nontechnology-intensive exports will be presented in order to facilitate comparison. The data for these industry groupings presented in this chapter will begin with an overview of the reliance of the five major trading nations upon exports of products from each industry group. It will then proceed to focus upon shift share analyses of U. S. exports from each of the industry groups in order to ascertain changes in the U. S. export position. Shift shares for the other major trading nations will be presented in Chapter 10.

Industrial Trade Patterns of Major Trading Nations

Table 9.5 presents the proportion of technology-intensive exports represented by exports from each of the four industry groups for the United States, France, Germany, the United Kingdom, and Japan. The figures indicate that most of the countries' technology-intensive exports consist primarily of products from the chemicals and machines and transport equipment groups, although Japan has consistently had a high percentage of exports from the miscellaneous machinery group. The basic manufactures exports occupy a small percentage of all countries' exports primarily because there is only one four-digit SITC product group within this category that is considered to be technology intensive.

The distinguishing feature between the United States and the other four countries in terms of the distribution of its technology-intensive exports among these four industry groupings is its relatively heavy reliance upon exports of machines and transport equipment. While all of the five nations maintain a large proportion of their technology-intensive exports from this group, the United States has always been particularly reliant upon these types of goods (Branson and Junz 1971, p. 289). Almost three quarters of U. S. technology-intensive exports in 1974 were from the machines and transport equipment industries. For the most part, the proportion of the other nations' exports from this industry group varied between 40 percent and 50 percent. In addition, U. S. exports of machines and transport equipment have increased substantially as a percentage of U. S. technology-intensive exports since 1963. In 1963 exports from this group were 60.2 percent of this nation's total technology-intensive exports, whereas by 1974 that figure had risen to 71.3 percent.

The other industry grouping that accounted for a consistently large percentage of technology-intensive exports from the five nations is chemicals. Technology-intensive chemicals exports have represented more than 30 percent of exports from France, Germany, and the United Kingdom throughout all of the years of the study, with the exception of the United Kingdom in 1972. The United States, however, is characterized by a diminishing percentage of chemical exports

TABLE 9.5

Percentage of Technology-Intensive Exports from Industry Groups for Major Trading Nations

	SITC Code	Industry Group	United States	France	Germany	United Kingdom	Japan
1963	5	Chemicals	27.2	40.3	39.4	31.9	28.8
	6	Basic Manufactures	1.8	4.3	2.3	3.1	3.9
	7	Machines and Transport Equipment	60.2	45.9	41.6	53.2	44.5
	8	Miscellaneous Manufactures	10.8	9.4	16.7	11.8	22.8
1968	5	Chemicals	16.2	39.3	40.7	31.8	22.7
	6	Basic Manufactures	1.0	5.1	4.3	3.1	6.0
	7	Machines and Transport Equipment	70.1	45.8	40.8	51.9	47.4
	8	Miscellaneous Manufactures	12.7	9.8	14.2	13.2	23.9
1972	5	Chemicals	14.1	34.1	37.6	28.0	21.0
	6	Basic Manufactures	0.7	4.6	5.0	3.2	4.8
	7	Machines and Transport Equipment	72.8	50.7	44.0	55.1	51.0
	8	Miscellaneous Manufactures	12.4	10.6	13.3	13.7	23.2
1974	5	Chemicals	16.0	42.0	44.1	36.2	28.1
	6	Basic Manufactures	1.3	4.4	4.9	2.8	4.6
	7	Machines and Transport Equipment	71.3	44.1	39.6	49.0	46.3
	8	Miscellaneous Manufactures	11.4	9.5	11.4	12.0	20.9

Source: Compiled by the authors.

among its total technology-intensive exports. Whereas in 1963 chemicals represented 27.2 percent of U.S. technology-intensive exports, by 1974 that figure had dropped to 16.0 percent. Between 1972 and 1974, there was a noticeable increase in the proportion of technology-intensive chemicals exports by all of the five nations. The United States showed the smallest gain, rising slightly less than 2 percent. The other four nations, however, all had increases of about 7 percent in the proportion of technology-intensive exports which came from the chemicals group. For the most part, the rise in the proportion of chemicals exports corresponded directly with a similar decrease in the percentage of their exports of machines and transport equipment. The shift that occurred in chemicals between 1972 and 1974 is probably associated with the price increases for petroleum which took place during that period.

The figures in Table 9.6 portray the proportion of nontechnology-intensive exports among the products employed in the study which each of the nations devotes to products from the four industry groupings. Unlike the comparable data for the technology-intensive exports, few differences of any great magnitude exist between the United States and the other four nations with regard to the manner in which this nation's nontechnology-intensive exports are distributed. All five of the countries export primarily products from the machines and transport equipment industry group. Exports from the other industry groups are minor in comparison. Here again, though, an increase can be seen in the proportion of nontechnology-intensive exports between 1972 and 1974 that are associated with the chemicals group in each nation. While the percentage figures remain small in contrast to the machines and transport equipment group, the percentage from chemicals more than doubled for Germany and increased at somewhat lesser rates for the other nations.

In summary, Tables 9.5 and 9.6 depict the United States as being predominantly reliant upon exports of products from the machines and transport equipment industry group. While the other nations are approximately equal in their reliance upon these exports for the nontechnology-intensive products employed in the study, they do not approach the United States' level of reliance within the technology-intensive category. The other nations place greater emphasis upon chemicals for technology-intensive exports than does the United States, which is characterized by a decreasing proportion of its technology-intensive trade from within that industry group. Chemicals, however, have been accounting for an increasing proportion of most nations' trade since 1972 due probably to the increased price of petroleum. The manner in which these tendencies are translated into the changes that have occurred in the United States' position with regard to technology-intensive and nontechnology-intensive exports is discussed below.

TABLE 9.6

Percentage of Nontechnology-Intensive Exports from Industry Groups for Major Trading Nations

	SITC Code	Industry Group	United States	France	Germany	United Kingdom	Japan
1963	5	Chemicals	8.2	6.8	3.4	4.8	1.6
	6	Basic Manufactures	4.2	8.6	3.0	4.5	14.5
	7	Machines and Transport Equipment	87.1	83.9	93.2	90.4	83.7
	8	Miscellaneous Manufactures	0.5	0.7	0.4	0.3	0.1
1968	5	Chemicals	5.8	7.9	4.0	5.4	1.2
	6	Basic Manufactures	3.2	9.3	3.5	4.2	14.1
	7	Machines and Transport Equipment	90.6	82.3	91.9	90.1	84.6
	8	Miscellaneous Manufactures	0.5	0.5	0.6	0.3	0.1
1972	5	Chemicals	3.4	5.6	1.9	4.2	0.5
	6	Basic Manufactures	3.2	8.5	3.9	4.8	10.8
	7	Machines and Transport Equipment	92.9	85.2	93.6	90.6	88.7
	8	Miscellaneous Manufactures	0.5	0.7	0.6	0.4	0.0
1974	5	Chemicals	5.0	7.2	4.0	7.3	0.8
	6	Basic Manufactures	4.0	9.1	4.8	5.5	8.8
	7	Machines and Transport Equipment	90.5	82.8	90.7	86.7	90.3
	8	Miscellaneous Manufactures	0.4	0.8	0.5	0.5	0.0

Source: Compiled by the authors.

Shift Share within Industrial Groupings

Technology-Intensive Exports

Table 9.7 presents the net shift and market share figures for U.S. technology-intensive exports from 1963 to 1974. In addition, the table shows the simple growth rate that U.S. exports within each industry group experienced during this period and the corresponding export growth rate registered by the combined 21 nations that were employed in the study. When taken in conjunction with the proportion of exports data presented above, these data provide further insights into the technology-intensive trade position of the United States.

The figures in Table 9.7 indicate that the industry group that is primarily responsible for the declining overall position of U.S. technology-intensive exports is chemicals. From 1963 to 1974, the U.S. market share dropped from 22.9 percent to 9.4 percent; while over the same time period, chemicals exports had dropped from 27.2 percent of U.S. technology-intensive exports to 16.0 percent (see Table 9.5). The growth rate of U.S. exports in this category was less than one-third of the growth rate of the 21 countries combined. The extent of the relative losses which the United States incurred in technology-intensive chemicals exports is reflected in the large net shift figure of -65.7, which indicates that almost two-thirds of the 21 nations' losses in this category could be attributed to the United States. If U.S. technology-intensive chemicals exports had grown at the rate of the combined 21 nations, the amount of these exports would have been greater than $9 billion instead of the actual amount of $3,740,651.

Table 9.7 also contains data that indicate that the United States lost substantial market share in exports from the basic manufactures category. This category, however, represents only a small fraction of total U.S. technology-intensive exports and the losses would therefore not have a large impact on the overall U.S. position.

While the United States also experienced losses in the machines and transport equipment and miscellaneous manufactures categories, these losses were small compared to the other two categories. U.S. market share in both categories dropped no more than 2 percent, and the U.S. growth rate almost kept pace with the combined nations' growth rate. The ability to keep pace was particularly important in the machines and transport equipment category, since exports from within that industry group represent such a large proportion of this nation's technology-intensive exports. However, it must also be noted that the world growth rate for exports from these latter two industry groups was significantly slower than the growth rate for basic manufactures and chemicals during the period of the study. It appears that the United States was keeping pace (or nearly so) only in the industries

TABLE 9.7

1963 to 1974 United States Technology-Intensive Export Shifts by Industry Group

SITC Code	Industry Group	1974 Exports (thousands of U.S. dollars)	Market Share Percent 1963	Market Share Percent 1974	Percent Net Shift	U.S. Annual Growth Rate (in percent)	OECD Annual Growth Rate (in percent)
5	Chemicals	3,740,651	22.9	9.4	-65.7	17.1	54.5
6	Basic Manufactures	293,582	16.8	7.3	-35.0	22.5	63.0
7	Machines and Transport Equipment	16,659,965	33.7	32.1	-15.0	43.4	45.9
8	Miscellaneous Manufactures	2,663,504	21.1	19.1	-13.3	37.8	42.7

Source: Compiled by the authors.

experiencing relatively low rates of growth—a further factor in the deteriorating overall position of the United States.

The U.S. export position within the four industry groups during the post-devaluation years is shown in Table 9.8. The data indicate

TABLE 9.8

1972 to 1974 United States Technology-Intensive Export Shifts by Industry Group

SITC Code	Industry Group	1972-1974 Change in Market Share	Percent Net Shift	U.S. Annual Growth Rate (in percent)	OECD Annual Growth Rate (in percent)
5	Chemicals	-0.79	-19.8	54.3	62.6
6	Basic Manufactures	3.39	49.7	116.6	39.3
7	Machines and Transport Equipment	2.93	59.8	40.4	31.7
8	Miscellaneous Manufactures	.74	25.2	34.8	31.0

Source: Compiled by the authors.

that U.S. export growth outpaced the combined nations' export growth within every industry group but chemicals. In the chemicals category U.S. growth continued to lag behind world growth with the result that the United States lost market share in technology-intensive chemicals exports even during times of relatively low prices. Since the combined nations' growth in chemicals was considerably greater than the corresponding growth within the other industry groups, the losses that the United States had in this category were probably largely responsible for the poorer-than-expected performance of this nation in technology-intensive exports as a whole from 1972 to 1974.

Within the remaining three industry groups, the United States performed well from 1972 to 1974. Of particular importance is the performance in machines and transport equipment, since that category represents such a large percentage of U.S. technology-intensive exports. In this category U.S. market share rose from 29.2 percent in 1972 to 32.1 percent in 1974. The net shift figure of 59.8 indicates that this nation accounted for almost 60 percent of world gains in this area. The impressive performance with regard to basic manufactures would have had only a small impact on the overall technology-intensive export performance due to the small amount of exports involved. However, the recovery of some market share in the miscellaneous manufactures category would have had a positive effect on the overall U.S. position, since exports of those products account for over 10 percent of total U.S. technology-intensive exports.

Nontechnology-Intensive Exports

Table 9.9 presents the market share, growth rate, and net shift figures for U.S. nontechnology-intensive exports in the four industry groups from 1963 to 1974. The table indicates certain differences in the patterns of these exports when compared to the comparable data for technology-intensive exports. First, the market share losses were generally greater for the nontechnology-intensive exports than for the technology-intensive exports. In the latter category of exports the United States experienced substantial losses within only two of the four industry groups. In contrast, all of the industry groups were characterized by substantial market share losses from 1963 to 1974. In most cases market shares in 1974 were about half of their 1963 values and U.S. growth rates were less than half of the growth rates for the combined 21 nations.

Similar to the figures for technology-intensive exports, the largest absolute loss in U.S. market share of the nontechnology-intensive exports from 1963 to 1974 was associated with chemicals, while machines and transport equipment exports had a relatively small loss. The United States accounted for almost all of the relative losses in nontechnology-intensive chemicals exports between 1963 and 1974, as reflected by the net shift value of -85.8. Its market share over that time period dropped from 38.6 percent to 19.3 percent. In 1963, U.S. exports of nontechnology-intensive chemicals were more than twice as great as those of any other nation. By 1974, Germany had eclipsed the United States for the number one position in this category. With regard to machines and transport equipment, the losses incurred in this category were not as great as in the other nontechnology-intensive categories. However, the losses were greater than found within the technology-intensive machines and transport equipment exports.

The 1972 to 1974 figures for U.S. nontechnology-intensive exports are presented in Table 9.10. They show that the United States rebounded significantly in all but one of the industry groups from 1972 to 1974. United States' basic manufactures exports and exports of machines and transport equipment grew at rates greater than that of the combined 21 nations. However, in neither of these groups of exports

TABLE 9.9

1963 to 1974 United States Nontechnology-Intensive Export Shifts by Industry Group

SITC Code	Industry Group	1974 Exports (thousands of U.S. dollars)	Market Share Percent		Percent Net Shift	U.S. Annual Growth Rate (in percent)	OECD Annual Growth Rate (in percent)
			1963	1974			
5	Chemicals	1,188,087	38.6	19.3	-85.8	13.0	35.0
6	Basic Manufactures	945,581	20.1	10.9	-49.7	25.2	53.9
7	Machines and Transport Equipment	21,331,418	24.2	17.2	-37.5	28.0	43.1
8	Miscellaneous Manufactures	89,190	24.2	11.4	-52.2	16.3	44.8

Source: Compiled by the authors.

TABLE 9.10

1972 to 1974 United States Nontechnology-Intensive Export Shifts by Industry Group

SITC Code	Industry Group	1972-1974 Change in Market Share	Percent Net Shift	U.S. Annual Growth Rate (in percent)	OECD Annual Growth Rate (in percent)
5	Chemicals	5.24	21.7	85.3	48.1
6	Basic Manufactures	2.31	39.5	63.4	39.0
7	Machines and Transport Equipment	.99	21.0	38.5	32.9
8	Miscellaneous Manufactures	-1.29	-22.6	21.6	29.2

Source: Compiled by the authors.

were the market share gains as great for the period as in the technology-intensive exports within the same industry groups (see Table 9.8). In direct contrast to the technology-intensive exports, nontechnology-intensive chemicals grew at a rate considerably greater than the rate of the combined nations, and U.S. market share increased more than 5 percent from 1972 to 1974. The one category of nontechnology-intensive exports in which the United States experienced a relative loss from 1972 to 1974, miscellaneous manufactures, cannot be considered important due to the small proportion of U.S. nontechnology-intensive exports (0.4 percent in 1974) accounted for by this category.

Shift Shares at the Two-Digit SITC Level

The preceding analyses of U.S. exports at the one-digit SITC level of disaggregation indicate that this nation's relative trade gains and losses have tended to be tied to certain industry groups rather than to all technology-intensive industries. The following discussion provides a brief analysis of relative U.S. gains and losses at a further level of disaggregation. The two-digit SITC codes refer to more spe-

U. S. TECHNOLOGY-INTENSIVE EXPORT POS / 185

cific industries rather than to broad industry groups. It will be seen that although relative losses tend to characterize certain broad industry groups (one-digit SITC), they do not necessarily reflect all of the individual industries within those groups. The opposite also applies for those industry groups in which the United States had relative export gains over the time period of the study.

Two-Digit Technology-Intensive Products

The market share, net shift and growth rate figures from 1963 to 1974 for technology-intensive products at the two-digit SITC level are presented in Table 9.11. In addition, Table 9.11 presents the value of 1974 U. S. exports of the products from each industry in order to provide an indication of the magnitude of U. S. exports from each category. With regard to technology-intensive exports from chemicals industries (SITC group 5), the two-digit data generally confirm the results obtained from the one-digit analyses. Exports from all but one of the chemicals divisions suffered substantial relative losses from 1963 to 1974. Some of these losses, however, tended to be more dramatic than others. For instance, in category 51, which in absolute terms represented the second largest category of U. S. chemicals exports, U. S. export growth over the time period averaged only 4.6 percent per year, versus a growth rate for the combined nations of 59.1 percent per year. As a result, U. S. market share in this category dropped from 21.3 percent in 1963 to 4.3 percent in 1974. The other major U. S. chemicals exports experienced similar, though not so dramatic, setbacks from 1963 to 1974. The exception is fertilizers, SITC 56, in which the United States showed an increase in market share during the period.

The other notable finding with respect to 1963 to 1974 U. S. technology-intensive exports concerns the industries within the machines and transport equipment group (SITC 7). It will be recalled that this industrial group showed one of the smallest losses from 1963 to 1974 when analyzed at the one-digit level. The two-digit data, however, indicate that the relative competitiveness of the United States in this group is industry specific. Two of the three major industries within this category, nonelectric machinery and transport equipment, actually experienced relative export gains from 1963 to 1974. On the other hand, the United States had a drop in market share in the third associated industry, electrical machinery. Thus, the overall loss which occurred within the machines and transport equipment group could be largely attributed to that one industry.

The 1972 to 1974 figures for U. S. technology-intensive exports at the two-digit level of disaggregation are shown in Table 9.12. The data for the more specific components of the overall chemicals category provide further clarification of the net loss recorded in that area

TABLE 9.11

1963 to 1974 United States Technology-Intensive Export Shifts Within Two-Digit SITC Classifications

SITC Code	Industry	1974 Exports (thousands of U.S. dollars)	Market Share Percent 1963	Market Share Percent 1974	Percent Net Shift	U.S. Annual Growth Rate (in percent)	OECD Annual Growth Rate (in percent)
51	Chemical Elements, Compounds	722,400	21.3	4.3	-71.8	4.6	59.1
53	Dyes, Tanning, Color Products	119,750	8.5	5.8	-27.3	25.1	41.0
54	Medicinal, Etc., Products	639,686	26.9	13.5	-95.1	13.7	35.9
55	Perfume, Cleaning, Etc., Products	41,584	36.1	10.1	-96.8	1.4	28.0
56	Fertilizers, Manufactured	332,658	14.6	16.3	7.2	33.9	29.4
58	Plastic Materials, Etc.	1,618,344	24.7	13.2	-53.8	38.6	80.2
59	Chemicals NES*	266,229	42.2	18.5	-94.1	11.5	37.6
65	Textile Yarn, Fabric, Etc.	293,582	16.8	7.3	-35.0	22.5	63.0
71	Machinery, Non-Electric	5,742,251	26.4	29.5	23.2	57.5	50.6
72	Electrical Machinery	5,151,298	25.9	21.1	-33.8	36.9	47.3
73	Transport Equipment	5,766,416	64.5	72.0	43.5	39.4	34.2
86	Instruments, Watches, Clocks	2,266,263	22.0	20.4	-10.5	35.5	38.8
89	Miscellaneous Manufactured Goods NES*	397,241	16.1	13.9	-11.6	56.8	67.1

*Not Elsewhere Specified.
Source: Compiled by the authors.

TABLE 9.12

1972 to 1974 United States Technology-Intensive Export Shifts Within Two-Digit SITC Classifications

SITC Code	Industry	1972–1974 Change in Market Share	Percent Net Shift	U.S. Annual Growth Rate (in percent)	OECD Annual Growth Rate (in percent)
51	Chemical Elements, Compounds	-2.20	-29.0	32.0	73.5
53	Dyes, Tanning, Color Products	1.20	41.5	59.3	36.4
54	Medicinal, Etc., Products	.06	1.8	32.9	32.1
55	Perfume, Cleaning, Etc., Products	.37	6.6	40.0	36.2
56	Fertilizers, Manufactured	-1.95	-9.4	118.5	138.2
58	Plastic Materials, Etc.	.11	2.6	66.7	65.3
59	Chemicals NES*	4.28	50.4	88.3	55.9
65	Textile Yarn, Fabric, Etc.	3.39	49.7	116.6	39.3
71	Machinery, Non-Electric	1.75	38.3	32.2	26.8
72	Electrical Machinery	2.03	43.6	44.8	35.2
73	Transport Equipment	8.61	88.2	46.1	34.2
86	Instruments, Watches, Clocks	.26	11.3	34.6	33.0
89	Miscellaneous Manufactured Goods NES*	1.86	28.0	36.1	24.1

*Not Elsewhere Specified.
Source: Compiled by the authors.

by the United States from 1972 to 1974. Most of the loss could be attributed to SITC 51, chemical elements and compounds. In addition, fertilizers (SITC 56) also show a loss from 1972 to 1974, which is somewhat surprising considering that this industry was the only chemicals category to register a market share increase from 1963 to 1974. The remaining chemicals industries remained generally static from 1972 to 1974, not losing market share, but also not registering any significant gains, with the exception of SITC 59, chemicals not elsewhere specified, for which U.S. exports actually registered a market share increase.

All of the remaining two-digit technology-intensive categories experienced relative gains from 1972 to 1974, most resulting in a market share increase of greater than 1 percent. The largest market share increase occurred with regard to transport equipment (SITC 73) where the United States increased its market share by 8.61 percent—a substantial rise particularly considering the size of the total export market for those products ($16.9 billion for the 21 nations). The two remaining SITC 7 categories also had notable increases during the post-devaluation period, including electrical machines which was the only SITC 7 technology-intensive industry to register a loss from 1963 to 1974. From the standpoint of the United States, it seems particularly important that exports of technology-intensive machines and transport equipment compete well internationally, since exports from that industry group comprise such a large percentage of total U.S. technology-intensive exports. While the United States does appear to be competing effectively in this area, the data suggest that its competitiveness is attributable largely to the 1971 dollar devaluation. A comparison of Tables 9.11 and 9.12 indicates that for SITC 73 exports the difference between the 1963 and 1974 market shares is more than accounted for by the increase in market share which occurred between 1972 and 1974. Similarly, more than half of the differential between the 1963 and 1974 U.S. market shares associated with SITC 71 occurred from 1972 to 1974. With respect to SITC 72, the loss which the United States experienced from 1963 to 1974 would have been much greater without the more than 2 percent market share gain registered from 1972 to 1974. It would appear, therefore, that the 1971 dollar devaluation was directly responsible for the United States' ability to increase its international competitiveness with respect to machines and transport equipment.

Two-Digit Nontechnology-Intensive Products

Table 9.13 shows the figures for the two-digit SITC nontechnology-intensive exports from 1963 to 1974. The data in the table indicate that the U.S. losses between these two years spanned almost all of the associated two-digit categories. The three categories for which

TABLE 9.13

1963 to 1974 United States Nontechnology-Intensive Export Shifts Within Two-Digit SITC Classifications

SITC Code	Industry	1974 Exports (thousands of U.S. dollars)	Market Share Percent		Percent Net Shift	U.S. Annual Growth Rate (in percent)	OECD Annual Growth Rate (in percent)
			1963	1974			
52	Coal, Petroleum, Etc., Chemicals	83,133	67.3	25.9	-90.6	2.5	20.9
54	Medicinal, Etc., Products	71,227	23.9	26.0	16.0	46.4	41.8
55	Perfume, Cleaning, Etc., Products	85,059	14.1	11.0	-21.3	33.2	44.9
57	Explosives, Pyrotechnic Products	49,764	22.2	23.2	6.2	22.2	20.8
59	Chemicals NES*	898,904	41.0	19.6	-88.4	12.4	35.8
62	Rubber Manufactures NES *	544,090	21.0	12.4	-44.8	21.8	42.9
65	Textile Yarn, Fabric, Etc.	252,851	18.0	7.1	-55.8	30.0	89.8
66	Nonmetal Mineral Manufactures NES*	148,640	20.1	20.2	.8	33.7	33.3
71	Machinery, Non-Electric	10,157,036	29.3	21.0	-53.1	21.4	33.4
72	Electrical Machinery	1,821,639	20.5	15.2	-33.5	31.8	45.9
73	Transport Equipment	8,697,796	19.3	14.7	-17.2	38.7	53.5
81	Plumbing, Heating, Lighting Equipment	49,107	22.0	8.3	-49.6	10.3	41.9
89	Miscellaneous Manufactured Goods NES*	40,083	33.0	20.4	-45.6	31.4	56.3

*Not Elsewhere Specified.

Source: Compiled by the authors.

190 / THE UNITED STATES AND WORLD TRADE

the United States experienced gains from 1963 to 1974 (SITC 54, 57, 66) were relatively minor in terms of export volume. It should be noted that with regard to SITC 7, machines and transport equipment, the United States had losses in all three of the two-digit categories. This finding is in contrast to the technology-intensive exports from the same industry, for which the United States registered its most substantial gains during the 1963 to 1974 period.

The 1972 to 1974 figures for nontechnology-intensive products at the two-digit level of disaggregation are presented in Table 9.14. While the United States lost market share in two of the chemicals categories and in both of the miscellaneous manufactures categories (SITC 81 and 89), all of these categories tended to represent a small portion of the total nontechnology-intensive exports. Most of the chemicals categories experienced significant gains from 1972 to 1974. This was particularly the case for the residual chemicals category, SITC 59, from which the United States derived the vast majority of its nontechnology-intensive chemicals exports. The fast growth that occurred in this latter category was responsible for the overall positive gain that the United States registered in its nontechnology-intensive chemicals exports. The three two-digit categories associated with machines and transport equipment also showed gains from 1972 to 1974. These gains, however, were not as great as those registered by the technology-intensive exports from the same category; nor were they as large as the gains for some of the nontechnology-intensive chemicals products and basic manufactures. The comparatively modest gains made within the machines and transport equipment category, and particularly within the two-digit transport equipment group (SITC 73) probably retarded the U.S. comeback in nontechnology-intensive exports following the devaluation, since this category is by far the largest among the nontechnology-intensive products.

Shift Shares at the Four-Digit SITC Level

The four-digit SITC is the highest level of disaggregation for which the international trade data are available. The market share and net shift figures for the technology-intensive exports of the United States for 1963 to 1974 are presented at the end of this volume in Appendix D, Table D.1. This appendix also includes the 1972 market share information. The corresponding data for the U.S. nontechnology-intensive exports are presented in Table D.2. For purposes of presentation of the four-digit data in the present chapter, the product categories were divided into three groups on the basis of the 1963 to 1974 market share information. The first group consisted of those product categories for which the United States posted market share

TABLE 9.14

1972 to 1974 United States Nontechnology-Intensive Export Shifts Within Two-Digit SITC Classifications

SITC Code	Industry	1972-1974 Change in Market Share	Percent Net Shift	U.S. Annual Growth Rate (in percent)	OECD Annual Growth Rate (in percent)
52	Coal, Petroleum, Etc., Chemicals	-10.40	-69.4	85.3	139.0
54	Medicinal, Etc., Products	-.00	-.0	37.5	37.1
55	Perfume, Cleaning, Etc., Products	2.12	62.2	52.0	31.9
57	Explosives, Pyrotechnic Products	2.74	36.0	39.4	28.4
59	Chemicals NES*	6.56	19.4	100.7	50.0
62	Rubber Manufactures NES*	2.68	38.2	68.4	42.5
65	Textile Yarn, Fabric, Etc.	2.54	35.7	87.9	38.3
66	Nonmetal Mineral Manufactures NES*	.50	8.8	27.9	25.5
71	Machinery, Non-Electric	1.19	34.4	42.8	37.1
72	Electrical Machinery	1.06	30.2	47.8	40.5
73	Transport Equipment	.77	11.4	33.0	28.2
81	Plumbing, Heating, Lighting Equipment	-.33	-6.8	23.0	25.4
89	Miscellaneous Manufactured Goods NES*	-6.93	-48.9	20.0	43.1

*Not Elsewhere Specified.
Source: Compiled by the authors.

gains of greater than 2 percent from 1963 to 1974. The second group was comprised of product categories for which the United States exports remained within plus or minus 2 percent in terms of market share from 1963 to 1974. The third group then contained those product groups that the United States had an export market share loss of greater than 2 percent from 1963 to 1974.

The process of dividing the product groups into categories in which the United States gained, remained the same, or lost in terms of export market share was then repeated for the 1972 to 1974 data. The one difference in the assignment process between the 1963 to 1974 data and the 1972 to 1974 data was that for the latter period a cutoff point of plus or minus 1 percent was used to distinguish between the products for which this country gained, remained the same, or lost with respect to export market share. This general procedure was used for classifying both technology-intensive and nontechnology-intensive U. S. exports.

On the basis of this assignment process, two matrices were constructed; one matrix for technology-intensive exports and the second for nontechnology-intensive exports (see Tables 9.15 and 9.16). Each of these nine-cell matrices represents a cross-classification of the product categories in which the United States gained, remained the same, or lost market share from 1963 to 1974 and from 1972 to 1974. The horizontal alignment of cells refers to the market share changes in the former period. Thus, if one reads across the top three cells in the matrix, all of the product categories listed in those cells are product categories for which the United States gained more than two percent in market share from 1963 to 1974. Similarly, the vertical alignment of cells portrays the product categories for which U. S. export market share gained, remained the same, and decreased from 1972 to 1974.

The purpose of these matrices is to present in as concise a fashion as possible the changes in position that occurred in the U. S. export position at this high level of data disaggregation. The individual cells of the matrices show the general performance levels of each product category over the two time periods. For instance, the top left cell shows those product categories for which the United States posted export market share gains during both periods, the top center cell shows the product categories for which the United States posted gains from 1963 to 1974, but for which market share remained fairly static from 1972 to 1974, etc.

Four-Digit Technology-Intensive Products

Table 9.15 presents the matrix for U. S. technology-intensive exports. It can be seen that for the 1963 to 1974 period, the United

TABLE 9.15

U.S. Technology-Intensive Exports: 1963 to 1974 and 1972 to 1974 Market Share Changes of Four-Digit SITC Categories

		Changes in 1972-1974 U.S. Market Share		
		Gains ($\Delta > 1\%$)	No Change ($\Delta \pm 1\%$)	Losses ($\Delta < -1\%$)
Changes in 1963 to 1974 U.S. Market Share	Gains ($\Delta > 2\%$)	513.4 561.2 581.9 711.5 711.6 729.3 734.1 861.3 861.4 891.2	711.4 714.9 861.1	513.6 515.1 515.2 515.3 729.7 862.3
	No Change ($\Delta \pm 2\%$)	513.5 722.1 861.5 862.4	724.2 864.1	561.1
	Losses ($\Delta < -2\%$)	513.3 531.0 541.1 599.2 651.6 711.3 711.8 714.1 714.3 729.5 734.9 861.2 861.7 861.8	513.2 532.3 541.3 541.4 541.6 541.7 551.2 581.1 581.2 581.3 719.63 722.2 724.1 724.9 863.0 891.1	513.1 714.2 861.6 861.9

Source: Compiled by the authors.

States registered losses in several more product groups than was the case for gains. This finding was to be expected on the basis of the material presented thus far. However, it should also be noted that the losses for 1963 to 1974 included many product categories from the industry groups (one-digit SITC) that had registered overall gains during the period. Several products from the nonelectric machines and transport equipment industries experienced losses from 1963 to 1974. In addition, among the product categories for which the United States registered 1963 to 1974 gains were several chemicals products. The change in the U. S. export position in technology-intensive products, therefore, was not as industry-specific as the one- and two-digit data had suggested.

The 1972 to 1974 figures presented in the matrix shown in Table 9.15 indicate that during those years the United States either gained market share or remained relatively constant in most instances. More than 80 percent of the product groups are listed within those two categories for 1972 to 1974. In most cases, however, the products for which the United States lost market share from 1963 to 1974 had either remained constant or market share had also declined from 1972 to 1974. Such was the case particularly for chemical products, but also for products from other categories. Some technology-intensive chemical products for which the United States had gained market share from 1963 to 1974 experienced losses from 1972 to 1974. This finding might suggest that for these products the United States had lost its international competitiveness following the devaluation. Such products, however, are clearly in the minority.

Four-Digit Nontechnology-Intensive Products

The matrix presented in Table 9.16 shows the comparable data for nontechnology-intensive products. Similar to the technology-intensive findings, the 1963 to 1974 nontechnology-intensive data show several more products for which the United States lost market share than gained. Also similar to the technology-intensive results, however, the losses and gains cut across almost all of the industry groups. Perhaps surprisingly, one product category for which the United States gained market share over both time periods is SITC 7321, passenger cars. This is a product category for which the United States has not been known as an international competitor, yet this country has managed to increase its market share through the years of the study.

When cross tabulated with the 1963 to 1974 findings, the 1972 to 1974 figures indicate some of the same tendencies for nontechnology-intensive products as they did for technology-intensive products. The figures indicate that for most of the products categories in which the United States lost 1963 to 1974 market share, the market share either

TABLE 9.16

U.S. Nontechnology-Intensive Exports: 1963 to 1974 and 1972 to 1974 Market Share Changes of Four-Digit SITC Categories

		Changes in 1972-1974 U.S. Market Share		
		Gains ($\Delta > 1\%$)	No Change ($\Delta \pm 1\%$)	Losses ($\Delta < -1\%$)
Changes in 1963 to 1974 U.S. Market Share	Gains ($\Delta > 2\%$)	571.2 571.4 664.4 664.8 667.4 711.7 731.3 732.1 735.9	541.9 723.1 726.1 729.1	571.3 621.0 664.7 731.7 733.4
	No Change ($\Delta \pm 2\%$)	629.3 712.2 718.2 719.1	521.1 599.5 719.2 732.9 735.3	731.4
	Losses ($\Delta < -2\%$)	553.0 571.1 599.7 599.9 629.1 629.9 653.5 664.6 711.2 712.9 717.1 718.1 718.3 719.3 719.4 719.8 725.0 729.2 731.2 731.6 732.4 812.2	629.4 664.5 712.3 715.1 717.2 717.3 718.4 718.5 719.5 719.7 726.2 729.6 729.9 731.5 732.3 812.1	521.4 599.6 663.5 664.2 711.1 712.5 715.2 719.9 729.4 732.2 732.8 733.3 735.1 899.6

Source: Compiled by the authors.

TABLE 9.17

Associated Volumes and Percentages of U.S. Exports Which Gained, Lost, and Maintained Constant Market Share, 1963 to 1974 and 1972 to 1974

	1974 Export Total	1974 Export Percent
Technology-Intensive Exports, 1963 to 1974		
Gained Market Share	11,475,463	49.13
Constant Market Share	1,577,665	6.75
Lost Market Share	10,304,561	44.12
Technology-Intensive Exports, 1972 to 1974		
Gained Market Share	13,822,903	59.18
Constant Market Share	7,636,143	32.69
Lost Market Share	1,898,643	8.13
Nontechnology-Intensive Exports, 1963 to 1974		
Gained Market Share	3,605,298	15.30
Constant Market Share	3,130,956	13.29
Lost Market Share	16,822,752	71.41
Nontechnology-Intensive Exports, 1972 to 1974		
Gained Market Share	9,981,016	42.37
Constant Market Share	6,979,492	29.63
Lost Market Share	6,598,498	28.01

Source: Compiled by the authors.

remained static or decreased from 1972 to 1974. Some additional data with respect to the volume of exports represented by the individual product categories, however, suggest that the situation may be more serious in the case of nontechnology-intensive exports. Table 9.17 shows the percentage of 1974 technology-intensive and nontechnology-intensive exports which are represented by the three types of market share changes noted in the matrix. These percentages are produced for both the 1963 to 1974 and 1972 to 1974 product categories for which the United States had gains, no change, or losses in export market share. The figures show that technology-intensive product categories for which the United States gained market share from 1963 to 1974 represented 49.1 percent of total technology-intensive exports. The comparable figure for 1963 to 1974 nontechnology-intensive exports is 15.3 percent. Thus, the relatively few technology-intensive gains from 1963 to 1974 involved products which represent a substantial portion of U.S. trade in those goods, but the same cannot be said for the nontechnology-intensive products. A comparison of the 1972 to 1974 figures for technology-intensive and nontechnology-intensive exports suggests the same conclusion. The United States appears to be losing market share in products that are more critical to its export position in nontechnology-intensive products than in technology-intensive products.

Summary

The analyses of the changes that have occurred in the U.S. export position at varying levels of aggregation have provided an indication of the pattern associated with the U.S. export position in technology-intensive products. While at higher levels of aggregation, the negative changes that had occurred in the U.S. export position seemed to be industry-specific, the more disaggregated data indicated that losses occurred within all industries in both the technology-intensive and nontechnology-intensive categories. The data also suggested that the 1971 dollar devaluation was very important to the United States, since it was responsible for the preservation of the U.S. export position in many instances. Indeed, many of the overall gains that were registered from 1963 to 1974 for particular products or industries could be attributed directly to the post-1971 years. Yet the devaluation did not cause the dramatic turnaround in U.S. technology-intensive exports that might have been expected. Most of the product categories that had lost market share over the 1963 to 1974 period either also lost during the 1972 to 1974 period or, as was more often the case, remained relatively static. Although U.S. technology-intensive exports appeared to be stronger than nontechnology-intensive exports following the devaluation, the findings do not suggest that the United States is regaining the position it previously held with respect to technology-intensive exports.

U.S. IMPORTS OF TECHNOLOGY-INTENSIVE PRODUCTS

The preceding analyses have been exclusively concerned with U.S. exports of technology-intensive and nontechnology-intensive products. However, an analysis of the import patterns associated with these products can provide an additional dimension to the study of the changes which have occurred in the U.S. export position in these products. It should be expected that a decline in U.S. exports of technology-intensive products would be accompanied by a corresponding increase in the U.S. market share for imports of those products. This is particularly the case since the export data suggested that in many instances a price effect was in operation. If a decrease in U.S. export market share could be attributed to relatively high U.S. prices, then imports of the relatively low-priced foreign goods into the United States should increase.

The following discussion provides an analysis of the changes that have occurred in U.S. import market share for technology-intensive and nontechnology-intensive products. The analyses will not be at the level of disaggregation of the similar export analyses; only the totals and one-digit SITC figures will be examined. At this level of aggregation, however, it is possible to discern the associated import trends. It will be seen that the findings do not coincide with the above-mentioned expectations, and that these results provide further implications for the U.S. export position.

U.S. Imports versus Other Major Trading Nations

When the market shares and net shifts of total U.S. technology-intensive and nontechnology-intensive imports are compared with those of the other major trading nations, the results appear very much as expected given the changes that had occurred in the U.S. export position. Table 9.18 presents the 1963 to 1974 figures for technology-intensive imports of the five major trading nations. The data show that each of the five nations increased its share of total technology-intensive imports, which suggests the growing importance of these five markets for technology-intensive products. These increases would also reflect the increasing propensity of the industrialized states to trade among themselves. As noted in Chapter 2, trade among the industrialized countries is increasing more rapidly than the trade of Third World countries either among themselves or with the industrialized nations.

The United States, however, far outpaced the other nations with respect to its rate of import growth and the resulting increase in import market share. The corresponding figures for nontechnology-intensive imports are shown in Table 9.19. Here again, the United States registered the largest gains in import market share, but the magnitude of the discrepancy between the United States and the other nations was considerably greater than in the case of technology-intensive

TABLE 9.18

1963 to 1974 Technology-Intensive Import Shifts of Major Trading Nations

Country	1974 Imports (thousands of U.S. dollars)	Market Share Percent		Percent Net Shift	Annual Growth Rate (in percent)
		1963	1974		
United States	10,576,960	8.1	12.5	45.5	93.3
France	8,769,399	9.1	10.3	13.2	67.1
Germany	10,233,243	10.0	12.1	22.1	71.9
United Kingdom	8,246,751	8.5	9.7	12.8	67.4
Japan	4,940,719	5.5	5.8	3.7	62.1

Source: Compiled by the authors.

TABLE 9.19

1963 to 1974 Nontechnology-Intensive Import Shifts of Major Trading Nations

Country	1974 Imports (thousands of U.S. dollars)	Market Share Percent		Percent Net Shift	Annual Growth Rate (in percent)
		1963	1974		
United States	18,176,302	7.8	19.5	79.3	130.5
France	8,429,603	8.3	9.1	5.2	52.0
Germany	7,742,521	7.8	8.3	3.5	50.6
United Kingdom	6,154,726	5.5	6.6	7.3	57.7
Japan	2,616,054	3.6	2.8	-5.5	34.3

Source: Compiled by the authors.

products. Other than the United States, only the United Kingdom increased its import market share by more than 1 percent, and Japan's share even dropped slightly. Conversely, U.S. import market share more than doubled, to the point that by 1974 the United States accounted for almost 20 percent of the 21 nations' imports of the nontechnology-intensive products used in the study.

The import market shares in some instances did not behave as might be expected during the 1972 to 1974 time period. The data for this period are presented in Tables 9.20 and 9.21 for technology-intensive and nontechnology-intensive exports, respectively. U.S. import market share for both types of products decreased during these years following the dollar devaluation. However, market share for technology-intensive imports fell more sharply than for nontechnology-intensive imports, despite the presumed higher price elasticity of the latter goods. The most curious aspect of these data concerns the import market shares of Germany through the 1972 to 1974 period. Despite the revaluation of the mark, German import market share declined. The decline that occurred for nontechnology-intensive imports was close to that registered by the United States, while the decline in technology-intensive market share was negligible. Japan behaved more in accordance to the expectations one would have for a nation with a revalued currency. Japan's import market share for both types of goods rose markedly from 1972 to 1974.

U.S. Import Shares within Industry Groups

While the findings with regard to total technology- and nontechnology-intensive import market share correspond reasonably well with the expectations for the United States, when these data are analyzed within industry groups some anomalies arise. Table 9.22 presents the 1963 to 1974 import market shares and net shift values for technology-intensive and nontechnology-intensive products. The most notable finding that appears with respect to both types of products is that the greatest growth in import market share occurs in the industry group for which the U.S. export market share declined relatively little from 1963 to 1974: machines and transport equipment. Within the technology-intensive portion of that industry group, the United States registered the smallest loss in export market share from 1963 to 1974 (see Table 9.7). The same was true with respect to nontechnology-intensive exports (see Table 9.9). However, the figures in Table 9.22 indicate that it was within the machines and transport equipment group that the United States registered the largest increase in import market share from 1963 to 1974. This finding applied to both the technology-intensive and nontechnology-intensive categories.

TABLE 9.20

1972 to 1974 Technology-Intensive Import Shifts of Major Trading Nations

Country	1972-1974 Change in Market Share	Percent Net Shift	Annual Growth Rate (in percent)
United States	-3.13	-75.3	21.9
France	.27	6.5	42.2
Germany	-.10	-2.4	39.0
United Kingdom	.71	17.1	46.8
Japan	.78	18.9	53.7

Source: Compiled by the authors.

TABLE 9.21

1972 to 1974 Nontechnology-Intensive Import Shifts of Major Trading Nations

Country	1972-1974 Change in Market Share	Percent Net Shift	Annual Growth Rate (in percent)
United States	-1.90	-36.7	20.2
France	.49	9.5	31.3
Germany	-1.34	-26.0	16.3
United Kingdom	.43	8.3	32.3
Japan	.73	14.2	54.0

Source: Compiled by the authors.

TABLE 9.22

1963 to 1974 United States Technology-Intensive and Nontechnology-Intensive Import Shifts by Industry Group

	SITC Code	Industry Group	1974 Imports (thousands of U.S. dollars)	Market Share Percent 1963	Market Share Percent 1974	Percent Net Shift	U.S. Annual Growth Rate (in percent)	OECD Annual Growth Rate (in percent)
Technology Intensive	5	Chemicals	1,215,146	3.8	4.0	2.1	68.2	64.5
	6	Basic Manufactures	143,516	0.0	5.5	25.8	∞	58.0
	7	Machines and Transport Equipment	7,232,393	9.1	18.0	64.7	118.9	55.3
	8	Miscellaneous Manufactures	1,985,905	16.6	17.6	11.1	54.9	51.0
Non-technology Intensive	5	Chemicals	282,526	5.3	5.7	4.0	45.9	41.9
	6	Basic Manufactures	856,147	7.5	12.9	32.2	121.7	66.3
	7	Machines and Transport Equipment	17,011,853	8.0	21.0	79.5	134.6	45.9
	8	Miscellaneous Manufactures	19,097	.6	2.8	11.0	308.4	55.8

Source: Compiled by the authors.

In the former category U.S. import market share almost doubled, while in the latter category market share increased more than two and one-half times.

It will be recalled that the United States experienced its largest export market share losses within the chemicals. Yet, the import data in Table 9.22 indicate that import market shares increased the least within this category for both technology-intensive and nontechnology-intensive products. In both cases import market share gains from 1963 to 1974 were less than 0.5 percent, while the export market share losses were -13.5 percent for technology-intensive products and -19.3 percent for nontechnology-intensive products (see Tables 9.7 and 9.9). The remaining two industry groups had import patterns that were more in conformance with expectations, since export market share losses were roughly approximated by import market share gains. The lack of conformity between exports and imports within the chemicals and machines and transport equipment is particularly important, however, because of the large proportion of total exports and imports that are represented by these two industry groups. In 1974 these two industry groups represented 87.3 percent of U.S. technology-intensive exports and 79.9 percent of technology-intensive imports. The corresponding figures for the nontechnology-intensive products employed in the study are 95.6 percent for exports and 95.2 percent for imports.

The market share and net shift figures for 1972 to 1974 U.S. imports, presented in Table 9.23, show some of the same patterns as the 1963 to 1974 figures. Over this time period U.S. technology-intensive chemicals exports lost market share, despite the dollar devaluation. Table 9.23 indicates that the U.S. market share of technology-intensive imports also decreased between these years. The 1972 to 1974 figures for machines and transport equipment are not as anomalous as the corresponding 1963 to 1974 figures. Even here, however, when this industry group's import and export shifts are contrasted with the comparable shifts which occurred within miscellaneous manufactures the same type of anomaly appears: machines and transport equipment had larger export shifts but smaller negative import shifts than miscellaneous manufactures. The 1972 to 1974 import figures for nontechnology-intensive products shown in Table 9.23 are more in accordance with expectations, given the nature of the export figures. In general, the products that had large positive export shifts had large negative import shifts, and vice versa.

The import figures within the industry groups for the United States raise certain questions about the competitiveness of U.S. exports, particularly technology-intensive exports. The import figures suggest that the United States may not be losing markets in technology-intensive exports due to a lack of price competitiveness or to a lack

TABLE 9.23

1972 to 1974 United States Technology-Intensive and Nontechnology-Intensive Import Shifts by Industry Group

	SITC Code	Industry Group	1972-1974 Change in Market Share	Percent Net Shift	U.S. Annual Growth Rate (in percent)	OECD Annual Growth Rate (in percent)
Technology Intensive	5	Chemicals	-.95	-29.3	38.7	59.4
	6	Basic Manufactures	-9.93	-86.3	-21.8	28.0
	7	Machines and Transport Equipment	-1.97	-60.3	23.8	31.4
	8	Miscellaneous Manufactures	-4.03	-80.3	15.4	29.8
Non-technology Intensive	5	Chemicals	-3.77	-29.6	8.3	45.9
	6	Basic Manufactures	-4.61	-76.8	16.7	39.8
	7	Machines and Transport Equipment	-1.36	-26.3	20.6	24.7
	8	Miscellaneous Manufactures	.13	2.3	29.1	24.9

Source: Compiled by the authors.

of uniqueness of the products. If U. S. products were not price-competitive on the international market, then U. S. imports of these products should increase. If other nations were producing better technology-intensive products than the United States, then imports should also increase. Since U. S. imports did not increase to the extent that its exports decreased, it is possible that other explanations besides price and quality may largely account for the deterioration in the U. S. technology-intensive export position.

The alternative explanations for the change in the U. S. technology-intensive export position will be explored in Chapter 11 which presents the conclusions of the study of technology-intensive trade. Before such conclusions can be reached, however, it is necessary to consider the changes that have occurred in the technology-intensive export positions of the other major trading nations on a more disaggregated basis. These findings are presented in Chapter 10.

10

TECHNOLOGY-INTENSIVE EXPORT POSITION OF OTHER MAJOR TRADING NATIONS

The preceding chapter provided an analysis of the United States' position in technology-intensive and nontechnology-intensive exports. It was seen that this position has changed substantially since 1963, and that the 1971 dollar devaluation did not, in an overall fashion, create the dramatic reversal in the downward trend of U.S. technology-intensive exports that might have been expected. It was noted, however, that large variations existed in industry and product export performance for the United States.

In order to provide a more comprehensive understanding of the changes that have occurred in international technology-intensive exports, the present chapter presents the industry-specific export data for France, West Germany, the United Kingdom, and Japan. The data for Germany and Japan will be presented down to the two-digit SITC level, whereas the data for France and the United Kingdom will be analyzed only at the one-digit SITC level. The reason for these differential analyses is that in Chapter 9 Germany and Japan were seen to account for the largest percentage net shift in technology-intensive exports. The detailed findings from these two countries, therefore, could give a clearer understanding of the changes that have occurred in the United States' technology-intensive export position.

GERMAN EXPORT POSITION

Analysis of the overall positions of the five major trading nations in Chapter 9 indicated that from 1963 to 1974 West Germany had tended to maintain a relatively stable market share for both technology-intensive and nontechnology-intensive exports. That nation had a small

POSITION OF OTHER MAJOR TRADING NATIONS / 207

gain in the former category and a small loss in the latter. However, from 1972 to 1974, Germany showed a gain in both categories of exports. The following analysis of German exports on a more disaggregated basis indicates that these patterns are not constant across all industries or product categories, and that the overall findings are often reflective of a limited number of industries or products.

One-Digit SITC Analysis

Table 10.1 presents the market share, net shift, and growth rate figures for German technology-intensive and nontechnology-intensive exports at the one-digit SITC level from 1963 to 1974. In addition, total 1974 exports from each industry group are presented in the table in order to provide an indication of the relative importance of exports from the individual industry groups. The reason for the stable German export position over this time period was the small, but positive, market share changes that took place with respect to the two industry groups that contain the overwhelming majority of German technology-intensive exports, chemicals and machines and transport equipment. While the other two industry groups were more dynamic, they did not represent a large proportion of German exports, and therefore had little influence on the overall results.

In the case of the 1963 to 1974 nontechnology-intensive export findings, the data in Table 10.1 indicate that the small overall loss incurred by German exports over this period was directly attributable to one industry group, machines and transport equipment. Exports from this group accounted for more than 90 percent of German nontechnology-intensive exports, and therefore the small loss that occurred in this category worked to overwhelm the gains registered in the other three nontechnology-intensive groups.

The 1972 to 1974 one-digit SITC findings for Germany are presented in Table 10.2. Here it can be seen that all of the industry groups contributed to the overall gain that German technology-intensive exports registered from 1972 to 1974. Even the miscellaneous machinery group (SITC 8) gained market share over this period, although German exports in this category had lost market share from 1963 to 1974. In addition, the 1972 to 1974 change in the market share for technology-intensive machines and transport equipment is slightly greater than the change that occurred over the entire 1963 to 1974 period, and more than one-third of the 1963 to 1974 market share difference in chemicals can be attributed to the 1972 to 1974 period. Despite the revaluation of the mark that occurred throughout this latter period, Germany was able to increase its market share in technology-intensive exports across all industry groups.

TABLE 10.1

WEST GERMANY: 1963 to 1974 Technology-Intensive and Nontechnology-Intensive Export Shifts by Industry Group

	SITC Code	Industry Group	1974 Exports (thousands of U.S. dollars)	Market Share Percent 1963	Market Share Percent 1974	Percent Net Shift	German Annual Growth Rate (in percent)	OECD Annual Growth Rate (in percent)
Technology Intensive	5	Chemicals	9,682,912	22.2	24.3	10.1	60.6	54.5
	6	Basic Manufactures	1,072,877	14.6	26.8	45.0	123.0	63.0
	7	Machines and Transport Equipment	8,680,771	15.5	16.7	11.5	50.2	45.9
	8	Miscellaneous Manufactures	2,512,288	21.9	18.0	-25.1	33.7	42.7
		Total Technology-Intensive Exports	21,948,848	18.6	20.0	11.3	53.2	48.8
Non-technology Intensive	5	Chemicals	1,276,858	15.4	20.7	23.6	50.4	35.0
	6	Basic Manufactures	1,531,131	14.1	17.7	19.5	70.2	54.0
	7	Machines and Transport Equipment	29,084,890	25.1	23.4	-9.1	39.7	43.1
	8	Miscellaneous Manufactures	157,220	16.0	20.0	16.2	58.4	44.8
		Total Nontechnology-Intensive Exports	32,058,103	24.0	22.9	-5.9	41.0	43.3

Source: Compiled by the authors.

TABLE 10.2

WEST GERMANY: 1972 to 1974 Technology-Intensive and Nontechnology-Intensive Export Shifts by Industry Group

	SITC Code	Industry Group	1972-1974 Change in Market Share	Percent Net Shift	German Annual Growth Rate (in percent)	OECD Annual Growth Rate (in percent)
Technology Intensive	5	Chemicals	.73	18.3	66.6	62.6
	6	Basic Manufactures	2.10	30.1	47.2	39.3
	7	Machines and Transport Equipment	1.40	27.9	39.5	31.7
	8	Miscellaneous Manufactures	.85	28.8	35.6	31.0
		Total Technology-Intensive Exports	1.63	45.5	49.6	41.0
Non-technology Intensive	5	Chemicals	9.81	40.7	137.0	48.1
	6	Basic Manufactures	2.74	46.9	55.9	39.0
	7	Machines and Transport Equipment	.32	6.8	34.5	32.9
	8	Miscellaneous Manufactures	-1.31	-23.0	24.8	29.2
		Total Nontechnology-Intensive Exports	0.80	16.7	37.2	33.8

Source: Compiled by the authors.

The findings in Table 10.2 indicate that from 1972 to 1974 market share gains were also generally the case for German exports of the nontechnology-intensive products employed in the study. The only industry group for which German exports experienced a market share loss was miscellaneous manufactures; and exports from this group comprised only 0.5 percent of 1974 nontechnology-intensive exports from Germany. Machines and transport equipment exports (SITC 7), the only nontechnology-intensive industry group in which German exports decreased their market share from 1963 to 1974, actually registered a slight increase from 1972 to 1974. German nontechnology-intensive chemicals exports showed the most dramatic market share increase from 1972 to 1974, 9.8 percent. Since the difference between the 1963 and the 1974 German market shares for nontechnology-intensive chemicals was only 5.3 percent, the 1972 to 1974 market change figure indicates that German chemicals exports of these goods were decreasing from 1963 to 1972, but showed a resurgence after 1972. Once again, all of these market share increases occurred despite the revalued Mark.

Two-Digit SITC Analysis

Table 10.3 presents the market share, growth rate, and net shift figures for German technology-intensive exports from 1963 to 1974 at the two-digit SITC level. The data shown in the table indicate that the tendency for German technology-intensive exports to maintain their market share between these two years was not industry specific: across all industries there was a tendency to maintain a rather constant market share. Such consistency was particularly the case for the industries that are characterized by the largest volumes of exports from Germany. SITC 51, 58, 71, and 72 all had 1974 export levels of greater than three billion dollars, and in each case the German market share increased, but only slightly. The only major German technology-intensive export industry that lost market share from 1963 to 1974 was SITC 86, instruments, watches, and clocks. Here, German market share decreased by 3.6 percent. The German industries that had the more dramatic market share gains or losses tended to be those that had relatively smaller volumes of exports. Thus, Germany's stable position with respect to technology-intensive exports cannot be attributed to any particular industry. In most of that nation's major export industries, growth occurred at about the same rate as that for the combined OECD nations.

The relative stability that characterized the German industries with regard to technology-intensive exports was not present for the nontechnology-intensive exports used in the study. Table 10.1 shows

TABLE 10.3

WEST GERMANY: 1963 to 1974 Technology-Intensive Export Shifts Within Two-Digit SITC Classifications

SITC Code	Industry	1974 Exports (thousands of U.S. dollars)	Market Share Percent 1963	Market Share Percent 1974	Percent Net Shift	German Annual Growth Rate (in percent)	OECD Annual Growth Rate (in percent)
51	Chemical Elements, Compounds	4,110,303	23.0	24.3	5.4	63.0	59.1
53	Dyes, Tanning, Color Products	833,880	37.0	40.5	34.9	45.8	41.0
54	Medicinal, Etc., Products	897,244	15.5	19.0	25.0	46.3	35.9
55	Perfume, Cleaning, Etc., Products	44,263	5.6	10.8	19.3	62.5	28.0
56	Fertilizers, Manufactured	183,387	14.7	9.0	-24.1	14.5	29.4
58	Plastic Materials, Etc.	3,202,060	26.0	26.1	0.3	80.5	80.2
59	Chemicals NES*	411,775	20.7	28.7	31.8	55.7	37.6
65	Textile Yarn, Fabric, Etc.	1,072,877	14.6	26.8	45.0	123.0	63.0
71	Machinery, Nonelectric	3,913,082	18.8	20.1	9.9	54.8	50.6
72	Electrical Machinery	4,547,347	18.2	18.6	3.2	48.8	47.3
73	Transport Equipment	220,342	3.6	2.8	-4.9	24.0	34.2
86	Instruments, Watches, Clocks	2,054,600	22.1	18.5	-24.9	31.0	38.8
89	Miscellaneous Manufactured Goods NES*	457,688	20.2	16.0	-22.1	51.4	67.1

*Not Elsewhere Specified.
Source: Compiled by the author.

that German nontechnology-intensive exports had a small loss in world market share from 1963 to 1974. The industry figures presented in Table 10.4, however, suggest that this loss was largely attributable to one industry, transport equipment. That industry accounted for 36 percent of German nontechnology-intensive exports in 1974, yet from 1963 to 1974 Germany suffered a market share loss of almost 7 percent, from 26.4 percent in 1963 to 19.5 percent in 1974. The primary export of this industry is automobiles, a fact which indicates that German loss of world automobile markets is responsible for retarding that nation's export growth in the nontechnology-intensive sector. The other industry which accounted for a large proportion of German nontechnology-intensive exports, nonelectric machinery, recorded a market share gain from 1963 to 1974. This industry accounted for slightly more than 40 percent of nontechnology-intensive German exports in 1974, and between 1963 and 1974 Germany increased its market share by 2.7 percent. With regard to the remaining nontechnology-intensive exports, most showed market share increases, and many of these increases were substantial. However, the magnitude of exports of machines and transport equipment tended to overwhelm these gains when all industries were aggregated.

The 1972 to 1974 German market share and net shift figures for technology-intensive exports are shown in Table 10.5. It was previously shown that total German technology-intensive exports had a large market share increase over this period. The data in the table indicate that, once again, these technology-intensive export gains were not industry specific, but characterized almost all of the industries' exports. Some of the larger gains were recorded by those industries that had the largest export volumes, SITC 51, 71, and 72. Only two industries, SITC 53 and 54, had decreases in market share over the period, and the decrease for the latter was marginal. In addition, all of the industries which had market share losses from 1963 to 1974 (see Table 10.3) showed gains from 1972 to 1974. When the 1963 to 1974 and the 1972 to 1974 figures are compared, they indicate that Germany had experienced several market share losses from 1963 to 1972, but that many of these losses were recaptured from 1972 to 1974. The recapturing of market share was most noticeable in the case of technology-intensive export industries that had the largest volume of exports, such as machinery, plastics, and chemical elements and compounds.

Table 10.6 shows that German nontechnology-intensive exports also gained market share from 1972 to 1974 in most instances, although the overall gain was not as great as that for German technology-intensive exports. Once again, the primary influence on the 1972-1974 overall results for nontechnology-intensive exports came from the two industries, nonelectric machinery and transport equipment, that ac-

TABLE 10.4

WEST GERMANY: 1963 to 1974 Nontechnology-Intensive Export Shifts Within Two-Digit SITC Classifications

SITC Code	Industry	1974 Exports (thousands of U.S. dollars)	Market Share Percent 1963	Market Share Percent 1974	Percent Net Shift	German Annual Growth Rate (in percent)	OECD Annual Growth Rate (in percent)
52	Coal, Petroleum, Etc., Chemicals	63,953	7.2	19.9	27.9	74.5	20.9
54	Medicinal, Etc., Products	67,920	21.6	24.8	24.8	49.6	41.8
55	Perfume, Cleaning, Etc., Products	92,143	8.7	11.9	22.5	64.9	44.9
57	Explosives, Pyrotechnic Products	48,340	25.0	22.5	-16.3	17.9	20.8
59	Chemicals NES*	1,004,502	16.1	21.9	23.7	51.8	35.8
62	Rubber Manufactures NES*	859,646	14.9	19.6	25.0	59.7	42.9
65	Textile Yarn, Fabric, Etc.	557,204	11.7	15.7	20.6	124.0	89.8
66	Nonmetal Mineral Manufactures NES*	114,281	15.2	15.5	2.0	34.4	33.3
71	Machinery, Non-Electric	13,176,269	24.5	27.2	17.6	38.4	33.4
72	Electrical Machinery	2,953,563	22.7	24.7	12.7	50.9	45.9
73	Transport Equipment	11,536,389	26.4	19.5	-25.8	37.3	53.5
81	Plumbing, Heating, Lighting Equipment	125,628	14.4	21.3	25.2	66.5	41.9
89	Miscellaneous Manufactured Goods NES*	31,592	22.2	16.1	-22.1	38.4	56.3

*Not Elsewhere Specified.
Source: Compiled by the authors.

TABLE 10.5

WEST GERMANY: 1972 to 1974 Technology-Intensive Export Shifts Within Two-Digit SITC Classifications

SITC Code	Industry	1972-1974 Change in Market Share	Percent Net Shift	German Annual Growth Rate (in percent)	OECD Annual Growth Rate (in percent)
51	Chemical Elements, Compounds	1.9	24.6	84.2	73.5
53	Dyes, Tanning, Color Products	-1.0	-34.1	34.9	36.4
54	Medicinal, Etc., Products	-0.2	-5.7	31.8	32.1
55	Perfume, Cleaning, Etc., Products	1.4	24.4	49.5	36.2
56	Fertilizers, Manufactured	2.3	10.9	201.7	138.2
58	Plastic Materials, Etc.	0.8	19.0	69.3	65.3
59	Chemicals NES*	1.9	22.0	63.8	55.9
65	Textile Yarn, Fabric, Etc.	2.1	30.1	47.2	39.3
71	Machinery, Nonelectric	1.8	38.7	34.7	26.8
72	Electrical Machinery	1.5	32.9	43.4	35.2
73	Transport Equipment	0.5	5.3	54.3	34.2
86	Instruments, Watches, Clocks	0.5	22.6	35.9	33.0
89	Miscellaneous Manufactured Goods NES*	1.8	26.6	33.9	24.1

*Not Elsewhere Specified.
Source: Compiled by the authors.

TABLE 10.6

WEST GERMANY: 1972 to 1974 Nontechnology-Intensive Export Shifts Within Two-Digit SITC Classifications

SITC Code	Industry	1972-1974 Change in Market Share	Percent Net Shift	German Annual Growth Rate (in percent)	OECD Annual Growth Rate (in percent)
52	Coal, Petroleum, Etc., Chemicals	4.4	29.2	192.8	139.0
54	Medicinal, Etc., Products	1.1	33.6	41.4	37.1
55	Perfume, Cleaning, Etc., Products	0.1	3.4	33.2	31.9
57	Explosives, Pyrotechnic Products	0.8	11.1	31.9	28.4
59	Chemicals NES*	12.9	38.2	193.9	50.0
62	Rubber Manufactures NES*	3.2	45.0	60.7	42.5
65	Textile Yarn, Fabric, Etc.	2.3	32.9	54.3	38.3
66	Nonmetal Mineral Manufactures NES*	1.5	26.9	34.3	25.5
71	Machinery, Nonelectrical	0.3	9.8	38.7	37.1
72	Electrical Machinery	1.2	32.7	45.4	40.5
73	Transport Equipment	-0.5	-6.9	26.9	28.2
81	Plumbing, Heating, Lighting Equipment	-0.2	-4.8	25.1	25.4
89	Miscellaneous Manufactured Goods NES*	-4.4	-30.8	23.7	43.1

*Not Elsewhere Specified.
Source: Compiled by the authors.

216 / THE UNITED STATES AND WORLD TRADE

counted for more than three-fourths of these exports. The former industry had gained market share from 1972 to 1974, but only slightly. The latter industry lost some market share during the period. These two industries, therefore, had a depressing effect on nontechnology-intensive export growth from 1972 to 1974, whereas many of the other, lower volume, industries recorded large market share gains.

JAPANESE EXPORT POSITION

The findings reported in Chapter 9 indicated the spectacular growth of Japan in the international export market for manufactures. Japan's export growth has been spectacular in both absolute and relative terms. In the period covered by the present study, Japan has become the third largest exporter of technology-intensive products; it is also the third largest exporter of the nontechnology-intensive products used in the study. Japan's market share has more than doubled for both technology-intensive and nontechnology-intensive exports from 1963 to 1974. Also from 1963 to 1974, Japan was characterized by the largest percentage net shift figure, indicative of the fact that Japan had captured more export market share in the product categories employed in the study than any of the other OECD nations. The following discussion provides further insights into the pattern of Japanese export growth by presenting the findings pertaining to these exports at the one and two-digit SITC levels.

One-Digit SITC Analysis

Table 10.7 shows the market share, percent net shift, and growth rate figures for Japanese exports within the one-digit SITC classifications for the 1963 to 1974 time period. These figures are shown for both technology-intensive exports and nontechnology-intensive exports. With regard to technology-intensive exports, it can be seen that substantial growth occurred within all of the industry groups. All industries except chemicals at least doubled their share of the world export market from 1963 to 1974, and chemicals almost doubled its market share. Therefore, Japan's growth as a technology-intensive exporter was not industry specific; this growth occurred across all major industry groups. In addition, the percent net shift values indicate that Japan was the primary market share gainer within two of the industry groups, machines and transport equipment and miscellaneous manufactures. Within both of these technology-intensive categories, Japan had a net shift value of greater than 60 percent, which indicates that for all of the nations which recorded gains in market share, Japan alone accounted for more than 60 percent of these gains.

TABLE 10.7

JAPAN: 1963 to 1974 Technology-Intensive and Nontechnology-Intensive Export Shifts by Industry Group

	SITC Code	Industry Group	1974 Exports (thousands of U.S. dollars)	Market Share Percent 1963	Market Share Percent 1974	Percent Net Shift	Japanese Annual Growth Rate (in percent)	OECD Annual Growth Rate (in percent)
Technology Intensive	5	Chemicals	3,625,547	4.9	9.1	20.4	109.0	54.5
	6	Basic Manufactures	598,915	7.5	15.0	27.5	134.3	63.0
	7	Machines and Transport Equipment	5,967,743	5.0	11.5	62.8	116.7	45.9
	8	Miscellaneous Manufactures	2,700,996	9.0	19.4	67.0	102.1	42.7
		Total Technology-Intensive Exports	12,893,201	5.6	11.8	49.7	111.9	48.8
Non-technology Intensive	5	Chemicals	172,785	1.5	2.8	5.6	71.4	35.0
	6	Basic Manufactures	1,847,344	14.3	21.3	38.1	85.1	54.0
	7	Machines and Transport Equipment	18,930,082	4.8	15.2	55.6	158.3	43.1
	8	Miscellaneous Manufactures	4,673	1.3	0.6	-2.8	15.7	44.8
		Total Nontechnology-Intensive Exports	20,958,362	5.1	15.0	53.5	146.1	43.3

Source: Compiled by the authors.

The figures for nontechnology-intensive Japanese exports presented in Table 10.7 suggest a different pattern than existed for Japan's technology-intensive exports. One industry group, machines and transport equipment, accounts for the vast majority of the nontechnology-intensive exports. It is within this industry group that Japan experienced the largest growth for nontechnology-intensive exports. Market share for machines and transport equipment more than tripled from 1963 to 1974, from 4.8 percent in 1963 to 15.2 percent in 1974. Within the remaining nontechnology-intensive industry groups, the growth did not match that of machines and transport equipment. One industry group, miscellaneous manufactures, even lost market share from 1963 to 1974, although the volume of Japanese nontechnology-intensive exports in this category is miniscule. With regard to chemicals, Japan increased its market share but still remained a relatively minor exporter of nontechnology-intensive goods from that industry group. Other than machines and transport equipment exports, the only industry group for which Japan registered a noticeable market share increase is basic manufactures. Therefore, unlike technology-intensive exports, Japan's spectacular growth from 1963 to 1974 in exports of the nontechnology-intensive goods used in the study was highly industry specific. The overwhelming majority of its growth can be traced to one industry group— machines and transport equipment.

The 1972 to 1974 figures for Japanese technology-intensive and nontechnology-intensive exports are presented in Table 10.8. With regard to technology-intensive exports from 1972 to 1974, it can be seen that Japan felt the effects of its revalued currency to a much greater extent than Germany. For three of the four industry groups, Japanese exports suffered a loss in market share from 1972 to 1974. The only industry group for which technology-intensive exports did not lose market share, chemicals, just barely managed to keep pace with world export growth. The result was a large overall net loss recorded by Japanese technology-intensive exports from 1972 to 1974.

The 1972 to 1974 figures for nontechnology-intensive Japanese exports are, once again, considerably different than for the technology-intensive exports. Overall, Japan showed an increase in market share for nontechnology-intensive exports from 1972 to 1974. The figures in Table 10.8, however, show that this increase can be attributed to exports of machines and transport equipment. Market share for nontechnology-intensive exports from this industry group increased by 2.5 percent from 1972 to 1974 despite the revaluation of the yen. Exports of nontechnology-intensive goods from chemicals industries also rose during this period, but were more than compensated for by the losses which Japanese exports incurred in basic manufactures. Therefore, the substantial market share gains recorded by Japan in machinery and transport equipment exports appear to have prevented

TABLE 10.8

JAPAN: 1972 to 1974 Technology-Intensive and Nontechnology Intensive Export Shifts by Industry Group

	SITC Code	Industry Group	1972-1974 Change in Market Share	Percent Net Shift	Japanese Annual Growth Rate (in percent)	OECD Annual Growth Rate (in percent)
Technology Intensive	5	Chemicals	.04	1.1	63.6	62.6
	6	Basic Manufactures	-1.50	-21.3	-31.9	39.3
	7	Machine and Transport Equipment	-.76	-15.5	27.2	31.7
	8	Miscellaneous Manufactures	-1.20	-40.9	26.8	31.0
		Total Technology-Intensive Exports	-.91	-25.3	35.0	41.0
Non-technology Intensive	5	Chemicals	1.08	4.5	110.5	48.1
	6	Basic Manufactures	-2.45	-42.0	30.3	39.0
	7	Machines and Transport Equipment	2.50	53.1	49.7	32.9
	8	Miscellaneous Manufactures	-.23	-4.0	7.8	29.2
		Total Nontechnology-Intensive Exports	2.10	45.3	47.9	33.8

Source: Compiled by the authors.

220 / THE UNITED STATES AND WORLD TRADE

Japanese nontechnology-intensive exports from experiencing the losses which characterized that nation's technology-intensive exports from 1972 to 1974.

Two-Digit SITC Analysis

The data at the two-digit SITC level provide further clarification of the trends in Japanese exports noted above. Table 10.9 presents the market share, percent net shift, and growth rate figures for Japanese technology-intensive exports from 1963 to 1974 at the two-digit level of classification. The figures show that the consistency in market share gains across industry groups that occurred at the one-digit level of classification is generally maintained when the data are further disaggregated. Japan registered market share gains within each of the two-digit SITC categories. Some variance existed between industries in the size of the gains that occurred, but most of the industries approximately doubled their market shares. There were only two industries, SITC 54 and 73, for which market share increased by less than 1 percent, and these two industries are minor ones in terms of the volume of technology-intensive exports they generate for Japan.

The corresponding 1963 to 1974 figures for Japanese nontechnology-intensive exports are presented in Table 10.10. The data in this table provide a further breakdown of the industry-specific nature of Japanese nontechnology-intensive exports. These exports are composed primarily of goods from two industries, nonelectrical machinery and transport equipment. The third component of SITC 7, electrical machinery, does not comprise a substantial portion of Japanese nontechnology-intensive exports, at least not to the extent of the other two components of that group. Market shares for both nonelectrical machinery and transport equipment exports more than tripled from 1963 to 1974. However, growth of nontechnology-intensive exports from the other industries did not occur at nearly this pace. In fact, Japan lost market share in nontechnology-intensive exports from five of the 13 industries for which data were gathered. These five industries, however, had only small export volumes and export market shares.

Table 10.11 presents the Japanese technology-intensive exports and associated market share changes, net shifts, and growth rates from 1972 to 1974 at the two-digit SITC level of disaggregation. While the one-digit data indicated market share losses across the four industry groups, the two-digit data shows considerable variation in the changes that occurred in the market shares for Japanese technology-intensive exports within the individual industries. The two industries that had the largest volumes of technology-intensive exports in 1974,

TABLE 10.9

JAPAN: 1963 to 1974 Technology-Intensive Export Shifts Within Two-Digit SITC Classifications

SITC Code	Industry	1974 Exports (thousands of U.S. dollars)	Market Share Percent 1963	Market Share Percent 1974	Percent Net Shift	Japanese Annual Growth Rate (in percent)	OECD Annual Growth Rate (in percent)
51	Chemical Elements, Compounds	1,856,987	5.4	11.0	23.3	128.9	59.1
53	Dyes, Tanning, Color Products	101,091	1.6	4.9	33.4	147.5	41.0
54	Medicinal, Etc., Products	128,136	2.4	2.7	2.0	41.1	35.9
55	Perfume, Cleaning, Etc., Products	7,665	0.6	1.9	4.9	115.7	28.0
56	Fertilizers, Manufactured	440,436	12.7	21.5	37.2	56.0	29.4
58	Plastic Materials, Etc.	1,032,612	4.8	8.4	16.9	147.9	80.2
59	Chemicals NES*	58,620	2.1	4.1	8.0	83.0	37.6
65	Textile Yarn, Fabric, Etc.	598,915	7.5	15.0	27.5	134.3	63.0
71	Machinery, Nonelectric	1,441,994	1.5	7.4	44.9	277.5	50.6
72	Electrical Machinery	4,494,711	9.7	18.4	61.7	98.5	47.3
73	Transport Equipment	31,038	0.3	0.4	0.3	40.9	34.2
86	Instruments, Watches, Clocks	1,748,513	7.9	15.8	54.0	86.6	38.8
89	Miscellaneous Manufactured Goods NES*	952,483	16.1	33.3	91.2	148.9	67.1

*Not Elsewhere Specified

Source: Compiled by the authors.

TABLE 10.10

JAPAN: 1963 to 1974 Nontechnology-Intensive Export Shifts Within Two-Digit SITC Classifications

SITC Code	Industry	1974 Exports (thousands of U.S. dollars)	Market Share Percent 1963	Market Share Percent 1974	Percent Net Shift	Japanese Annual Growth Rate (in percent)	OECD Annual Growth Rate (in percent)
52	Coal, Petroleum, Etc., Chemicals	8,781	1.2	2.7	3.3	58.7	20.9
54	Medicinal, Etc., Products	8,870	4.4	3.2	-8.6	28.8	41.8
55	Perfume, Cleaning, Etc., Products	10,954	3.6	1.4	-15.5	12.0	44.9
57	Explosives, Pyrotechnic Products	4,189	5.5	2.0	-22.6	1.7	20.8
59	Chemicals NES*	139,991	0.9	3.1	9.1	151.3	35.8
62	Rubber Manufactures NES*	532,722	9.6	12.2	13.7	57.2	42.9
65	Textile Yarn, Fabric, Etc.	1,263,152	30.0	35.5	28.3	108.1	89.8
66	Nonmetal Mineral Manufactures NES*	51,470	4.6	7.0	14.0	55.8	33.3
71	Machinery, Nonelectric	4,132,858	2.8	8.5	36.5	120.4	33.4
72	Electrical Machinery	1,266,391	6.3	10.6	27.2	83.8	45.9
73	Transport Equipment	13,180,905	7.0	22.3	57.5	189.6	53.5
81	Plumbing, Heating, Lighting Equipment	3,152	1.3	0.5	-2.9	11.6	41.9
89	Miscellaneous Manufactured Goods NES*	1,521	1.2	0.8	-1.6	32.8	56.3

*Not Elsewhere Specified.
Source: Compiled by the authors.

TABLE 10.11

JAPAN: 1972 to 1974 Technology-Intensive Export Shifts Within Two-Digit SITC Classifications

SITC Code	Industry	1972-1974 Change in Market Share	Percent Net Shift	Japanese Annual Growth Rate (in percent)	OECD Annual Growth Rate (in percent)
51	Chemical Elements, Compounds	-1.5	-19.7	59.2	73.5
53	Dyes, Tanning, Color Products	0.4	13.6	44.4	36.4
54	Medicinal, Etc., Products	0.0	-0.0	32.6	32.1
55	Perfume, Cleaning, Etc., Products	-0.1	-1.2	33.6	36.2
56	Fertilizers, Manufactured	14.0	67.7	491.1	138.2
58	Plastic Materials, Etc.	-1.7	-40.0	46.8	65.3
59	Chemicals NES*	-1.1	-12.4	34.7	55.9
65	Textile Yarn, Fabric, Etc.	-1.5	-21.3	31.9	39.3
71	Machinery, Nonelectric	0.1	2.1	28.3	26.8
72	Electrical Machinery	-2.1	-44.5	27.1	35.2
73	Transport Equipment	-0.3	-3.4	-3.9	34.2
86	Instruments, Watches, Clocks	0.6	26.5	36.9	33.0
89	Miscellaneous Manufactured Goods NES*	-6.0	-90.3	13.3	24.1

*Not Elsewhere Specified.
Source: Compiled by the authors.

TABLE 10.12

JAPAN: 1972 to 1974 Nontechnology-Intensive Export Shifts Within Two-Digit SITC Classifications

SITC Code	Industry	1972-1974 Change in Market Share	Percent Net Share	Japanese Annual Growth Rate (in percent)	OECD Annual Growth Rate (in percent)
52	Coal, Petroleum, Etc., Chemicals	1.0	6.7	249.2	139.0
54	Medicinal, Etc., Products	-0.7	-23.7	21.4	37.1
55	Perfume, Cleaning, Etc., Products	-1.1	-32.5	-3.5	31.9
57	Explosives, Pyrotechnic Products	-1.3	-17.2	-2.6	28.4
59	Chemicals NES*	1.8	5.2	184.6	50.0
62	Rubber Manufactures NES*	-0.7	-10.1	37.9	42.5
65	Textile Yarn, Fabric, Etc.	-4.9	-69.3	28.0	38.3
66	Nonmetal Mineral Manufactures NES*	-0.7	-12.1	19.2	25.5
71	Machinery, Nonelectric	1.4	41.2	55.1	37.1
72	Electrical Machinery	-0.9	-24.4	34.2	40.5
73	Transport Equipment	4.7	70.5	49.8	28.2
81	Plumbing, Heating, Lighting Equipment	-0.3	-5.2	1.6	25.4
89	Miscellaneous Manufactured Goods NES*	-0.2	-1.2	26.9	43.1

*Not Elsewhere Specified.
Source: Compiled by the authors.

SITC 51 and 72, experienced sizeable market share losses from 1972 to 1974. However, some of the other industries which had relatively large volumes of technology-intensive exports kept pace with world export growth during this period, such as SITC 71 and 86. There was also the case of SITC 56 (manufactured fertilizers) in which Japanese exporters recorded a gain of 14 percent in market share. Thus, Japanese technology-intensive exports from 1972 to 1974 were not as consistently retarded as the one-digit SITC figures suggested. The technology-intensive exports of many industries either maintained or increased their international positions during this time. However, the industries that had the greatest volumes of technology-intensive exports tended to be characterized by the largest losses.

The 1972 to 1974 figures for nontechnology-intensive Japanese exports at the two-digit level of disaggregation are presented in Table 10.12. These figures provide further verification of the previous findings related to Japanese nontechnology-intensive exports from 1972 to 1974 at the one-digit level of classification. With the exceptions of nonelectrical machinery and transport equipment (SITC 71 and 73), Japanese nontechnology-intensive exports from all but two industries lost market share over this period. However, nontechnology-intensive exports of nonelectrical machines and transport equipment both registered large gains from 1972 to 1974. The gains were particularly large for the latter industry, which registered a 4.7 percent increase in market share in an area in which world exports are extremely high. Thus, while most Japanese nontechnology-intensive exports behaved in a manner consistent with the expectations one might have for a nation that had recently experienced a currency revaluation, nonelectrical machinery and transport equipment behaved in a contrary fashion. The export performance of goods from these industries might suggest the existence of some form of subsidy from the Japanese government to support export prices. While other rationales are possible, export subsidization would seem the most likely explanation for the export expansion that occurred at the same time prices were rising.

UNITED KINGDOM EXPORT POSITION

Throughout all the portions of this book, it has been noted that the United Kingdom's position in the international economy is deteriorating at a rapid pace. This deterioration was noted with regard to the number of nations for which the United Kingdom provided the largest export market and for the degree of dependence which British trading partners had upon the U.K. market. It was also noted in Chapter 9 that at the highest level of aggregation, the United Kingdom's share of technology-intensive and nontechnology-intensive export markets had been declining throughout the period of the study. The following discussion briefly presents the changes that have occurred in the United Kingdom's technology-intensive and nontechnology-intensive export position at the one-digit SITC level of disaggregation.

The 1963 to 1974 market share, net shift, and growth rate figures for the United Kingdom for both technology-intensive and nontechnology-intensive exports are presented in Table 10.13. These figures indicate that the United Kingdom lost market share within all industry groups for both types of exports from 1963 to 1974. With regard to technology-intensive exports, the data show some variation in the magnitude of the losses associated with the different industry groups. The largest percentage market share loss is associated with basic manufactures, SITC 6, where market share fell from 13 percent in 1963 to 7 percent in 1974. Despite the size of this loss, however, the change in market share within SITC 6 cannot be viewed as having a large impact upon the United Kingdom's technology-intensive export position. SITC 6 is the United Kingdom's smallest technology-intensive export category in terms of volume. Also, despite the large drop in market share, the United Kingdom registered a percent net shift of only -22.1, which suggests that the market for these exports was quite dynamic and that several other nations also had lost market share.

In terms of the volume of exports involved, the United Kingdom's largest loss in the technology-intensive category occurred with regard to SITC 7, machines and transport equipment. It is from this industry group that the United Kingdom derived the greatest amount of its technology-intensive exports, and within that group U.K. export market share had fallen from 13.1 percent in 1963 to 9.4 percent in 1974. The net shift value of -36.3 indicates that the United Kingdom accounted for more than one-third of all market share losses for technology-intensive exports of machines and transport equipment. The United Kingdom's exports of technology-intensive goods from the remaining two industries, chemicals and miscellaneous manufactures, also recorded market share losses. These losses, however, were not as great as the losses associated with basic manufactures and machines and transport equipment.

The data that pertain to nontechnology-intensive U.K. exports shown in Table 10.13 also indicate considerable variance between industry groups with respect to the magnitude of the market share losses incurred. The most dramatic loss of nontechnology-intensive export markets occurred with respect to machines and transport equipment. Exports from this industry group accounted for 86.7 percent of the United Kingdom's nontechnology-intensive exports in 1974, yet U.K. market share of these exports had dropped from 16.7 percent in 1963 to 7.4 percent in 1974. Thus, if the United Kingdom had been able to maintain its 1963 market share through the period of the study, its

TABLE 10.13

UNITED KINGDOM: 1963 to 1974 Technology-Intensive and Nontechnology-Intensive Export Shifts by Industry Group

	SITC Code	Industry Group	1974 Exports (thousands of U.S. dollars)	Market Share Percent 1963	Market Share Percent 1974	Percent Net Shift	U.K. Annual Growth Rate (in percent)	OECD Annual Growth Rate (in percent)
Technology Intensive	5	Chemicals	3,578,436	11.8	9.0	-14.0	39.2	54.5
	6	Basic Manufactures	281,031	13.0	7.0	-22.1	29.9	63.0
	7	Machines and Transport Equipment	4,853,795	13.1	9.4	-36.3	30.2	45.9
	8	Miscellaneous Manufactures	1,184,965	10.2	8.5	-11.0	34.2	42.7
		Total Technology-Intensive Exports	9,898,227	12.3	9.0	-26.4	33.6	48.8
Non-technology Intensive	5	Chemicals	773,770	15.2	12.5	-11.6	27.5	35.0
	6	Basic Manufactures	588,087	14.4	6.8	-41.4	20.6	54.0
	7	Machines and Transport Equipment	9,203,314	16.7	7.4	-49.4	14.1	43.1
	8	Miscellaneous Manufactures	50,276	8.9	6.4	-10.2	29.7	44.8
		Total Nontechnology-Intensive Exports	10,615,801	16.5	7.6	-47.9	15.1	43.3

Source: Compiled by the authors.

1974 nontechnology-intensive machines and transport equipment exports would have been more than twice their actual value. A market share drop of almost the same magnitude as machines and transport equipment occurred with respect to basic manufactures. The impact of the reduction of market share for nontechnology-intensive basic manufactures, however, was not nearly as great as the associated impact for machines and transport equipment, since the volume of exports was considerably smaller. The remaining two industry groups, chemicals and miscellaneous manufactures, did not experience losses of the same magnitude as occurred for basic manufactures and machines and transport equipment.

The changes that occurred in the United Kingdom's export position from 1972 to 1974 are shown in Table 10.14. It should be expected that there would be very little difference between the 1972 to 1974 U.K. data and the 1963 to 1974 U.K. data. The former time period was a critical period for the United States, Japan, and Germany, since the currencies of these three nations were undergoing fundamental realignments from 1972 to 1974. The British pound had been in the process of realignment throughout most of the 1963 to 1974 period, and thus a dramatic change in the United Kingdom's export position should not be anticipated following 1971. The figures presented in Table 10.14 correspond to this expectation. The United Kingdom lost market share from 1972 to 1974 in technology-intensive exports that roughly corresponded to the proportion of the 1963 to 1974 losses that would be expected if the losses occurred evenly throughout the eleven year period. The one possible exception is technology-intensive exports from the miscellaneous machinery group for which the United Kingdom experienced more than half of its 1963 to 1974 market share loss during the 1972 to 1974 period.

The changes that occurred in the United Kingdom's export position for nontechnology-intensive products from 1972 to 1974 are less consistent than was the case for technology-intensive products. The figures in Table 10.14 show that U.K. market share actually increased for nontechnology-intensive exports of chemicals and miscellaneous manufactures. While the increase for the latter industry group was very small, nontechnology-intensive chemicals exports had a relatively large market share increase, 2.8 percent, particularly if the short amount of time involved is considered. Yet, these gains were more than offset by the continued market share loss which the United Kingdom experienced with respect to nontechnology-intensive exports of machines and transport equipment. Nontechnology-intensive exports of machines and transport equipment behaved in much the same manner from 1972 to 1974 as most of the United Kingdom's technology-intensive exports during the period: market share dropped proportionate to the decreases that occurred during the 1963 to 1974 period.

TABLE 10.14

UNITED KINGDOM: 1972 to 1974 Technology-Intensive and Nontechnology-Intensive Export Shifts by Industry Group

	SITC Code	Industry Group	1972-1974 Change in Market Share	Percent Net Shift	U.K. Annual Growth Rate (in percent)	OECD Annual Growth Rate (in percent)
Technology Intensive	5	Chemicals	-.54	-13.6	56.7	62.6
	6	Basic Manufactures	-1.50	-22.1	24.0	39.3
	7	Machine and Transport Equipment	-1.10	-22.3	23.7	31.7
	8	Miscellaneous Manufactures	-1.10	-36.5	22.4	31.0
		Total Technology-Intensive Exports	-.96	-26.7	32.7	41.0
Non-technology Intensive	5	Chemicals	2.78	11.5	76.5	48.1
	6	Basic Manufactures	-.43	-7.4	34.2	39.0
	7	Machines and Transport Equipment	-1.41	-29.9	20.1	32.9
	8	Miscellaneous Manufactures	.11	1.9	31.0	29.2
		Total Nontechnology-Intensive Exports	-1.20	-24.9	23.2	33.8

Source: Compiled by the authors.

FRENCH EXPORT POSITION

The outstanding characteristic of French exports throughout the period of the study has been their ability to maintain their position in the international market. The figures presented in Table 10.15 show the extent to which French technology-intensive and nontechnology-intensive exports have retained their market shares from 1963 to 1974. During this period French technology-intensive chemicals exports retained the identical market share. The other major French technology-intensive export industry group, machines and transport equipment, gained slightly in market share, as did miscellaneous manufactures. The only French industry group to record a market share loss from 1963 to 1974 was basic manufactures. This loss, however, did little to affect the French position due to the relatively small volume of exports involved.

French nontechnology-intensive exports showed somewhat less consistency from 1963 to 1974 than that nation's technology-intensive exports. The nontechnology-intensive export figures for France reported in Table 10.15 indicate relatively large market share increases for two of the industry groups, chemicals and miscellaneous manufactures. Nontechnology-intensive exports from these industry groups, however, did not constitute a large portion of French trade in these goods. The French industry group having the greatest amount of nontechnology-intensive exports, machines and transport equipment, remained relatively static in market share from 1963 to 1974, as did French market share for basic manufactures.

The 1972 to 1974 market share, net shift and growth rate figures for French technology-intensive and nontechnology-intensive exports are presented in Table 10.16. Once again, these figures show France maintaining a remarkable level of consistency in its export market shares, particularly when compared with the comparable data from the other major trading nations. With regard to technology-intensive exports, French exports did not record any market share changes of greater than ± 0.2 percent from 1972 to 1974. The growth rates of French technology-intensive exports within each of the industry groups came very close to approximating the growth rate for combined nations employed in the study. The 1972 to 1974 figures for French nontechnology-intensive exports shown in Table 10.16 indicate that these exports were more dynamic than technology-intensive exports during the period. The most serious loss was that connected with nontechnology-intensive exports of machines and transport equipment. Although French exports from this industry group lost only 0.45 percent of market share from 1972 to 1974, the large volume of nontechnology-intensive exports from that group was primarily responsible for the overall loss incurred by French nontechnology-intensive exports over

TABLE 10.15

FRANCE: 1963 to 1974 Technology-Intensive and Nontechnology-Intensive Export Shifts by Industry Group

	SITC Code	Industry Group	1974 Exports (thousands of U.S. dollars)	Market Share Percent 1963	Market Share Percent 1974	Percent Net Shift	French Annual Growth Rate (in percent)	OECD Annual Growth Rate (in percent)
Technology Intensive	5	Chemicals	3,459,590	8.7	8.7	0.0	54.2	54.5
	6	Basic Manufactures	366,261	10.6	9.2	-5.3	53.3	63.0
	7	Machines and Transport Equipment	3,632,046	6.6	7.0	3.8	49.2	45.9
	8	Miscellaneous Manufactures	780,683	4.7	5.6	5.5	52.1	42.7
		Total Technology-Intensive Exports	8,238,580	7.2	7.5	2.8	51.6	48.8
Non-technology Intensive	5	Chemicals	856,778	10.0	13.9	17.3	52.4	35.0
	6	Basic Manufactures	1,074,747	12.8	12.4	-2.0	52.2	54.0
	7	Machines and Transport Equipment	9,797,141	7.2	7.9	3.5	48.0	43.1
	8	Miscellaneous Manufactures	92,927	9.5	11.8	9.4	58.2	44.8
		Total Nontechnology-Intensive Exports	11,829,016	7.7	8.5	4.2	48.7	43.3

Source: Compiled by the authors.

TABLE 10.16

FRANCE: 1972 to 1974 Technology-Intensive and Nontechnology-Intensive Export Shifts by Industry Group

	SITC Code	Industry Group	1972–1974 Change in Market Share	Percent Net Shift	French Annual Growth Rate (in percent)	OECD Annual Growth Rate (in percent)
Technology Intensive	5	Chemicals	.03	.7	63.5	62.6
	6	Basic Manufactures	-.14	-2.1	38.5	39.3
	7	Machines and Transport Equipment	-.17	-3.6	30.2	31.7
	8	Miscellaneous Manufactures	.06	2.1	32.4	31.0
		Total Technology-Intensive Exports	.06	1.6	42.2	41.0
Non-technology Intensive	5	Chemicals	.83	3.4	54.8	48.1
	6	Basic Manufactures	-.37	-6.3	37.0	39.0
	7	Machines and Transport Equipment	-.45	-9.5	28.9	32.9
	8	Miscellaneous Manufactures	1.95	34.2	45.3	29.2
		Total Nontechnology-Intensive Exports	-0.30	-7.1	31.1	33.8

Source: Compiled by the authors.

the period. Still, when the changes that occurred in the French non-technology-intensive export position over the 1972 to 1974 period are compared with the corresponding changes for the other major trading nations, they are indeed minor.

U.S., GERMAN, AND JAPANESE EXPORT POSITIONS COMPARED

The preceding discussion suggests that the greatest challenge to the export position of the United States comes primarily from Japan and Germany. The United Kingdom is certainly not threatening the U.S. export position, since that nation appears to be in a state of decline of a greater magnitude than the United States. France, on the other hand, is maintaining its export position, although it does not appear to be doing so at the expense of other nations. Germany and Japan, however, are in many cases increasing their export positions, and such increases are at the expense of other nations, probably the United States and the United Kingdom.

In order to provide some indication of the extent to which Germany and Japan are responsible for the changes that have occurred in the U.S. export position for technology-intensive and nontechnology-intensive products, a series of correlation analyses were run on the net shifts which these three nations recorded during the periods of the study. Correlation coefficients (Pearson's r) were calculated between the net shifts that occurred at the four-digit SITC level of disaggregation within each industry group. Thus, net shifts at the four-digit level within the chemicals industry group were correlated between the United States and Japan and between the United States and Germany, and so on within each industry group. One industry group within both the technology-intensive and the nontechnology-intensive categories could not be used in the correlation analysis due to an insufficient number of product categories. The technology-intensive group contained only one SITC 6 product category, while the nontechnology-intensive group contained only three SITC 8 product categories. In addition, the nontechnology-intensive SITC 7 group was divided into the three two-digit components of that category for the correlation analyses, due to the overriding importance of that group within nontechnology-intensive exports and to the large number of product categories contained by each of the associated two-digit groups. While such correlations do not indicate causality in the changes in export position that occurred, they may suggest the possibility of a relationship between changes in the U.S. position and the changes in the positions of Germany and Japan. A high negative correlation between the net shift values of the United States and the net shift values of Germany

TABLE 10.17

1963 to 1974 U.S. Net Shifts Correlated With German and Japanese Net Shifts

	SITC Code	Industry	Number of Product Categories	U.S./ Germany r	U.S./ Japan r
Technology Intensive	5	Chemicals	38	-.32	-.18
	7	Machines and Transport Equipment	20	-.06	-.28
	8	Miscellaneous Manufactures	15	-.35	-.00
Non-technology Intensive	5	Chemicals	12	-.55	-.57
	6	Basic Manufactures	14	-.51	-.31
	71	Machinery, Nonelectric	25	-.40	.05
	72	Electrical Machinery	9	-.63	-.46
	73	Transport Equipment	20	-.10	.15

Source: Compiled by the authors.

and/or Japan could indicate the extent to which U.S. export markets are being lost to one or both of those nations. However, the small number of cases that exist within most of the industry groups make the results of these analyses only suggestive rather than definitive.

The correlation values found to exist between the 1963 to 1974 net shift figures of the United States and West Germany and the United States and Japan are presented in Table 10.17 for both technology-intensive products and nontechnology-intensive products. With regard to technology-intensive products, it can be seen that some relationships exist between the net shifts of the United States and the other two nations, but these relationships cannot be considered strong. The highest correlations exist between the United States and Germany for SITC 5 (chemicals) and SITC 8 (miscellaneous manufactures), yet r values of -.32 and -.35 do not suggest that German exports of these products expanded primarily at the expense of U.S. exports. The correlations between the Japanese and U.S. net shifts do not exceed -.3, also too low to suggest that the general increase of Japanese export markets came primarily at the expense of U.S. export markets. Yet the correlation values do tend to be negative ones, and most are at a level that suggests some association between U.S. export market losses and the gains of the other two nations.

The correlation values found to exist between the nations for net shifts of nontechnology-intensive products are more dramatic than those associated with technology-intensive goods. Table 10.17 shows that for chemicals Japan and Germany had r values with the United States of -.57 and -.55 respectively. It was in the chemicals group that the United States experienced the greatest market share loss from 1963 to 1974, and it appears that its losses in this area were related to many of the German and Japanese gains. Likewise, Germany and to a lesser extent Japan have high negative correlations with the United States with regard to the net shift values associated with exports of basic manufactures (SITC 6). Within the machines and transport equipment industry group (SITC 7), the highest correlations exist with respect to exports of electrical machinery (SITC 72). In this case both Japan and Germany have high negative correlations with the United States. Yet electrical machinery represented the smallest category of U.S. exports within SITC 7. For the largest U.S. export category within that group, nonelectric machinery (SITC 71), the United States shows a relatively high negative correlation with Germany and virtually no correlation with Japan. The third SITC 7 group, transport equipment, was the group for which the United States had the smallest negative net shift. This small net shift value is reflected in the relatively low correlation values between the United States and Germany and Japan.

In summary, the correlation analysis between the United States and Germany and Japan which employed the 1963 to 1974 net shift values has indicated some relationship between U.S. export losses and the gains of the other two nations for technology-intensive products, but not a strong one. Conversely, the corresponding analyses for nontechnology-intensive exports yielded several relatively high negative correlations between the United States and the two other nations. Germany, particularly, showed strong negative correlations with the United States, while Japan did to a lesser extent.

The correlation values associated with the 1972 to 1974 net shift figures are presented in Table 10.18. It will be recalled that between these two years the United States increased its market shares for exports from several of the product categories. Therefore, negative net shift values shown in this table could in many cases (but not all) suggest that U.S. gains have come at the expense of Japan or Germany. With regard to technology-intensive exports, the table shows that all of the correlation values are negative, which should

TABLE 10.18

1972 to 1974 U.S. Net Shifts Correlated With German and Japanese Net Shifts

	SITC Code	Industry	Number of Product Categories	U.S./ Germany r	U.S./ Japan r
Technology Intensive	5	Chemicals	38	-.06	-.15
	7	Machines and Transport Equipment	20	-.25	-.19
	8	Miscellaneous Manufactures	15	-.09	-.44
Non-technology Intensive	5	Chemicals	12	-.45	-.40
	6	Basic Manufactures	14	-.18	-.05
	71	Machinery, Nonelectric	25	-.47	-.25
	72	Electrical Machinery	9	.30	-.64
	73	Transport Equipment	20	-.05	.17

Source: Compiled by the authors.

be expected given the positions of the three nations in international trade. Yet most of the r values are relatively small. The only association of any strength exists between the United States and Japan for miscellaneous manufactures. Otherwise, none of the r values exceed -.25. These findings suggest that although some association exists between the United States and Germany and Japan in terms of the net shifts that those nations experienced from 1972 to 1974, the relationship is not strong. Apparently many of the shifts that the United States had during that time are also related to many of the other OECD nations.

The correlation values in Table 10.18 for the 1972 to 1974 non-technology-intensive net shifts tend to be higher than those for the technology-intensive net shifts, yet lower than the corresponding 1963 to 1974 values. Relatively high negative correlations exist between the United States and Germany for chemicals (SITC 5) and nonelectric machinery (SITC 71). High negative correlations exist between the

United States and Japan for chemicals and for electrical machinery (SITC 72). Otherwise, the r values tend to be low, with virtually no relationship being indicated with regard to exports of nontechnology-intensive basic manufactures or transport equipment for the 1972 to 1974 period.

SUMMARY

This chapter has analyzed the positions of the United States' primary competitors in the international market with respect to technology-intensive and nontechnology-intensive exports. It has shown that West Germany and particularly Japan are the most dynamic nations in terms of their growth in both areas. In general, Japan has increased its market shares at a faster pace than Germany, yet Japan experienced more negative consequences from the 1971 currency realignment than did Germany. In the face of the revaluation of the Mark, Germany managed to increase its market share in many cases, whereas Japan lost market share in most export industries following the revaluation of the yen. The United Kingdom has also been dynamic in terms of market share changes, but in a negative direction. Over both time periods studied, the United Kingdom lost market share consistently for both technology-intensive and nontechnology-intensive exports, although the losses in the former category were somewhat less. France, on the other hand, has shown a remarkable ability to parallel OECD export growth in almost all of the industry groups studied, both technology-intensive and nontechnology-intensive exports.

When the U. S. net shift values for the individual product categories were correlated with the corresponding values for Germany and Japan, the results showed a less than strong relationship for technology-intensive exports. In most cases some relationship was indicated, but the magnitude of the correlation values did not suggest that the export growth of Germany and Japan came primarily at the expense of the United States, at least across all product categories. Conversely, the correlations that existed between the net shift values for the nontechnology-intensive exports were considerably stronger. These findings suggested a relatively high level of association between the changes which occurred in U. S. export shares and those experienced by Germany, particularly in the 1963 to 1974 period. To a lesser extent, these relatively high correlations also existed between the United States and Japan for nontechnology-intensive exports. Overall, these findings suggest that within the nontechnology-intensive group, Germany has had a more pronounced impact upon U. S. exports across all product categories, whereas Japan's impact has been upon more selected product categories.

The findings that have been presented in Chapters 9 and 10 will be summarized in the next chapter. These findings will also be integrated with the main tenets of the previous literature that was discussed in Chapter 7. In addition, the next chapter explores some of the potential explanations for the changes that have occurred in the U. S. position and addresses the policy issues which could arise from these changes.

11

IMPLICATIONS FOR U.S. TECHNOLOGY-INTENSIVE TRADE

The previous chapters have provided insights into many facets of the changes in export markets for manufactures, particularly technology-intensive products, and the positions of the major trading nations in these markets over time. Before any attempt is made to interpret the results from Part II, however, a number of caveats are necessary. First, there remains the possibility that the categories used for technology-intensive and nontechnology-intensive manufactures were not totally inclusive ones. For example, some nontechnology-intensive items may have been included within the technology-intensive group. Such misallocations of exports could have a cumulative effect in any analysis. A related difficulty is the possibility that some products that were technology-intensive ones in 1963 might have been nontechnology-intensive in 1974 due to standardization that occurred in the interim. Finally, the impact of domestic markets was not directly incorporated into the analyses, although the consideration of U. S. import shares did provide some indications of events in this area.

Notwithstanding the above cautionary statements, it is still clear that the position of the United States in world markets for both technology-intensive and nontechnology-intensive manufactures has changed. While the above caveats are necessary to bear in mind when evaluating the exact magnitudes of such changes, the general trends remain clear. In order to evaluate the results from this portion of the study, the role of technology intensity in conferring comparative advantage, particularly for the United States, will be considered in light of the findings of the preceding chapters. Possible explanations for the trends will then be discussed, along with the policy areas that are affected by the trends.

TECHNOLOGY INTENSITY AND COMPARATIVE ADVANTAGE

The United States

As the results of the analyses have indicated, U. S. technology-intensive manufactures have had a decreasing share of world export markets. This long-term decline was at least temporarily halted by the devaluation of the dollar. Yet, even with the devaluation, U. S. market shares in most export categories were much lower in 1974 than they had been in 1963. This general trend of decline reflects the presence of a number of factors. The economic resurgence of Germany, Japan and many of the other industrialized countries is undoubtedly a major cause of the diminishing U. S. share of trade in technology-intensive manufactures. Also, in the case of Western Europe, the Common Market with its tariff and nontariff barriers may have led to trade advantages for the member nations at the expense of the United States. The result of these and other forces has been that the dominance the United States once enjoyed in technology-intensive export markets is being eroded. In 1974 German exports of these goods approached the U. S. level, and Japanese technology-intensive exports were at almost half the U. S. level. Since these two nations are only a fraction of the economic size of the United States, it is difficult to conclude that this nation still maintains a comparative advantage over Japan and Germany in the production of technology-intensive goods.

U. S. Comparative Advantage

Despite the general decline in its technology-intensive export position, the findings suggest that U. S. comparative advantage still lies in the production of high technology products. In 1974 its share of the world export market for technology-intensive goods was greater than its export market share for the nontechnology-intensive products employed in the study. Likewise, when the data were disaggregated they showed that U. S. technology-intensive exports from three of the four industry groups experienced smaller losses from 1963 to 1974 than the nontechnology-intensive exports from the same industry groups. In addition, the technology-intensive exports from these same three industry groups had larger market share gains from 1972 to 1974 than the corresponding nontechnology-intensive exports.

The U. S. comparative advantage in the production of technology-intensive products is also suggested by the analysis of import market shares. From 1963 to 1974 the U. S. market share for total nontechnology-intensive imports increased at a faster rate than the increase for total technology-intensive imports. Within the one-digit industry groups the findings for technology-intensive and nontechnology-intensive imports were somewhat mixed, and a clear trend could not be discerned. Still, with the exception of the imports of the industry group with the smallest import volume (miscellaneous manufactures), the market shares of the nontechnology-intensive imports had larger positive net shifts than the corresponding technology-intensive imports.

The import patterns of the other major trading nations provide a further indication of the relative reliance placed by the United States upon the production of technology-intensive goods. Unlike the United States, the import market shares of the United Kingdom, Japan, France, and Germany rose faster for technology-intensive goods than for nontechnology-intensive goods. Japan even decreased its market share for nontechnology-intensive imports. Apparently, the United States is capable of providing its own technology-intensive products to a relatively greater extent than the other major trading nations.

All of the preceding findings point to the continuance of the U.S. comparative advantage in the production of technology-intensive goods. Technology-intensive goods represent a larger proportion of U.S. manufactured exports and a smaller portion of U.S. manufactured imports than is the case for the other major trading nations. Yet, one question referring to a possible paradox arising out of the findings remains unanswered: How are Japan and Germany capable of having seeming advantages in the production (at least for export) of both technology-intensive and nontechnology-intensive goods? This is a major point to keep in mind, since these two nations have increased their export markets in both areas, whereas the United States has lost in both areas, only less so for technology-intensive goods. Some of the possible explanations for this pehnomenon will be presented later in this chapter.

Industry-Specific Export Losses

The more detailed analyses of U.S. export share changes indicated that the decline in this country's technology-intensive export position tended to be attributable to one specific industry group. Of the four broad industry groups represented in the study, the chemical industry was found to be primarily responsible for the poor overall performance of U.S. technology-intensive exports. Exports of chemicals showed the largest negative net shifts for both technology-intensive and nontechnology-intensive exports. In fact, the reason that total U.S. technology-intensive exports had a larger negative net shift value than total U.S. nontechnology-intensive exports can be traced directly to chemicals exports. Chemicals represented a considerably larger proportion of U.S. technology-intensive exports than nontechnology-intensive exports. Thus, market share losses within chemicals exports had a larger impact on the total net shift of technology-intensive exports.

The decline of U. S. chemicals exports, both technology-intensive and nontechnology-intensive, represents a major change in the U. S. export position since the 1960s. Exports of chemicals have been noted as being an area in which the United States was highly competitive in the 1950s (Balassa 1964, pp. 110-1). It is also significant that from 1953 to 1965 worldwide exports of chemicals had one of the highest growth rates among manufactured goods (Chou 1967, p. 281). It appears, therefore, that the United States is losing market share in what has been one of the most dynamic export industries.

There was some suggestion in the findings that the decline in the U. S. technology-intensive export position cannot be totally attributed to economic factors. The analysis of the U. S. import position with regard to technology-intensive products indicated that increases in U. S. imports were not as large as the corresponding decreases that occurred in U. S. exports. This lack of congruence was particularly noticeable within the chemical industry group, the group largely responsible for the sizable negative net shift the United States experienced for technology-intensive exports. While the technology-intensive export market share for U. S. chemicals dropped substantially from 1963 to 1974, the U. S. import market share remained virtually unchanged. It would appear, therefore, that factors other than price were responsible for the U. S. decline in this area.

Other Countries

The shift-share analyses of trends for the other countries provide a basis for the comparison of the recent U. S. performance. For quite different reasons, the performance of France and the United Kingdom cannot be considered the principal cause for the export market losses of the United States. Germany and Japan, however, have increased their shares noticeably in many areas in which the United States has incurred losses.

France has maintained a relatively static share of the export market for both technology-intensive and nontechnology-intensive manufactures from 1963 to 1974. Net shifts have been relatively small, but positive. In this sense, France has performed better than the United States. While total export volumes are smaller, reflecting in part a smaller economy, France has maintained its position relative to other states, an accomplishment not approached by the United States. Between 1972 and 1974, France suffered a market share loss in nontechnology-intensive manufactures, perhaps reflecting gains by the

United States and Germany in that area. In the technology-intensive area, however, France had a positive net shift. While this gain was not as large as that of the United States, it could reflect increased comparative advantage in the export of these types of products.

The United Kingdom has failed to maintain its relative position in world markets for exports of manufactures. It lost market shares for both technology-intensive and nontechnology-intensive items, both at the aggregate level and at the level of almost every one-digit SITC code. Unlike the United States, the United Kingdom did not show any signs of either recovery or stability in the period from 1972 to 1974. The United Kingdom apparently has maintained some comparative advantage in technology-intensive goods since its losses in the nontechnology areas have been greater overall. This trend, however, did not hold true for the period from 1972 to 1974. The United Kingdom apparently has maintained some comparative advantage in technology-intensive goods since its losses in the nontechnology areas have been greater overall. This trend, however, did not hold true for the period from 1972 to 1974. Perhaps some of the U. S. gains in technology-intensive products in this period came at the expense of the United Kingdom, or perhaps the technology advantage once held by the United Kingdom is being lost.

Germany has a pattern that also indicates some comparative advantage arising from technology intensity. Export share for such manufactures rose while shares for nontechnology-intensive manufactures experienced a small overall decline. For the period from 1972 to 1974, however, export shares rose for both categories. Thus, the recovery of the United States in this period was not at the expense of Germany. In fact, Germany was the only other country to experience increases in both aggregate technology-intensive and nontechnology-intensive classifications in the 1972 to 1974 period. The increases related to technology-intensive exports for this period were more substantial than those in the nontechnology-intensive area. The 1963 to 1974 shifts for both technology-intensive and nontechnology-intensive exports, however, were not large. Yet it appears that within certain industry groups, especially among nontechnology-intensive exports, U. S. losses were closely related to German gains. Even though Germany is the leading exporter of nontechnology-intensive manufactures, that nation appears to be placing increased emphasis upon technology-intensive exports and may thus be developing more of a comparative advantage in that area.

Japan is clearly the country that has achieved the most dramatic gains in export share from 1963 to 1974. It had large net shifts during this 11-year period in both the technology-intensive and nontechnology-intensive areas, with the gains in the nontechnology-intensive categories being slightly larger. From 1972 to 1974, there was a negative net shift in the technology-intensive exports, while nontechnology-intensive exports showed a large gain due to Japan's increased exports of transport equipment. Of the five major trading nations, Japan experienced the most pronounced consequences from the currency realignments of the early 1970s. While Japan showed large increases in almost every technology-intensive category from 1963 to 1974, the reverse was true for the 1972 to 1974 period—losses occurred in almost every technology-intensive category. These findings make it difficult to evaluate the general area of Japan's comparative advantage. It appears that Japan has been developing its high technology capacities since 1963, but the currency realignments that have occurred since 1971 have retarded that nation's growth in this area.

World Trends

The five major industrialized countries taken as a group appear to be maintaining comparative advantage better in technology-intensive exports. Their share of nontechnology-intensive manufactures fell from 78.1 percent to 70.8 percent from 1963 to 1974, while technology-intensive exports declined from 71.5 percent to 69.6 percent. Thus, while shares were lost in both areas, the shift in the case of technology-intensive exports was much less. The fact that total market shares for the group were virtually the same in both export categories in 1974 might suggest that the relative advantage is the same. The trend indicates, however, that technology-intensive manufactures will be a more important source of comparative advantage for the five major trading countries in the future. The increased reliance of the major trading nations upon technology-intensive exports will probably continue despite the fact that from 1972 to 1974 these nations' export share of nontechnology-intensive goods increased while their share of technology-intensive exports remained constant. As additional competitors enter the international market, their capacities will probably be in the nontechnology-intensive sector, while the major trading nations are more likely to retain their technology-intensive advantages.

EXPLANATIONS OF SHIFTS IN TECHNOLOGY-INTENSIVE EXPORT MARKETS

The decline of the U.S. share of technology-intensive and nontechnology-intensive export markets was to be expected in a world of reviving economic competitors. It appears, however, that several other forces may be involved in explaining the lost export shares of the United States. These additional factors are particularly important in explaining the decreasing relative advantage that the United States has in the technology-intensive area, the area upon which the continued competitiveness of U. S. exports largely depends. The possible causal factors will therefore be discussed with emphasis upon the forces affecting high technology items. In this respect the product life cycle will first be discussed in some depth, followed by comments on other possible causes.

The Product Life Cycle

The product life cycle may be an important component of the decline in the U. S. share of technology-intensive exports. While new products may be replacing old ones in the export mix of the United States, it is to be expected that the volume of exports for the new products will be initially low compared to lost volumes for old products. Those products for which there is a large world demand would be the ones for which standardization, with decreasing technology intensity, would be most suitable. Since standardization leads to new entrants into the world market, it would naturally make inroads into the market share of the United States, the original export leader for many products.

Notwithstanding other contributory factors, the United States would be most likely to suffer market share losses due to the workings of the product life cycle. After World War II, the United States had inherent trade advantages due to both its large size and the lack of internal destruction during the course of the war. With the recovery of Europe and Japan, these advantages were bound to decrease. The first markets in which the product life cycle would anticipate erosion would be the markets for nontechnology-intensive products. Following this, it would be expected that losses would occur in markets for high technology manufactures for which high trade volume existed, thus making standardization worthwhile for the recovering nations.

The above possibilities are supported by the findings in Chapter 9 for the 1963 to 1974 period. West Germany had a larger share of nontechnology-intensive export markets than the United States by 1968, whereas in 1974 it had not quite equalled the U. S. totals for technology-intensive exports. Similarly, Japan's nontechnology-intensive exports in 1974 were closer to the U. S. shares than was the case for technology-intensive exports. These findings provide support for the operation of a product life cycle, since they show that the recovering nations have captured nontechnology-intensive markets to a greater extent than they have captured technology-intensive markets. There is also some evidence to support the idea that nations would first enter high-volume technology-intensive markets. Japan's largest technology-intensive net shifts occurred within two of the highest volume technology-intensive industries, electrical and nonelectrical machinery.

If the above aspects of the product life cycle have been operative, export shares of technology-intensive products may achieve a relative stability for the United States. Such stability would be achieved through the expansion of exports of new products for which standardization is not yet relevant. Of course, such expansion will then lead to standardization in many cases and the consequent lessening of export shares. These losses, however, could be replaced by the invention, expansion of production, and then export of yet newer products. Such a cycle can only now begin to appear since the United States held such an initially large, perhaps unnaturally large, share of the export markets in the years after World War II. If U.S. exports have now become concentrated in this nation's most competitive fields, such a replacement cycle may come into effect and be a relatively stable one. This occurrence is based on the premise that U.S. export shares have, in fact, stabilized, a premise that is only weakly supported by the findings of the study. The achievement of such stability also rests upon a <u>ceteris paribus</u> assumption which the discussion in the following section will draw into question.

Other Possible Causes

The product life cycle provides a theoretical perspective that helps to explain many of the changes that have occurred in the U.S. export position during the period of the study. Yet it cannot be considered the sole, or even the primary, factor involved in determining the decline experienced by the United States in technology-intensive export markets. Several other forces have also been contributing to the U.S. decline since 1963 and can help to explain portions of the results that were obtained. While it is impossible to know the extent that each of these forces contributed to the U.S. decline, it is important to recognize them and to understand the relationship they have to the U.S. technology-intensive export position. Five such forces are considered individually below: the European Economic Community; research and development expenditures in the United States; the relative lack of U.S. government support for exports; the lack of an export mentality among U.S. businesses; and the expansion of multinational corporations.

<u>The European Economic Community</u>

The EEC has undoubtedly had a large impact on the competiveness of U.S. exports both within and outside of its boundaries. Within its boundaries, the EEC tariff schedule tends to protect resident manufacturers from substitute products from abroad (Tullock 1973, p. 39). EEC producers are able to operate behind these tariff walls, and the imports of other nations naturally assume higher prices. These EEC tariff barriers may provide part of the explanation for Germany's ability to increase its technology-intensive and nontechnology-intensive market shares in the face of the revaluation of the mark. The relatively lower prices of U. S. goods following 1971 could have been irrelevant within the EEC, since EEC tariffs could have brought these prices above the level of German prices. Thus, Germany would have been able to continue its export expansion inside the Common Market.

The EEC could have impacted U. S. exports to nations outside of the community through its creation of a large internal market for manufacturers located within the community. The creation of this large market could have facilitated the development of economies of scale in European manufacturing industries. Such economies of scale could have reduced the prices of some goods produced in the EEC which would thus make such goods more competitive internationally. The large internal market and the resultant economies of scale have traditionally provided U. S. manufacturers with a competitive advantage in certain industries. That the EEC now also contains a market of this magnitude could have eroded U. S. advantages in certain areas.

Research and Development in the United States

Several indicators exist that suggest that the United States is losing its superiority in basic research and development (R&D) activities. For instance, the percent of U. S. GNP that is devoted to R&D expenditures fell dramatically and consistently during the years of the present study, while the corresponding expenditures by Japan and Germany increased substantially. In 1964 U. S. research and development expenditures represented 3.0 percent of U. S. GNP, but they fell consistently after that time to 2.3 percent of GNP in 1974. Conversely, Germany's R&D expenditures in 1964 amounted to only 1.4 percent of GNP, while in 1974 they had surpassed the United States at 2.4 percent of GNP. Similarly, the percentage of Japan's GNP devoted to R&D expenditures rose from 1.2 percent in 1963 to 1.9 percent in 1973 (National Science Foundation 1976). It is highly probable that the reduction in proportionate U. S. research and development expenditures coupled with the increases by Germany and Japan was responsible for at least part of the deterioration of the U. S. technology-intensive position from 1963 to 1974. If these trends in R&D expenditures continue, then the United States will probably continue to lose its markets abroad for technology-intensive products.

Another indicator of the decline of U. S. research and development superiority is the number of scientists and engineers per 10,000 population that are engaged in R&D activities. Here again the United States has been losing ground relative to Japan and Germany. The U. S. figure for this indicator dropped slightly between 1964 and 1973, from 25 to about 24. On the other hand, the number of scientists and engineers in Germany per 10,000 population who were engaged in R&D rose from five in 1964 to 15 in 1973, while in Japan the figure went from 12 to 17 (National Science Foundation 1976). Thus, while the United States has remained fairly static in terms of the proportion of its population engaged in R&D, Japan, and especially Germany, have grown rapidly. If the United States continues to lose its relative R&D superiority in terms of the manpower engaged in its pursuit, there can be little doubt that this nation will lose more of its advantage in the production of high technology products.

Several other indicators are available that suggest the diminution of U. S. research and development superiority in the world (National Science Foundation 1976). The two just given, however, are sufficient to illustrate the point that the decline that has occurred in U. S. technology-intensive export markets is probably related to the reduction of resources that the United States is devoting to R&D activities and the corresponding increases by Germany and Japan. If these trends continue, then the stability that may have been achieved in technology-intensive export markets that was suggested by the product life cycle is clearly an overly optimistic assessment of the situation.

U. S. Government Support of Exports

The U. S. government has traditionally had a more "arm's length" relationship with domestic businesses than is true for the governments of Japan and Germany. The differences in philosophies of government-business interaction between these nations extends into the support that is provided to export industries in the three nations. The U. S. government has given exporters relatively little encouragement except through the provision of information and permission for "collusion" among U. S. firms under certain specified export conditions. In fact, it has been generally noted that in the United States the government has to date been unable to set economic priorities and allocate resources in such a way as to encourage exports and international trade in general (Quinn 1966, p. 126). The findings of the study, however, suggest that the governments of Japan and possibly Germany have taken a more active role in assisting their export industries. It is difficult to imagine how the Japanese were able to dramatically expand their sales of nontechnology-intensive transport equipment after 1971, a time when their markets for practically all other goods were contracting, without some assistance from the government. Likewise, the ability of German exports to increase their market shares in the face of the revaluation of the mark can probably be explained by more than just the protective barriers of the EEC, possibly through active support of the German government using subsidies or other methods of assistance. Here again is a situation where inaction by the United States, coupled with positive action by Germany and Japan, could work to continue the erosion of U. S. export market shares.

Export Attitudes of U. S. Businesses

In conjunction with the lack of active U. S. government support for its exporters, there exists a lack of an export mentality among U. S. businesses. According to Rostow (1978), "as a nation, we do not have the export-or-die mentality that suffuses some of the countries of Western Europe and Japan, as well as such successful smaller nations as South Korea and Taiwan." Since U. S. businesses are not geared toward exports, it is possible that part of the reason for the deterioration of the U. S. export position is due to the lack of aggressiveness by U. S. firms in seeking export markets. Thus, the U. S. decline may not be entirely related to factors pertaining to inherent comparative advantage, but may be partially attributable to a lethargic attitude by U. S. businessmen toward exports.

Some of the findings in the present study are consistent with this explanation for the U. S. decline in export markets. For one, it should be noted that although the United States lost market share in most export categories, the absolute volume of U. S. exports in the majority of these categories grew throughout the period of the study. The declines were caused by the fact that U. S. exports grew at a slower rate than the exports of the other nations. Since U. S. exports in most areas continued their absolute growth, it means that this nation may have remained competitive in many product categories, despite this nation's market share losses. It could have been a lack of aggressiveness on the part of U. S. businesses that retarded this nation's growth. A second finding that is consistent with the argument is the fact that U. S. imports in most industry groups did not increase at the same level as the corresponding exports decreased. Thus, it appears that U. S. producers were capable of supplying domestic needs at competitive prices without increased competition from imported goods. If this was the case, then it is also possible that U. S. goods could have sold competitively on international markets, but that U. S. producers did not actively seek to cultivate those markets.

U. S.-Based Multinational Corporations

Labor unions in the United States have long been critical of U. S.-based multinational corporations with respect to these firms' propensity to export U. S. jobs and technology, and in turn diminish the markets for U. S. exports (Goldfinger 1973). This is indeed a complex issue that does not have a clear-cut answer. Yet it is highly probable that the transfer of capital, skills, and technology by these firms through their direct investment and licensing activities abroad has had some negative impact on U. S. export markets for technology-intensive goods. Although these firms will argue that their investments tend to be defensive, such as investments in the EEC to avoid the tariff barriers, and that these investments tend to create additional export markets for U. S. goods (Harvey and Kerin 1976), it is difficult to argue with the findings of the present study. During the 1963 to 1974 period, while U. S. export market shares for technology-intensive goods were decreasing substantially, the book value of foreign private direct investment by U. S. firms went from $40.6 billion in 1963 to $118.6 billion in 1974 (Survey of Current Business 1966, 1976). Furthermore, it has been noted that the subsidiaries that U. S. firms create abroad tend to have a disproportionate share of their sales in highly research-oriented product categories (Gruber, et al. 1967, p. 31). Thus, there seems to be a close relationship between the expansion of U. S. private direct investment abroad and the decline in the U. S. share of export markets for technology-intensive products.

While it is impossible to point to any specific findings of the present study that relate directly to lost U. S. exports due to foreign investment by the multinationals, the manner in which such firms could have affected U. S. export sales is clear. These firms are heavily involved in the transfer of technology through both the initiation of direct operations abroad and licensing activities with foreign firms. Transfers of technology from the United States to other nations could deprive this country of comparative advantage in products that had previously been produced more efficiently in the United States. The extent to which overseas expansion by U. S.-based multinationals has retarded U. S. export growth is not known for certain, although labor and management have both made estimates (Goldfinger 1973; Harvey and Kerin 1976). Not surprisingly, the estimates of the two groups are not the same. Yet is must be concluded that this expansion of U. S. firms overseas has had some negative impact upon U. S. exports as firms undertake foreign production of products which were previously exported from the United States.

Beyond the direct transfer of technology, multinationals can affect competition for U. S. exports through their transfer of management and the skills necessary to produce technology-intensive products. Management has long been a strength of U. S. business, and it has probably contributed to U. S. competitive advantage in many product areas. These managerial abilities are transferred by U. S. corporations to their foreign subsidiaries, usually through training indigenous personnel. Likewise, the technical skills required to work with multinationals' production processes are often transferred to local personnel. Thus, multinationals are often involved in upgrading the labor force of the nations in which they locate subsidiaries. Such transfers have positive impacts on the nations involved, but they can also result in lost U.S. export sales.

POLICY AREAS

The preceding discussion has suggested several policy areas that the U.S. government should consider if it places a high priority upon its position in the production and export of high technology products. Perhaps the most obvious area of potential improvement would involve the direction of more funds into research and development activities. The relative decline that the United States has experienced in this area, if continued, will undoubtedly have a long-term impact upon this nation's ability to retain an advantage in high technology goods.

The U.S. government may also have to reevaluate its passive position toward the stimulation of exports by U.S. businesses. If, in fact, the governments of other trading nations, and particularly of Germany and Japan, are actively involved in stimulating exports through direct or indirect subsidies, the U.S. government might also consider such actions. An active role played by foreign governments combined with the passive role played by the U.S. government has probably had the net effect of retarding U.S. export growth. Thus, the U.S. government may be forced into playing a more active role if this nation's exports are to expand at a rate that approximates the world rate.

Before the U.S. government becomes more actively involved in some form of export subsidization, it may first be necessary to stimulate interest in export activities among U.S. businesses. The passive role involved in providing information to firms that express an interest in exports may no longer be adequate. It may be more advisable for agencies such as the U.S. Department of Commerce to actively solicit export operations from firms that have an export potential. If firms are unaware of export opportunities, they are not likely to express much interest in foreign sales. If such opportunities are pointed out to them, and if technical assistance with regard to the many complexities of exporting is provided, then more interest may be generated from U.S. businesses.

The policy issues surrounding the control of the overseas activities of multinational corporations are multifaceted and extremely complex. In many respects, these activities serve U.S. interests abroad.

They involve U.S. businesses directly in the economies of foreign countries and thus provide a base through which U.S. influence can be exerted within those countries. Multinationals also contribute substantially to the U.S. balance of payments through the repatriation of foreign earnings. Yet, if these firms are involved in undercutting the U.S. position in the international economy through the diffusion of the basis of U.S. competitive advantage throughout the world, then it might be necessary to place some controls over their activities. This is an area that deserves considerable additional study before actual recommendations can be made. The studies that have been conducted to date in this area have tended to be self serving, such as studies by labor unions or management organizations. It will be necessary to obtain some more objective information in order to evaluate the impact that these corporations have had upon the U.S. position in world trade.

PART III

CONCLUSIONS AND IMPLICATIONS

12

EXPORT PATTERNS AND U.S. ECONOMIC INFLUENCE

The findings of Part I and Part II provide a perspective on the changing role of the United States in the world economy that is less than optimistic. The trading positions of the major countries in terms of market nodes and hierarchy positions and as exporters of technology-intensive products are closely related. In order to evaluate the results of the various analyses in the preceding chapters, the connections between the first and second portions of the study will be discussed. Then, an overall evaluation will be made of the position of the United States in the international economic community. The two areas are not conceptually distinct, and many overlaps exist. The connections between the two areas of trade have a bearing on the possible continued decline of the United States in the international economy. The chapter concludes with a discussion of the future prospects for the position of the United States.

TECHNOLOGY INTENSITY AND EXPORT MARKETS

The most obvious connection between export markets and export shares for manufactures appeared in the derivation of the hierarchies. Of those noncommunist countries included in both analyses, the ones with the largest export shares of technology-intensive and nontechnology-intensive products were also those nations that were key final or intermediate nodes in the hierarchies that were derived for various years in Part One. The United States, Germany, Japan, France, and the United Kingdom proved to be central as both markets for goods from other nations and as exporters of manufactures. Thus, by different selection processes, the relevant nations for each analysis proved to be the same. The importance of these key countries was thus made clear, as was the importance of the relationship between the two areas of trade.

Competitive Positions

There was a correspondence between the longitudinal results for the hierarchies and the changes in export shares among the OECD nations. The position of the United Kingdom was clearly on the wane as evidenced by the results of both sets of analyses. The hierarchy of the United Kingdom contained relatively fewer countries over time, and some of the losses were major trading states with high levels of exports. Similarly, that nation's export positions for both technology-intensive and nontechnology-intensive manufactures deteriorated. In both analyses the decline in the position of the United Kingdom appeared constant and the level of economic viability appeared to be declining rapidly.

In the case of France, the similarities of the findings are also remarkable. That country appeared to be maintaining a stable position in the international economic system, particularly after 1961. Changes in export shares were small over time, and the nations attached to France as a nodal market showed great consistency. The only major change for France in the study was its change from an independent node to an intermediate one by 1961. Since the export data did not start until 1963, it was not possible to determine if a similar correspondence was present for the earlier years.

Japan and Germany both displayed the greatest gains, both in terms of export shares and as hierarchical market nodes. Germany showed the greatest expansion in its hierarchical position between 1951 and 1961 with a smaller expansion between 1961 and 1971 and virtually no change between 1971 and 1976. The export position of Germany was strong at the start of 1963, and it clearly was much stronger in that year than it would have been in 1951. From 1963 to 1974 the gain in export shares paralleled that of the gains to the hierarchy. Relative export shares improved on the whole, although not in dramatic fashion, just as there were additions to the hierarchy; but the major expansion had occurred prior to that time.

The agreement between the two parts of the study for Japan is also present. The addition of new nations to the Japanese hierarchy has roughly paralleled the gains that country has made in terms of export shares. However, it might have been anticipated that the Japanese hierarchy would have shown more expansion, given the tremendous gains in export shares that that nation experienced. Such further expansion might be forthcoming in the future, since there might be a lag between the expansion of exports of manufactures and the gain of new nations as exporters.

The United States presents the most anomalous case with respect to the findings of the two parts of the study. The analysis of the U.S. hierarchy indicated that the number and strength of the nations attached to the United States remained approximately constant from 1961 to 1976. Conversely, the analysis of the U.S. export position clearly showed that the United States has experienced a significant decline in this area. The lack of correspondence between the two parts of the study is puzzling, but may not be as contradictory as might be assumed. Here again there may be a lag that exists between changes that occur in a nation's export position and the number of nations that are attached to its market. This idea will be explored in greater depth later in the chapter.

The differing time periods for the two sets of analyses have hindered making some direct comparisons between the findings of the two parts of the study. It seems clear that the United Kingdom's export position in 1951 was stronger than in later years. Likewise, France appeared to be in approximately the same export position in 1951 as in 1961 and thereafter, with the major exception being that France was not tied to a larger nation in 1951. Germany and Japan were in roughly similar positions in 1951. The German Federal Republic was formed in 1949, and the occupation of Japan did not officially end until 1952. These two countries also had only a few nations directly linked to them in the 1951 hierarchies. Although data on export shares were not available for this year, it is likely that these two countries held only small portions of the total exports for manufactures. In terms of both export position and positions as market nodes, Germany improved first. If the German pattern proves to be a parallel for Japan, continued improvement in Japan's hierarchical ties will occur.

Since data were unavailable for the Soviet Union, it is unclear what the relationship between exports and hierarchical position is for that country. Given the sheer size of its economy, it is probably the largest exporter of manufactures within its hierarchical group, although East Germany and Czechoslovakia also provide manufactures for export to the other East European countries and the USSR. These two countries might even be greater exporters of certain types of technology-intensive manufactures. Of course, the fact that the Soviet hierarchy is not supported by economic ties alone, but rather with actual or potential military control, makes direct analogy to the other hierarchical nodes difficult. Also, exports from one Eastern European country to another are at least partially determined in Moscow. Such decisions would affect the types of exports available. In fact, Rumania's increasingly strained relations with the Soviet Union originated with that state's refusal to be a supplier of raw materials for the USSR.

Dependence and Political Compliance

The connection between the export of manufactures and dependence on markets is probably not a direct one. For some theorists, however, technology has been considered to be part of dependence. A monopoly of technology has been postulated as one part of the means by which dependence is perpetuated by the industrialized states and development in the periphery is inhibited (Dos Santos 1971, pp. 231, 235; Rweyemamu 1969, p. 217; Gantzel 1973, p. 205). Hveem (1973, p. 322) felt that one aspect of a hierarchical international system included the control of technology by states at the top of the hierarchy. The results of the two parts of this study clearly indicate that those states at the top of the market hierarchies dominate at least the export of technology-intensive products. Gantzel (1973, pp. 205-06) felt that technology was one form of U.S. dominance over Western Europe. However, the results of the changing export shares for technology-intensive products would discount this argument. Although the United States may have had technical dominance in earlier periods, there is little indication that such dominance has continued to the present, at least not in all categories. Just as Western Europe has not been dominated by the United States in terms of market hierarchies, it also has been outside of U.S. technological dominance as well.

The need for increasing technological inputs for manufactures could work against the interests of Third World countries in some ways. Technological borrowing requires greater amounts of prerequisites in the form of skilled labor, capital, educated technicians, and sophisticated markets. In addition, as technological inputs in manufactures increase, the possibility of obtaining political compliance on the part of some states may also increase. Gantzel (1973, pp. 204-05) noted that the greater the technical resources of a nation, the more likely it would be to participate in the international system and exert influence. The presence of a high level of technology intensity, as evidenced by technology-intensive exports, provides at least one means of influencing other states.

The major exporting countries may be able to exert influence over other nations through the technological capabilities they possess. They could withhold essential spare parts in order to bring about desired political objectives. Plants and equipment in various countries have proven to be almost useless from a lack of spare parts that has resulted from changing political relationships. High technology items will not necessarily have interchangeable parts. In particular, countries that have shifted from western to communist sources, or vice versa, have often found that old equipment no longer is very useful. Thus, technology and dependence and political compliance do have some relationships to each other. The increasing use of technology permits at least one additional economic weapon to be deployed if a state desires to do so. Since the major exporters of high technology manufactures are also the major market nodes, the possibility of bringing additional pressure to bear is present.

The apparent diffusion of high technology capabilities from the United States to Japan and Germany could also have some associated positive consequences for Third World nations with respect to their dependency upon the dominant nations. When the United States held a position of overwhelming dominance as a supplier of technology-intensive products, many countries had little choice but to purchase these goods from the United States. As Japan and Germany have developed capabilities in this area, Third World countries increasingly are being provided with alternative sources of technology-intensive goods. While this situation does not solve the economic problems associated with dependency, it may reduce some of the more objectionable political consequences involved in being primarily dependent upon one country as a source of supply.

Hierarchical Positions and Export Shares

It has been shown that changes in the nodal market position of the various countries are related to changes in their export share positions. While declines or gains in both areas are probably mutually reinforcing, it is possible that gains in one area can be a causal factor for improvements in the other, and vice versa.

Before discussing a possible causal relationship, it should be noted that the strength of the economy of a given country may have an effect on both a nation's position in a hierarchy and the nation's ability to compete for export markets. In the case of the United States, domestic influences are important and could thus lead to problems or improvement in both areas. For the other dominant nations in the hierarchies, except the USSR, international factors are probably more important since international trade has traditionally been more important to their economic well being. For all countries, however, domestic factors have an important impact on trading relationships.

It is likely, controlling for domestic impacts, that the export position of a country affects its position as a market rather than its market position affecting its export shares. One reason that exports to major markets were chosen in Part One to derive the hierarchies was because import levels reflect, at least in part, the availability of foreign exchange earned from the sale of exports. The loss of export shares by the United States, particularly for technology-intensive manufactures where a comparative advantage has been assumed to exist, obviously will have an eventual impact on the ability of the United States to provide a market for other nations' products. The decreasing value of the dollar as a reserve currency may heighten this impact. Thus, the loss of export shares by the United States may have increased the viability of the nations with revalued currencies—Germany and Japan—as markets. The same situation may have been present for the United Kingdom. As U.K. products became less competitive on world markets, the value of the pound declined, and the United Kingdom was not able to provide the large market for many nations' goods that it once had. The case of Japan might also indicate that expanded export shares will lead to an expansion in the number of countries linked to Japan as a market node.

Exports may be related to hierarchical market positions in another sequence. Although the Third World countries with the exception of energy producers have less impact on trade than the industrialized states, their effect as a group is still present. The Western Hemisphere territories may have suffered a competitive setback for their exports by the preferences that are provided to former European colonies through associate membership in the EEC. If the exports of Western Hemisphere nations decline relative to the exports of the associate members, then imports must be curtailed. The United States could be hurt by this situation in two ways. While sources of imports of the Western Hemisphere countries are varied, a curtailment of their imports would probably have a larger impact on the United States than on its Western European competitors or Japan. Thus, less dollars are spent for imports from the United States. Also, a loss of export markets by Western Hemisphere nations may inhibit the development of these countries, thus limiting their ability to purchase imports, again much of which come from the United States. At the same time, exports from the EEC associate members may be rising relative to other areas of the world, and will very possibly lead to an increased demand for exports from the EEC countries, much of which could consist of technology-intensive products.

While the export position of the various countries and their positions as markets are related, it would appear that the export position is more important in that expanded exports lead to an enhanced importance as a market node, and vice versa. Thus, the decreasing export shares of the United States could lead to a decline in the number of countries dependent on its market.

PROSPECTS FOR THE FUTURE

It has become clear through the course of the present study that the position of the United States in the international economy has weakened considerably over time. The United States has gone from the position of being the overwhelmingly dominant economic power in the world to a position in which it is increasingly a regional power in the Western Hemisphere. The other regions of the world are coming under the influence of more geographically proximate powers such as the EEC or Japan. If the current trends that have been identified by this study continue, then the position of the United States should continue to decline in many areas.

The formation of the Common Market has obviously had, and will continue to have, a major impact on the position of the United States. While European economic recovery was bound to affect the United States, the EEC has increased that impact. The initial impacts of the Treaty of Rome may well have run their course. Even the admittance of the original associate members had a minimal effect on world trade patterns since the territories involved were former colonies of the full members with existing close economic ties. Future impacts, however, are likely to occur that will further affect the United States. The addition of the three new full members, particularly the United Kingdom, will change trade patterns. Also, the proliferation of new associate memberships should have further negative impacts on the U.S. position as a nodal market and on the export position of Latin America. Thus, the Common Market will probably continue to increase its collective economic position in the world, at least partially at the expense of the United States.

The original recovery of the European nations and the formation of the Common Market was welcomed by the United States, yet the long-term impacts may be extremely harmful to this country. The original improvements in these countries' trade positions came largely at the expense of the United Kingdom and the United States, although total U.S. and U.K. trade was also growing during this time. In the future, the position of the United States may deteriorate in absolute terms as well as relative ones when trade is adjusted for inflation. The United Kingdom may avoid these problems as a result of joining the EEC, but the United States does not have that option. The probable integration of the United Kingdom into the German hierarchy should have a further negative impact on the position of the United States, both as a market node and as an exporter.

The economic recovery of Japan has also contributed to the weakened position of the United States during the time period of the present study. However, the long-term prospects for the continuing impact of Japan on the U. S. position do not appear as negative as is the case for the EEC. Notwithstanding the economic progress of Japan, that country's continued ties to the U. S. market may reflect the effects of geographic proximity. The United Kingdom and other European states have major markets nearby as alternatives to the United States. In this sense, it will be more difficult for Japan to find new major markets than, for example, the United Kingdom, particularly since the EEC has maintained discriminatory tariff rates against Japanese goods. The effects of geographic proximity might also place limits on the extent to which the Japanese hierarchy can expand. Germany, France, and the United Kingdom are geographically close to the numerous states of Africa, Europe, and parts of west Asia, and the United States is relatively close to the Western Hemisphere countries. Japan, however, is proximate only to the relatively few Asian countries and the widely scattered nations and territories of Oceania. It is therefore likely that Japan will remain closely tied to the U. S. market for the foreseeable future.

A further area of concern for the United States is the possibility of the decrease in U. S. influence in the Western Hemisphere that may accompany the decline of its worldwide economic position. As mentioned above, a decrease in U. S. exports may lead to an eventual decrease in the viability of the U. S. market for other nations' exports. Such a course of events would have a major impact on the nations of Latin America, most of which depend heavily upon the U. S. market. The concurrent development of potential economic powers within Latin America, such as Brazil, could lead many of these nations to shift a portion of their exports to such new markets. Likewise, a weakened U. S. position could enhance the viability of the regional associations that exist within Latin America, such as the Andean Common Market. These events within the Western Hemisphere have already begun to occur, although their full effects will not be noticeable in the near future. The decreased reliance of Latin America upon the United States that could be associated with the general decline of the U. S. economic position in the world, however, may serve to hasten their occurrence.

It is possible to interpret the results from the present study in a more optimistic manner with regard to the future position of the United States. The hierarchy of the United States did not contract from 1971 to 1976, and the U. S. export position from 1972 to 1974 for both technology-intensive and nontechnology-intensive products did not decline. Such findings could be indicative of some stabilization occurring in the U. S. position. Within the context of the entire study, however, it is difficult to defend such an interpretation, particularly in light of the lag that was postulated to exist between U. S. export shares and the U. S. market for the exports of other countries. The most recent balance of payments statistics at the time of this writing show that the U.S. current account position is worsening. While the current account in 1976 registered a small deficit of $1.4 billion, in 1977 the United States recorded a current account deficit of more than $20 billion. Total U.S. exports in 1977 were only 5 percent higher than in 1976, less than the rate of inflation (Summary of Current Business 1978). Thus, this nation's international transactions are being increasingly financed through the liquidity accounts, and such a method of financing cannot continue indefinitely. It appears that the trend toward a diminishing role for the United States in world trade is continuing, and that the resurgence that occurred immediately following the dollar devaluation was only temporary.

While it is easy to blame the present U.S. current account problems on the energy situation and the huge sums being spent on oil, such an argument applies only to a point. Germany and Japan are more highly dependent on imports of oil than the United States, and yet those nations have been able to maintain surpluses in their trade balances. In addition, the use of the energy crisis and the oil exporters as scapegoats does not serve any positive purpose in altering the current state of affairs. The price of oil is something that is largely beyond the control of the United States. This nation can attempt to reduce consumption and to persuade the OPEC nations against further price increases, but the current high price of oil and the level of U.S. oil imports are not going to diminish in the near future. Therefore, short- and intermediate-term solutions to the problems faced by the United States do not seem to lie in this area much beyond those actions that are presently being proposed and debated.

Perhaps it is time for U.S. policy makers to realize that this nation cannot allow the status quo to exist with regard to U.S. trade policies and expect natural forces to rectify the situation. Such a rectification will not occur, if only because the governments of other nations are not permitting the natural forces associated with trade theory to operate. In a world where the United States was the unquestioned economic giant, such a "hands off" attitude toward the international operations of the private sector in this country may have been warranted. However, the United States no longer occupies that position, and its policies should reflect this new situation.

Several policy options seem to be available to the United States that might improve its current position in international trade, particularly its trade in the technology-intensive sector, some of which are better or more feasible than others. For instance, higher rates of inflation in the United States relative to Germany and Japan have certainly played a role in the decline of U.S. export shares. Yet, U.S. economic policy toward inflation must be tempered by numerous domestic political realities and, thus, cannot by itself be depended upon to provide the necessary adjustments. Another area of trade policy that is likely to receive attention, particularly as the U. S. balance of payments situation deteriorates, concerns the construction of additional trade barriers to discourage imports. New tariffs, however, would be counterproductive from the standpoint of the overall U. S. position in the world economy. In addition to all of the other economic deficiencies associated with higher tariffs, such barriers would probably work to reduce total U. S. trade and therefore further reduce U. S. export markets.

The types of policies that are needed by the United States are those that work in a positive direction to stimulate U. S. exports in those areas in which this nation retains a comparative advantage. Policies of this nature would have the most immediate, and the most lasting, impact on the U. S. export position. The findings presented in Part II of this volume suggested that although the United States has lost considerable market share in the export markets for technology-intensive goods, this nation appears to have retained its competitive advantage in the production of many technology-intensive products. It would seem, therefore, that policies that are directed toward improving the U. S. export position in these products would be most beneficial to this country.

The general policy measures that would have the largest impact upon U. S. technology-intensive exports were noted in Chapter 11 and will be only briefly restated here. First, it seems necessary for the U. S. government to provide increased incentives for the conduct of basic research and development in this country. It is through research and development activities that technology-intensive products and production processes are derived, and the worldwide decline of the United States in various R&D indicators foreshadows continued U. S. losses in technology-intensive export markets. Second, the government should actively undertake an extensive program to encourage U. S. producers of internationally-competitive goods to take advantage of export opportunities. It has been suggested that many such producers are either unaware of export opportunities or are unwilling to deal with the complexities of export operations. If government agencies actively became involved in these processes, exports could be stimulated. Third, the U. S. government should seriously consider some forms of subsidies to exporters in order to provide further incentives for firms to engage in these activities. Although subsidies of this nature are not consistent with the dominant economic philosophy of this country, they appear to be used by other governments at the expense of U. S. exports. It would therefore seem that some action by the United States is necessary to counteract the impact of other nations' subsidy programs.

Positive actions of the type noted above appear necessary if the United States is to regain some of its lost markets and retain its economic influence. A lack of action on the part of this country will continue its decline toward becoming an increasingly regional, as opposed to a world, economic power. The present trends suggest that economic power is shifting to the EEC and away from the United States. While it is difficult to imagine the EEC becoming as politically powerful as the United States, the close association that exists between economic and political power cannot be denied. Of course, this is not to suggest that the United States' position in high technology exports is the only area that substantially affects this country's position of international influence, or that it is even the most important area. However, the associations between high technology capabilities and economic influence are well established, as are the associations between economic influence and political influence. It therefore seems important that the United States take some initiative in this area if it is to retain a dominant position in the world.

APPENDIX A

COUNTRIES EMPLOYED IN HIERARCHY STUDY

TABLE A.1

Countries Employed in Hierarchy Study, 1951

Aden	Ethiopia	Liberia
Aden Protectorate	Falkland Islands	Libya
Afghanistan	Faeroe Islands	Macao
Albania	Fiji	Madagascar
Algeria	Finland	Malaya-Singapore
Anglo Egyptian Sudan	France	Maldive Islands
Angola	French Cameroon	Mauritius
Argentina	French Equatorial	Mexico
Australia	Africa	Mozambique
Austria	French Morocco	Naru
Belgian Congo	French Somali Coast	Netherlands
Belgium-Luxembourg	French West Africa	Netherlands Antilles
Bolivia	(including Togo)	New Guinea
Brazil	French West Indies	New Zealand
British Guiana	Germany, East	Nicaragua
British Honduras	Germany, Federal	Nigeria
British Perisan Gulf	Republic of	North Borneo
States	Gold Coast	Norway
British Somaliland	Greece	Nyasaland
British West Indies	Greenland	Oman
Brunei	Guatemala	Pakistan
Bulgaria	Haiti	Panama
Burma	Honduras	Pápua
Cameroun	Hong Kong	Paraguay
Canada	Hungary	Peru
Ceylon	Iceland	Philippines
Chile	India	Poland
China (Mainland)	Indochina	Portugal
China (Taiwan)	Indonesia	Portuguese Guinea
Colombia	Iran	Rhodesia, North
Costa Rica	Iraq	Rhodesia, South
Cuba	Ireland	Rumania
Cyprus	Israel	St. Thomas and
Czechoslovakia	Italy	Prince Islands
Denmark	Jamaica	Sarawak
Dominican Republic	Japan	Saudi Arabia
Dutch New Guinea	Jordan	Sierra Leone
Ecuador	Kenya	Somalia
Egypt	Korea, South	South Africa
El Salvador	Lebanon	Southwest Africa

(continued)

Table A.1 continued

Spain
Spanish Guinea
Spanish Morocco
Surinam
Sweden
Switzerland
Syria
Tanganyika
Thailand
Trinidad and Tobago
Trieste, Free Territory of
Tunisia
Turkey
Uganda
United Kingdom
United States
Uruguay
U. S. S. R.
Venezuela
Western Samoa
Yugoslavia

Source: Compiled by the authors.

TABLE A.2

Countries Employed in Hierarchy Study, 1961

Aden	Dominican Republic	Kenya
Aden Protectorate	Ecuador	Korea, South
Afghanistan	El Salvador	Kuwait
Albania	Ethiopia	Laos
Algeria	Faeroe Islands	Lebanon
Angola	Falkland Islands	Leeward Islands
Argentina	Fiji	Liberia
Australia	Finland	Libya
Austria	France	Malagasy Republic
Bahrain	Gabon	Malaya
Bahamas	Gambia	Maldive Islands
Barbados	Germany, East	Mali Republic
Belgium-Luxembourg	Germany, West	Malta
Bermuda	Ghana	Martinique
Bolivia	Gibralter	Mauritania
Brazil	Greece	Mauritius
British Honduras	Greenland	Mexico
Brunei	Guadeloupe	Morocco
Bulgaria	Guatemala	Mozambique
Burma	Guinea Republic	Naru
Cameroun	Guyana	Netherlands
Canada	Haiti	Netherlands Antilles
Central African Republic	Honduras	New Caledonia
	Hong Kong	New Guinea
Ceylon	Hungary	New Hebrides
Chad	Iceland	New Zealand
Chile	India	Nicaragua
China (Mainland)	Indonesia	Niger
China (Taiwan)	Iran	Nigeria
Colombia	Iraq	North Borneo
Congo, Brazzaville	Ireland	Norway
Congo, Leopoldville	Irian Barat	Oman
Costa Rica	Israel	Pakistan
Cuba	Italy	Panama
Cyprus	Ivory Coast	Papua
Czechoslovakia	Jamaica	Paraguay
Dahomey	Japan	Peru
Denmark	Jordan	Philippines

(continued)

Table A.2 continued

Poland	U.S.S.R.
Portugal	Venezuela
Portuguese Guinea	Vietnam, South
Qatar	Windward Islands
Reunion	Western Samoa
Rhodesia and Nyasaland	Yemen
Rumania	Yugoslavia
Ryukyus	Zanzibar
St. Pierre and Miquelon	
St. Thomas and Prince Islands	
Sarawak	
Saudi Arabia	
Senegal	
Sierra Leone	
Singapore	
Somali Coast	
Somalia	
South Africa	
Spain	
Sudan	
Surinam	
Sweden	
Switzerland	
Syria	
Tanganyika	
Thailand	
Togo	
Trinidad and Tobago	
Tunisia	
Turkey	
Uganda	
United Arab Republic	
United Kingdom	
United States	
Upper Volta	
Uruguay	

Source: Compiled by the authors.

TABLE A.3

Countries Employed in Hierarchy Study, 1971

Afars and Issas	Czechoslovakia	Ireland
Afghanistan	Dahomey	Israel
Albania	Denmark	Italy
Algeria	Dominican Republic	Ivory Coast
Angola	Ecuador	Jamaica
Argentina	Equatorial Guinea	Japan
Australia	Egypt	Jordan
Austria	El Salvador	Kenya
Bahamas	Ethiopia	Korea, South
Bahrain	Faeroe Islands	Kuwait
Barbados	Falkland Islands	Laos
Belgium-Luxembourg	Fiji	Lebanon
Bermuda	Finland	Leeward Islands
Bolivia	France	Liberia
Brazil	French Guiana	Libya
British Honduras	Gabon	Macao
British Solomon Islands	Gambia	Malagasy Republic
Bulgaria	Germany, East	Malawi
Brunei	Germany, West	Malaysia
Burma	Ghana	Maldive Islands
Burundi	Gibralter	Mali Republic
Cambodia	Gilbert and Ellice Islands	Malta
Cameroun	Greece	Martinique
Canada	Greenland	Mauritania
Cape Verde Islands	Guadeloupe	Mauritius
Central African Republic	Guatemala	Mexico
Chad	Guinea Republic	Morocco
Chile	Guyana	Mozambique
China (Mainland)	Haiti	Naru
China (Taiwan)	Honduras	Nepal
Colombia	Hong Kong	Netherlands
Congo, People's Republic	Hungary	Netherlands Antilles
Costa Rica	Iceland	New Caldeonia
Cuba	India	New Hebrides
Cyprus	Indonesia	New Guinea
	Iran	New Zealand
	Iraq	Nicaragua
		Niger

(continued)

Table A.3 continued

Nigeria
Norway
Oman
Pakistan
Panama
Papua
Paraguay
Peru
Philippines
Poland
Portugal
Portuguese Guinea
Qatar
Reunion
Rhodesia
Rumania
Rwanda
Ryukyus
St. Pierre and Miquelon
St. Thomas and Prince Islands
Saudi Arabia
Senegal
Seychelles Islands
Sierra Leone
Singapore
Somalia
South Africa
Spain
Sri Lanka
Sudan
Surinam
Sweden
Switzerland
Syria
Tanzania
Thailand
Togo
Trinidad and Tobago
Tunisia

Turkey
Uganda
United Arab Emirates
United Kingdom
United States
Upper Volta
Uruguay
U.S.S.R.
Venezuela
Vietnam, South
Western Samoa
Windward Islands
Yemen Arab Republic
Yemen, P.D.R.
Yugoslavia
Zaire
Zambia

TABLE A.4

Countries Employed in Hierarchy Study, 1976

Afghanistan	Czechoslovakia	Iran
Algeria	Denmark	Iraq
Angola	Djibouti	Ireland
Argentina	Dominican Republic	Israel
Australia	Ecuador	Italy
Austria	Egypt	Ivory Coast
Bahamas	El Salvador	Jamaica
Bahrain	Ethiopia	Japan
Barbados	Equatorial Guinea	Jordan
Belgium-Luxembourg	Faeroe Islands	Kenya
Belize	Falkland Islands	Korea, South
Benin, People's Republic of	Fiji	Kuwait
	Finland	Laos
Bermuda	France	Lebanon
Bolivia	French Polynesia	Leeward Islands
Brazil	Gabon	Liberia
British Solomon Islands	Gambia	Libya
	Germany, East	Macao
Bulgaria	Germany, West	Malagasy Republic
Brunei	Ghana	Malawi
Burma	Gibralter	Malaysia
Burundi	Gilbert and Ellice Islands	Maldive Islands
Cameroun		Mali Republic
Canada	Greece	Malta
Cape Verde Islands	Greenland	Martinique
Central African Empire	Guadeloupe	Mauritania
	Guatemala	Mauritius
Chad	Guiana, French	Mexico
Chile	Guinea-Bissau	Morocco
China (Mainland)	Guinea Republic	Mozambique
China (Taiwan)	Guyana	Naru
Colombia	Haiti	Nepal
Comoros Islands	Honduras	Netherlands
Congo, People's Republic	Hong Kong	Netherlands Antilles
	Hungary	New Caldeonia
Costa Rica	Iceland	New Hebrides
Cuba	India	New Zealand
Cyprus	Indonesia	Nicaragua

(continued)

Table A.4 continued

Niger	Trinidad and Tobago
Nigeria	Tunisia
Norway	Turkey
Oman	Uganda
Pakistan	United Arab Emirates
Panama	United Kingdom
Papua and New Guinea	United States
	Upper Volta
Paraguay	Uruguay
Peru	U.S.S.R.
Philippines	Venezuela
Poland	Western Samoa
Portugal	Windward Islands
Qatar	Yemen Arab Republic
Reunion	Yemen, P.D. Republic
Rumania	Yugoslavia
Rwanda	Zaire
St. Pierre and Miquelon	Zambia
St. Thomas and Prince Islands	
Saudi Arabia	
Senegal	
Seychelles Islands	
Sierra Leone	
Singapore	
Somalia	
South Africa	
Spain	
Sri Lanka	
Sudan	
Surinam	
Sweden	
Switzerland	
Syria	
Tanzania	
Thailand	
Timor	
Togo	
Tonga	

Source: Compiled by the authors.

APPENDIX B

PERCENTAGE OF EXPORTS TO LARGEST MARKETS

TABLE B.1

Percentage of Exports to Largest Markets

Country	1951	1961	1971	1976
North America				
Canada	59.1	54.6	66.0	64.7
Mexico	70.5	60.8	61.0	55.7
United States	17.2	17.4	23.5	21.0
Europe				
Austria	15.1	27.5	22.9	23.4
Belgium-Luxembourg	17.9	23.4	25.3	23.2
Denmark	38.2	24.8	18.9	17.1
Finland	27.3	21.6	19.0	20.2
France	11.4	15.2	21.1	16.9
Germany, West	10.0	9.4	12.5	13.1
Greece	19.9	18.9	20.2	21.6
Iceland	23.3	24.1	36.7	28.9
Ireland	83.9	74.4	65.9	48.7
Italy	13.5	17.9	22.7	19.0
Malta	N/A	26.1	40.4	24.5
Netherlands	15.6	23.1	33.7	31.0
Norway	19.8	20.7	18.8	29.4
Portugal	19.6	13.5	22.6	18.3
Spain	15.6	16.9	15.4	14.5
Sweden	18.9	15.7	13.5	11.3
Switzerland	12.7	17.9	15.2	15.6
Turkey	26.6	18.8	19.4	19.2
United Kingdom	12.0	7.8	11.9	9.6
Yugoslavia	18.4	12.6	14.7	23.5
South America, Central America and Other Western Hemisphere Countries				
Argentina	19.7	18.0	15.0	10.8
Bahamas	N/A	86.8	83.1	N/A
Barbados	N/A	50.8	33.8	30.9
Bolivia	65.6	49.2	45.8	26.6
Brazil	49.0	40.1	26.2	18.2
Chile	51.3	36.5	19.1	13.7

(continued)

Table B.1 continued

Country	1951	1961	1971	1976
Colombia	81.4	59.8	37.7	33.6
Costa Rica	76.9	58.3	40.7	39.5
Dominican Republic	50.2	62.3	74.4	69.5
Ecuador	60.0	61.1	40.7	44.0
El Salvador	86.1	33.7	22.8	36.6
Guadeloupe	N/A	99.0	75.6	84.9
Guatemala	87.8	53.3	30.7	33.0
Guyana	N/A	25.8	25.9	22.5
Haiti	59.5	53.2	65.0	75.3
Honduras	72.9	63.8	56.3	54.0
Honduras, British (Belize)	62.8	55.8	32.3	39.7
Jamaica	59.4	35.7	44.6	43.2
Martinique	N/A	100.0	94.9	70.4
Mexico	70.5	60.8	60.7	55.7
Netherlands Antilles	23.0	32.3	58.8	52.8
Nicaragua	55.5	47.2	35.2	31.2
Panama Republic	81.9	93.9	49.0	38.7
Paraguay	20.8	28.3	27.4	15.0
Peru	23.9	35.9	28.7	24.6
Surinam	77.8	74.6	40.6	33.5
Trinidad and Tobago	27.7	24.5	45.2	69.2
Uruguay	43.4	24.2	11.7	13.0
Venezuela	30.3	39.0	37.7	39.7
Middle East				
Bahrain	N/A	19.6	16.8	18.8
Cyprus	26.2	36.6	41.3	27.3
Egypt (United Arab Republic)	19.2	15.0	39.7	28.1
Iran	17.3	23.7	36.4	19.8
Iraq	26.5	18.9	22.5	17.5
Israel	32.4	16.0	19.4	18.1
Jordan	100.0	19.5	13.4	10.9
Kuwait	N/A	32.7	17.8	23.6
Lebanon	23.3	14.3	15.4	24.9
Oman	100.0	N/A	34.3	43.3
Qatar	N/A	31.9	31.9	20.9
Saudi Arabia	19.2	14.3	17.1	19.6
Syria	29.7	12.3	28.1	19.1
United Arab Emirates	N/A	N/A	44.6	27.6

Country	1951	1961	1971	1976
Yemen, People's Democratic Republic	27.2	12.0	11.7	70.9
Africa				
Algeria	68.3	81.9	26.0	42.5
Angola	17.6	19.4	31.2	48.7
Burundi	—	—	62.2	43.3
Cameroun	61.8	59.0	27.1	24.8
Central African Republic	—	77.5	51.9	38.2
Chad	—	74.9	16.6	16.7
Congo, People's Republic	—	30.7	23.7	23.1
Dahomey (Benin)	—	72.7	42.1	21.8
Ethiopia	9.1	39.8	43.9	27.9
French Equatorial Africa	73.2	—	—	—
French West Africa	72.1	—	—	—
Gabon	—	55.8	54.1	22.5
Gambia	N/A	51.7	38.9	29.8
Ghana (Gold Coast)	41.4	28.8	24.3	17.2
Guinea-Bissau (Portuguese Guinea)	100.0	N/A	75.0	76.2
Guinea Republic	—	20.3	28.1	27.3
Ivory Coast	—	51.7	33.4	25.2
Kenya (includes Uganda for 1951)	30.0	22.4	17.1	12.7
Liberia	N/A	36.1	22.3	24.4
Libya	73.6	35.9	24.0	26.6
Malagasy Republic (Madagascar)	73.2	54.4	34.2	28.8
Malawi	—	—	44.4	42.4
Mali Republic	—	59.2	34.7	32.3
Mauritania	—	100.0	21.5	22.8
Mauritius	61.0	81.1	52.1	68.0
Morocco	39.9	36.8	36.5	24.0
Mozambique	N/A	41.4	37.5	15.0
Niger	—	95.6	69.8	82.6
Nigeria	76.4	44.1	21.6	43.4
Reunion	N/A	92.5	83.1	75.8
Rhodesia	38.7	46.4	42.8	N/A
Rwanda	—	—	61.4	41.1

(continued)

Table B.1 continued

Country	1951	1961	1971	1976
Senegal	—	76.2	51.9	54.5
Sierra Leone	88.7	79.0	62.3	43.9
Somalia Republic	89.1	79.5	59.6	55.3
South Africa	56.6	32.9	26.8	14.6
Sudan (Anglo-Egyptian)	66.5	19.2	16.0	19.7
Tanzania (Tanganyika)	41.2	34.8	21.3	13.8
Togo	—	49.5	31.5	36.9
Tunisia	45.2	54.9	19.5	23.2
Uganda (includes Kenya for 1951)	30.0	16.4	21.8	33.4
Upper Volta	—	89.5	38.4	22.4
Zaire (Congo, People's Republic)	45.0	47.8	40.5	44.3
Zambia	58.0	N/A	20.5	22.9
Asia				
Afghanistan	29.9	30.3	28.2	18.4
Brunei	100.0	70.7	96.2	79.4
Burma	23.7	17.2	11.3	35.3
Ceylon (Sri Lanka)	30.8	29.2	17.1	10.8
China, Taiwan	48.3	28.9	43.4	37.5
Hong Kong	39.1	17.0	35.0	29.1
India	25.3	24.6	16.6	12.3
Indonesia	35.1	23.8	43.8	41.7
Japan	14.0	25.3	31.6	23.7
Korea, South	59.3	50.9	49.8	32.3
Laos	N/A	57.1	51.3	22.8
Macao	100.0	N/A	16.8	22.7
Malaysia (includes Singapore for 1951)	20.0	19.9	22.5	21.1
Nepal	N/A	N/A	16.0	61.0
Pakistan	22.5	14.5	10.1	8.3
Philippines	63.1	53.2	40.4	36.0
Ryukyus	N/A	87.4	85.1	N/A
Singapore	—	26.8	22.9	14.6
Thailand	29.3	13.7	24.8	25.7
Vietnam, South	37.9	36.1	43.9	—
Oceania				
Australia	32.7	19.7	27.8	33.7
Fiji	68.9	51.5	28.9	40.0

Country	1951	1961	1971	1976
New Caledonia	N/A	57.3	47.0	50.9
New Guinea (includes Papua in 1976)	95.8	N/A	42.7	32.6
New Hebrides	—	N/A	71.1	69.7
New Zealand	57.4	50.8	31.8	18.1
Papua	N/A	70.4	54.3	—

Source: Compiled by the authors.

APPENDIX C

PERCENTAGE OF GDP REPRESENTED BY EXPORT TO LARGEST MARKETS

TABLE C.1

Percentage of GDP Represented by Export to Largest Markets

Country	1951	1961	1971	1976
North America				
Canada	10.7	8.5	12.8	13.3
United States	.8	.7	1.0	1.4
Mexico	7.2	3.8	2.5	2.4
Europe				
Austria	2.1	4.7	4.4	4.9
Belgium-Luxembourg	5.8	7.7	11.2	10.0[1]
Denmark	9.5	5.8	4.0	4.0
Finland	6.9	4.1	4.0	4.6
France	1.3	1.6	2.7	2.8
Germany, West	1.2	1.5	1.9	3.0
Greece	0.8	1.1	1.2	2.5
Iceland	N/A	7.5	9.0	7.2[1]
Ireland	17.5	19.4	18.9	20.0
Italy	1.3	2.0	3.4	4.1
Malta	N/A	2.5	7.8	8.7[1]
Netherlands	5.4	8.1	17.5	13.9
Norway	4.7	3.9	3.8	7.4
Portugal	3.7	1.7	3.5	2.8[1]
Spain	0.8	1.0	1.2	1.2
Sweden	4.8	3.0	2.8	2.8
Switzerland	1.6	3.8	3.6	4.0
Turkey	1.9	1.1	1.1	0.9
United Kingdom	2.2	1.1	1.9	2.0
Yugoslavia	N/A	N/A	1.9	3.5[1]
South America, Central America, and Other Western Hemisphere Countries				
Argentina	1.8	1.2	1.2	0.6[1]
Barbados	N/A	16.1	8.7	9.1[1]
Bolivia	N/A	9.1	8.8	7.6[1]
Brazil	5.3	2.7	1.7	1.1[1]
Chile	5.4	4.1	1.9	3.2[1]
Colombia	9.1	5.6	3.4	3.5[1]

(continued)

Table C.1 continued

Country	1951	1961	1971	1976
Costa Rica	18.7	9.4	9.0	9.9
Dominican Republic	12.3	12.8	10.0	12.7
Ecuador	6.7	6.5	4.8	10.9
El Salvador	N/A	7.0	4.8	12.4
Guadeloupe	N/A	26.7	13.2	N/A
Guatemala	9.7	5.5	4.4	6.4
Guyana	N/A	11.9	14.5	20.0^1
Haiti	11.4	6.4	6.7	6.5^1
Honduras	10.0	10.9	16.1	18.4
Jamaica	11.4	8.8	10.9	8.6
Martinique	N/A	36.6	10.1	N/A
Nicaragua	8.9	8.0	7.3	9.3
Panama Republic	3.5	4.4	4.8	5.5
Paraguay	2.5	2.2	2.7	1.6
Peru	4.6	7.5	3.8	2.8
Surinam	N/A	29.3	22.1	15.2^2
Trinidad and Tobago	17.9	14.4	29.1	68.6^2
Uruguay	N/A	2.7	0.8	1.9^1
Venezuela	17.1	11.7	9.8	12.5^1
Middle East				
Cyprus	8.1	5.9	7.6	9.2
Egypt (United Arab Republic)	N/A	1.7	4.3	4.9^2
Iran	N/A	9.9	8.8	6.1
Iraq	5.1	7.2	8.3	11.1^1
Israel	2.5	1.3	2.9	3.5
Jordan	N/A	0.7	0.7	1.3^1
Kuwait	N/A	25.2	11.1	20.7^1
Lebanon	N/A	0.8	2.5	N/A
Saudi Arabia	N/A	6.7	13.4	16.2
Syria	3.5	1.2	2.7	3.5
Yemen, (People's Democratic Republic)	N/A	20.6	5.6	N/A
Africa				
Algeria	17.2	11.2	4.1	N/A
Cameroun	N/A	9.1	5.1	8.5^2
Central African Republic	—	6.7	8.1	N/A
Chad	—	7.6	1.9	N/A
Congo, People's Republic	—	4.7	7.2	N/A

Country	1951	1961	1971	1976
Dahomey (Benin)	—	6.7	9.2	3.5[1]
Ethiopia	N/A	3.1	2.9	2.4[2]
Gabon	—	20.3	23.2	18.9[2]
Gambia	N/A	12.9	14.7	11.0
Ghana	N/A	6.5	3.8	6.9[2]
Guinea Republic	—	4.9	4.6	N/A
Ivory Coast	—	14.2	9.6	8.3[1]
Kenya	N/A	4.1	3.0	3.0
Liberia	N/A	14.5	11.4	10.2[1]
Malawi	—	—	8.0	9.6
Mali Republic	—	2.1	3.0	N/A
Mauritania	—	1.1	10.5	N/A
Mauritius	22.1	30.7	16.9	40.5[1]
Morocco	N/A	7.0	4.9	3.8
Niger	—	6.9	7.3	N/A
Nigeria	15.2	6.4	7.4	N/A
Reunion	N/A	20.0	10.5	N/A
Rwanda	—	—	4.6	4.6[2]
Senegal	—	15.0	8.2	15.7
Sierra Leone	N/A	9.2	13.4	11.9[1]
Somalia Republic	N/A	18.1	9.6	N/A
South Africa	5.7	5.6	3.0	3.4
Sudan	N/A	2.8	2.8	1.3[1]
Togo	—	8.0	5.9	8.6[1]
Tunisia	N/A	9.8	2.9	4.1
Uganda	N/A	2.8	3.9	N/A
Zambia	N/A	N/A	8.4	8.3
Zaire	N/A	18.0	9.3	10.9[1]
Asia				
Burma	5.2	2.1	0.7	0.9[2]
Ceylon (Sri Lanka)	12.1	7.3	2.5	1.8
China (Taiwan)	6.0	3.2	13.9	17.7
Hong Kong	N/A	11.5	30.5	N/A
India	N/A	1.0	0.7	0.6[2]
Indonesia	N/A	2.8	5.4	9.6
Japan	1.3	2.1	3.4	2.3[1]
Korea, South	2.5	0.8	5.8	9.8

(continued)

Table C.1 continued

Country	1951	1961	1971	1976
Malaysia	—	7.8	9.2	10.2
Pakistan	N/A	0.7	0.6	0.7
Philippines	6.8	4.8	5.9	5.2
Singapore	N/A	N/A	19.0	16.8
Thailand	7.6	2.3	2.9	4.8
Vietnam, South	N/A	0.6	.05	N/A
Oceania				
Australia	7.5	2.9	3.9	5.1
Fiji	N/A	N/A	8.2	8.3
New Zealand	19.5	10.5	5.9	3.6[1]

[1]Based on 1975 trade and GDP figures.
[2]Based on 1974 trade and GDP figures.

Source: Compiled by the authors.

APPENDIX D

FOUR-DIGIT SITC PRODUCT CATEGORIES AND UNITED STATES MARKET SHARES AND PERCENT NET SHIFTS, 1963 TO 1974

TABLE D.1

Market Share and Percentage Net Shift for United States Technology-Intensive Exports, Four-Digit SITC Level

| SITC | Product Group | Market Share Percent | | | Percent Net Shift |
		1963	1972	1974	1963-1974
512.1	Hydrocarbons	9.99	0	0	-27.52
512.2	Alcohols, Phenols	29.82	0	0	-86.04
512.3	Ethers, Eporides	27.90	0	0	-83.83
512.4	Aldehyde, etc, funct cmpnds	8.24	0	0	-39.71
512.5	Organic Acids, etc.	11.37	0	0	-46.94
512.6	Inorganic Esters, etc.	0	0	0	—
512.7	Nitrogen, Functional Compounds	15.00	0	0	-68.33
512.8	Organic-Inorganic Compounds, etc.	3.05	0	0	-12.23
512.9	Other Organic Chemicals	78.25	0	0	-97.81
513.1	Gases, excluding Halogens	48.57	18.72	13.89	-70.20
513.2	Chemical Elements NES*	34.63	16.29	16.44	-46.03
513.3	Inorganic Acids, etc.	49.88	11.77	17.25	-93.20
513.4	Halogen, Sulfur Compounds, Nonmetallic	2.50	10.47	11.72	32.95
513.5	Metallic Oxide for Paint	10.88	7.93	11.37	3.52
513.6	Inorganic Bases, etc., NES*	14.86	20.82	17.19	6.33
514.1	Metal Compound of Inorganic Acid	36.74	0	0	-78.20

(continued)

Table D.1 continued

| SITC | Product Group | Market Share Percent | | | Percent Net Shift |
		1963	1972	1974	1963-1974
514.2	continuation of 514.1	17.13	0	0	-57.82
514.3	conclusion of 514.1	8.01	0	0	-34.86
514.9	Inorganic Chemical Products NES*	7.87	0	0	-21.57
515.1	Radioactive Elements, etc.	14.29	62.23	54.27	49.16
515.2	Stable Isotopes	0	85.96	61.07	80.01
515.3	Other Chemicals Assoc. with Radioactivity	0	80.98	66.94	95.69
531.0	Synthetic Dye, Nat. Indigo, LAKES	8.15	4.59	5.82	-23.59
532.3	Synthetic Tanning Products	21.43	5.73	5.50	-77.52
541.1	Vitamins, Provitamins	29.34	4.54	6.73	-64.33
541.3	Antibiotics	61.04	29.72	28.87	-95.25
541.4	Vegetable Alkaloids and Derivatives	4.83	1.56	1.60	-25.39
541.6	Glycosides, Glands, Sera	53.91	33.02	32.68	-74.35
541.7	Medicaments	18.04	9.83	9.62	-81.30
551.2	Synthetic Perfume Flavor Products	36.13	9.73	10.11	-96.85
561.1	Chemical Nitrogenous Fertilizer	7.80	11.54	6.64	-4.26
561.2	Chemical Phosphatic Fertilizer	34.84	37.29	49.13	51.42
581.1	Products of Condensation, etc.	28.01	13.67	13.13	-60.75
581.2	Products of Polymerizing, etc.	21.48	10.99	11.53	-41.59
581.3	Cellulose Derivatives, etc.	30.78	21.85	21.78	-66.13

581.9	Plastic Materials NES*	18.85	23.60	32.84	50.31
599.2	Pesticides, Disinfectants	42.18	14.24	18.52	-94.09
651.6	Yarn of Synthetic Fibres	16.81	3.95	7.34	-34.97
711.3	Steam Engines including Jet	22.64	0	14.01	-34.32
711.4	Aircraft Engines including Jet	5.12	39.53	39.23	98.02
711.5	Piston Engines Nonaircraft	24.74	25.88	27.01	12.28
711.6	Gas Turbines Nonaircraft	0	29.32	30.61	50.50
711.8	Engines NES*	23.71	5.83	6.93	-52.44
714.1	Typewriters, Cheque-writers	10.53	4.13	6.16	-22.36
714.2	Accounting Machines, Computers	19.17	36.72	10.83	-18.90
714.3	Statistical Machines	52.79	7.24	28.01	-97.99
714.9	Office Machines NES*	45.70	50.85	50.93	37.89
719.63	Nonelectric Machines NES*	30.72	18.34	18.81	-67.88
722.1	Electric Power Machinery	21.25	18.17	21.84	4.84
722.2	Switch Gear, etc.	21.24	17.31	16.47	-30.76
724.1	Television Receivers	14.28	8.85	8.83	-22.29
724.2	Radio Broadcast Receivers	1.70	2.36	1.86	0.77
724.9	Telecommunications Equipment NES*	35.15	18.43	18.95	-66.57
729.3	Transistors, Values, etc.	26.27	34.52	39.14	53.78
729.5	Electric Measuring, Controlling Equipment	39.63	29.16	30.93	-58.79
729.7	Particle Accelerators	0	51.24	37.33	47.99
734.1	Aircraft Heavier than Air	62.60	80.22	87.86	94.15
734.9	Aircraft Parts, etc.	66.32	42.52	44.47	-71.37
861.1	Optical Elements	7.47	11.03	10.33	11.21
861.2	Spectacles and Frames	10.23	4.60	6.07	-42.82
861.3	Optical Instruments	4.68	7.14	8.87	45.41
					(continued)

Table D.1 continued

| SITC | Product Group | Market Share Percent | | | Percent Net Shift |
		1963	1972	1974	1963-1974
861.4	Cameras Still, Flash APP	11.82	9.08	14.64	10.87
861.5	Cinema Cameras, Projectors, etc.	15.22	9.87	14.70	-3.24
861.6	Photographic Equipment NES*	31.50	28.47	26.54	-17.74
861.7	Medical Instruments NES*	41.86	29.14	30.73	-60.85
861.8	Meters, Counters, Nonelectrical	12.49	8.05	9.37	-23.38
861.9	Measuring, Controlling Instruments	30.35	29.87	27.32	-20.52
862.3	Chemical Photographic Goods, Retail	20.27	33.15	31.93	55.50
862.4	Photo Film Excluding DEV Cinema	28.73	27.79	29.06	2.83
863.0	Developed Cinema Film	39.91	31.40	31.62	-66.50
864.1	Watches, Movements, Cases	0.90	0.31	1.27	11.68
891.1	SND Recorders, Phonographs, PRTS	16.88	8.26	9.04	-30.54
891.2	Sound Recording Tape, Discs	12.26	24.55	26.15	52.82

*Not Elsewhere Specified.
Source: Compiled by the authors.

TABLE D.2

Market Share and Percentage Net Shift for United States Nontechnology-Intensive Exports, Four-Digit SITC Level

SITC	Product Group	Market Share Percent			Percent Net Shift 1963-1974
		1963	1972	1974	
521.1	Mineral Tar	3.53	2.31	2.92	-1.17
521.4	Coal Tar Distillation Products NES*	71.11	40.17	27.22	-90.05
541.9	Pharmaceutical Goods	23.92	26.04	26.02	16.04
553.0	Tire, Battery, and Accessory Dealers	14.05	8.88	11.00	-21.31
571.1	Prepared Explosives	41.41	15.82	25.08	-66.82
571.2	Fuses, Primers, Detonators	0	18.94	22.78	61.28
571.3	Pyrotechnic Products	0	37.29	29.11	73.29
571.4	Ammunition, Hunting, Sporting	0	19.47	21.11	49.01
599.5	Starch, Inulin, Gluten	10.64	9.27	9.63	-7.92
599.6	Chemicals from Wood, Resin	47.04	38.71	31.79	-82.40
599.7	Organic Chemical Products NES*	48.19	31.54	33.63	-66.24
599.9	Chemical Products, Preps NES*	44.86	1.90	14.53	-95.55
621.0	Materials of Rubber	4.77	16.27	14.86	43.41
629.1	Rubber Tires, Tubes	14.85	6.01	10.76	-21.22
629.3	Hygienic UNHRDND Rubber	29.16	24.29	28.65	-3.37
629.4	Rubber Belting	13.91	9.81	9.61	-20.81

(continued)

Table D.2 continued

| SITC | Product Group | Market Share Percent | | | Percent Net Shift |
		1963	1972	1974	1963-1974
629.9	Other Rubber Articles NES*	63.35	20.26	18.20	-97.21
653.5	Woven Synthetic Fabrics	18.02	4.57	7.11	-55.81
663.5	Mineral Insulating Products NES*	52.63	18.63	17.14	-94.14
664.2	Optical Glass Unworded, etc.	40.17	38.34	33.91	-33.83
664.4	Glass Surface-Ground, etc.	15.15	14.84	20.93	26.72
664.5	Cost, Rolled Class Unworked	12.53	1.42	1.69	-46.26
664.6	Glass Construction Products	22.81	11.38	16.07	-14.22
664.7	Safety Glass	17.56	32.75	25.49	21.02
664.8	Sheet Glass Metal-Coated	0	10.03	15.46	52.21
667.4	Synthetic PREC, SEMI-P. Stone	0	5.94	7.07	9.33
711.1	Steam Boilers	37.96	25.09	15.93	-54.44
711.2	Boiler House Plant NES*	42.01	22.38	34.38	-35.53
711.7	Nuclear Reactors	10.45	48.13	61.69	71.33
712.2	Harvesting ETC Machines	20.64	18.03	19.40	-9.47
712.3	Dairy Farm Equipment	31.85	15.04	14.78	-73.39
712.5	Tractors Non-Road	47.74	35.17	32.83	-42.63
712.9	Agriculture Machines NES*	75.81	33.19	35.17	-97.97
715.1	Machine Tools for Metal	19.50	11.32	11.19	-56.09
715.2	Metal Working Machinery NES*	44.31	21.15	19.90	-88.29

298

717.1	Textile Machinery	14.45	6.95	8.64	-35.89
717.2	Skin, Leather Working Machines	13.40	6.08	6.24	-29.46
717.3	Sewing Machines	14.48	9.56	9.28	-33.57
718.1	Paper ETC Mill Machinery	19.61	10.90	12.77	-39.73
718.2	Printing, Binding Machinery	21.25	17.89	19.67	-23.09
718.3	Food Machinery, Non-domestic	21.00	15.15	17.13	-31.49
718.4	Construction, Mining Machinery NES*	49.50	37.12	37.40	-53.67
718.5	Crushing etc, Glass Machinery	25.99	14.33	15.16	-68.41
719.1	Heating, Cooling Equipment	24.80	22.96	25.87	7.37
719.2	Pumps, Centrifuges	23.16	23.39	23.60	5.09
719.3	Mechanical Handling Equipment	43.17	23.94	25.17	-88.26
719.4	Domestic Appliances, Nonelectric	20.72	11.19	13.88	-35.93
719.5	Powered Tools NES*	20.67	17.46	16.61	-29.49
719.7	Ball, Roller, etc. Bearings	24.60	12.90	13.07	-42.03
719.8	Other Machines Nonelectric	26.11	17.04	18.63	-44.80
719.9	Machines Parts, Accessories NES*	19.83	14.87	13.57	-42.12
723.1	Insulated Wire, Cable	8.97	11.05	11.45	13.77
725.0	Domestic Electric Equipment	18.21	8.17	10.89	-29.86
726.1	Electro-Medical Equipment	7.85	35.43	35.08	81.09
726.2	X-Ray Apparatus	16.98	9.13	9.35	-43.10
729.1	Batteries, Accumulators	8.94	13.74	14.62	25.23
729.2	Electric Lamps, Bulbs	17.62	11.61	13.53	-38.00
729.4	Automotive Electric Equipment	31.84	23.06	21.54	-47.21
729.6	Electro-Mechanical Hand Tools	28.42	13.36	14.00	-59.10
729.9	Other Electrical Machinery	28.75	18.67	19.58	-50.77
731.2	Electric Locomotives Non-Self-Generating	20.39	1.52	9.25	-24.06
					(continued)

Table D.2 continued

| SITC | Product Group | Market Share Percent | | | Percent Net Shift |
		1963	1972	1974	1963-1974
731.3	Locomotives Not Steam, Not Electric	56.88	49.01	60.15	14.52
731.4	Mechanically Propelled Railway Cars	8.34	21.80	9.43	9.48
731.5	Passenger Cars No: Powered	6.10	0.80	0.33	-9.91
731.6	Freight Cars Not Powered	9.22	1.42	7.11	-5.08
731.7	Railway, Locomotive, Car Parts NES*	18.74	26.18	23.26	21.23
732.1	Passenger Motor Vehicle Excl. Buses	8.73	8.38	10.84	6.29
732.2	Buses	18.16	9.83	8.81	-29.09
732.3	Lorries, Trucks	26.55	16.98	17.28	-29.08
732.4	Special Motor Vehicles NES*	76.72	37.87	42.10	-96.88
732.5	Tractors for TR Trailers	0	0	0	—
732.6	Passenger Motor Vehicle Chassis	0	0	0	—
732.7	Lorry, Truck, Bus Chassis	0	0	0	—
732.8	Motor Vehicle Parts NES*	44.39	32.14	30.77	-56.51
732.9	Motorcycles etc. Parts	0.83	0.54	0.55	-0.67
733.3	Vehicles NES Nonmotor, Trailers	20.28	18.03	16.85	-28.13
733.4	Invalid Carriages Motorized	0.45	25.72	11.60	24.37
735.1	Warships	82.11	63.48	49.96	-98.69
735.3	Ships and Boats, Ncn-War	2.29	1.85	1.75	-1.57
735.9	Ships and Boats NES*	2.40	14.05	19.61	50.26

300

812.1	Central Heating Equipment	27.46	9.31	8.63	-57.39
812.2	Ceramic Plumbing Fixtures	11.25	6.44	7.50	-15.58
899.6	Heating, Orthopaedic Aids	32.97	27.31	20.38	-45.60

*Not Elsewhere Specified.
<u>Source</u>: Compiled by the authors.

REFERENCES

Adedeji, Adebayo. 1970. "Prospects of Regional Economic Co-operation in West Africa." Journal of Modern African Studies, Vol. 8, No. 2, pp. 213-31.

Adler, F. Michael. 1970. "The Relationship between the Income and Price Elasticities of Demand for United States Exports." Review of Economics and Statistics, Vol. 52, No. 3, pp. 313-19.

Aitken, Norman D. 1973. "The Effect of the EEC and EFTA on European Trade: A Temporal Cross Section Analysis." American Economic Review. Vol. 63 No. 5, pp. 881-92.

Alschuler, Lawrence R. 1976. "Satellization and Stagnation in Latin America." International Studies Quarterly, Vol. 20, No. 1, pp. 39-82.

Amin, Samir. 1973. "Underdevelopment and Dependence in Black Africa—Their Historical Origins and Contemporary Forms." Social and Economic Studies, Vol. 22, No. 1, pp. 177-96.

———. 1972. "Underdevelopment and Dependence in Black Africa—Origins and Contemporary Forms." Journal of Modern African Studies, Vol. 10, No. 4, pp. 503-24.

Arkhurst, Frederick S. 1970. "Problems of Economic Integration in Africa." In Africa in the Seventies and Eighties: Issues in Development, ed. Frederick S. Arkhurst, pp. 372-87. Praeger Special Studies in International Politics and Government. New York: Praeger.

Arrighi, Giovanni. 1970. "International Corporations, Labor Aristocracies, and Economic Development in Tropical Africa." In Imperialism and Underdevelopment: A Reader, ed. Robert I. Rhodes, pp. 220-67. New York: Monthly Review.

Balassa, Bela. 1969. "Country Size and Trade Patterns: Comment." American Economic Review, Vol. 59, No. 1, pp. 201-4.

_____. 1964. "Trade Liberalisation and 'Revealed' Comparative Advantage." Manchester School of Economic and Social Studies, Vol. 33, No. 2, pp. 99-123.

Baldwin, Robert E. 1971. "Determinants of the Commodity Structure of U.S. Trade." American Economic Review, Vol. 61, No. 1, pp. 126-46.

Baranson, Jack. 1976-77. "Technology Exports Can Hurt Us." Foreign Policy, No. 25, pp. 180-94.

Baumgartner, T., and T. R. Burns. 1975. "The Structuring of International Economic Relations." International Studies Quarterly, Vol. 19, No. 2, pp. 126-59.

Bechin, A. 1963. "Forms of International Economic Relations Which Influence Development of World Trade." In International Trade Theory in a Developing World: Proceedings of a Conference Held by the International Economic Association, eds. Roy Harrod and Douglas Hague, pp. 230-40. New York: St. Martin's.

Beckerman, W. 1956. "Distance and the Pattern of Intra-European Trade." Review of Economics and Statistics, Vol. 38, No. 1, pp. 31-40.

Berg, Elliot J. 1971. "Structural Transformation versus Gradualism: Recent Economic Development in Ghana and the Ivory Coast." In Ghana and the Ivory Coast: Perspectives on Modernization, eds. Philip Foster and Aristide R. Zolberg, pp. 187-230. Chicago: University of Chicago.

Bhagwate, Jagdish N. 1970. "Comments." In The Technology Factor in International Trade: A Conference of the Universities—National Bureau Committee for Economic Research, ed. Raymond Vernon, pp. 273-74. New York: National Bureau of Economic Research.

Birnberg, Thomas, and Stephen Resnick. 1973. "A Model of the Trade and Government Sectors in Colonial Economies." American Economic Review, Vol. 63, No. 4, pp. 572-87.

Blake, David H., and Robert S. Walters. 1976. The Politics of Global Economic Relations. Englewood Cliffs, New Jersey: Prentice-Hall.

Bodenheimer, Susanne. 1971. "Dependency and Imperialism: The Roots of Latin American Underdevelopment." In Readings in U.S. Imperialism, eds. K. T. Fann and Donald C. Hodges, pp. 155-81. Boston: Porter Sargent.

Brams, Stephen J. 1969. "The Structure of Influence Relationships in the International System." In International Politics and Foreign Policy, ed. James N. Rosenau, pp. 589-99. New York: Free Press.

———. 1966. "Transaction Flows in the International System." American Political Science Review, Vol. 60, No. 4, pp. 880-98.

Branson, William H. 1971. "U. S. Comparative Advantage: Some Further Results." Brookings Papers on Economic Activity, Vol. 3, pp. 754-59.

Branson, William H., and Helen B. Junz. 1971. "Trends in U. S. Trade and Comparative Advantage." Brookings Papers on Economic Activity, Vol. 2, pp. 285-338.

Brzenk, Eleanor T. 1964. "Patterns of Trade between the Common Market and Eastern Europe." East Lakes Geographer, Vol. 1, pp. 21-28.

Brewster, Havelock. 1973. "Economic Dependence: A Quantitative Interpretation." Social and Economic Studies, Vol. 22, No. 1, pp. 90-95.

Brzezinski, Zbigniew K. 1967. The Soviet Bloc: Unity and Conflict, revised and enlarged ed. Cambridge: Harvard University.

Cairncross, A. K. 1966. "International Trade and Developing Countries." In Problems in Economic Development, ed. E. A. G. Robinson, pp. 418-32. New York: St. Martin's.

Carlsson, Bo, and Lennart Ohlsson. 1976. "Structural Determinants of Swedish Foreign Trade: A Test of the Conventional Wisdom." European Economic Review, Vol. 7, No. 2, pp. 165-74.

Chase-Dunn, Christopher. 1975. "The Effects of International Economic Dependence on Development and Inequality: A Cross-National Study." American Sociological Review, Vol. 40, No. 6, pp. 720-33.

Chipman, John S. 1970. "Induced Technical Change and Patterns of International Trade." In The Technology Factor in International Trade: A Conference of the Universities—National Bureau Committee for Economic Research, ed. Raymond Vernon, pp. 95-127. New York: National Bureau of Economic Research.

Chou, K. R. 1967. "Present Trends in Trade." In International Development, eds. H. W. Singer, Nicholas de Kun, and Abbas Ordoobadi, pp. 279-83. New York: Oceana.

Condoni, Rene, Bruno Fritsch, Alex Melzer, F. J. Oertly, Luitgard Sieber, and Peter Walser. 1971. World Trade Flows, Integrational Structure and Conditional Forecasts, Vol. One. Research Monograph, New Series, Vol. 5. Zürich: Center for Economic Research, Swiss Federal Institute of Technology.

Cooper, Richard N. 1972-73. "Trade Policy is Foreign Policy." Foreign Policy, No. 9, pp. 18-36.

Coppock, Joseph D. 1962. International Economic Instability: The Experience after World War II. New York: McGraw-Hill.

Corbet, Hugh. 1971. "Commercial Realignments and Commonwealth Relations." In Commonwealth Policy in a Global Context, eds. Paul Streeten and Hugh Corbet, pp. 60-84. London: Frank Cass.

Cosgrove, Carol Ann. 1972. "The EEC and Its Yaounde Associates: A Model for Development." International Relations, Vol. 4, No. 2, pp. 142-55.

Dell, Sidney. 1970. "African Trade and Aid: Present Situation and Future Prospects." In Africa in the Seventies and Eighties: Issues in Development, ed. Frederick S. Arkhurst, pp. 341-71. Praeger Special Studies in International Politics and Government.

──────. 1963. Trade Blocs and Common Markets. New York: Knopf.

Dos Santos, Theotonio. 1971. "The Structure of Dependence." In Readings in U. S. Imperialism, eds. K. T. Fann and Donald C. Hodges, pp. 225-36. Boston: Porter Sargent.

Emmanuel, Arghiri. 1972. Unequal Exchange: A Study of the Imperialism of Trade, trans. Brian Pearce. London: Monthly Review.

Esseks, John D. 1971. "Economic Dependence and Political Development." Journal of Politics, Vol. 33, No. 4, pp. 1052-75.

Fareed, A. E. 1972. "Formal Schooling and the Human-Capital Intensity of American Foreign Trade: A Cost Approach." Economic Journal, Vol. 82, No. 326, pp. 629-40.

Fox, Annette Baker. 1971. "The Twenty and the One: Latin American Relations and the United States." In Small States in International Relations, eds. August Schou and Arne Olav Brundtland, pp. 157-70. Stockholm: Almqvist & Wikesell.

Frank, Andre Gunder. 1970. "On the Mechanisms of Imperialism: The Case of Brazil." In Imperialism and Underdevelopment: A Reader, ed. Robert I. Rhodes, pp. 89-100, New York: Monthly Review.

Freeman, Donald B. 1973. International Trade, Migration, and Capital Flows: A Quantitative Analysis of Spatial Economic Interaction, Department of Geography Research Paper No. 146. Chicago: University of Chicago.

Furtado, Celso. 1973. "The Brazilian 'Model.'" Social and Economic Studies, Vol. 22, No. 1, pp. 122-31.

Galtung, Johan. 1971. "A Structural Theory of Imperialism." Journal of Peace Research, Vol. 8, No. 2, pp. 81-118.

Gantzel, Klaus Jürgen. 1973. "Dependency Structures as the Dominant Pattern in World Society." Journal of Peace Research, Vol. 10, No. 3, pp. 203-15.

Girvan, Norman. 1973. "The Development of Dependency Economics in the Caribbean and Latin America: Review and Comparison." Social and Economic Studies, Vol. 22, No. 1, pp. 1-33.

Goldfinger, Nat. 1973. "The Case for the Hartke-Burke." Columbia Journal of World Business, Vol. 8, No. 1, pp. 22-26.

Green, Reginald Herbold, and K. G. V. Krishna. 1967. Economic Cooperation in Africa: Retrospect and Prospect. Nairobi: Oxford University.

Grotewold, Andreas. 1961. "Some Aspects of the Geography of International Trade." Economic Geography, Vol. 37, No. 4, pp. 309-19.

Grotewold, Andreas, and Lois Grotewold. 1957. "Some Geographic Aspects of International Trade." Economic Geography, Vol. 33, No. 3, pp. 257-66.

Grove, David L. 1969. "World Markets: The U.S. Position is Disturbing." Columbia Journal of World Business, Vol. 4, No. 3, pp. 19-27.

Gruber, William, Dileep Merta, and Raymond Vernon. 1967. "The R&D Factor in International Trade and International Investment of United States Industries." Journal of Political Economy, Vol. 75, No. 1, pp. 20-37.

Gruber, William H., and Raymond Vernon. 1970. "The Technology Factor in a World Trade Matrix." In The Technology Factor in International Trade: A Conference of the Universities—National Bureau Committee for Economic Research, ed. Raymond Vernon, pp. 233-72. New York: National Bureau of Economic Research.

Haberler, Gottfried. 1968. "International Trade and Economic Development." In Reshaping the World Economy: Rich and Poor Countries, ed. John A. Pincus, pp. 92-101. Englewood Cliffs, New Jersey: Prentice-Hall.

Harkness, Jon, and John F. Kyle. 1975. "Factors Influencing United States Comparative Advantage." Journal of International Economics, Vol. 5, No. 2, pp. 153-65.

Harvey, Michael G., and Roger A. Kerin. 1976. "Multinational Corporations versus Organized Labor: Divergent Views on Domestic Employment." California Management Review, Vol. 18, No. 3, pp. 5-13.

Herman, Leon M. 1969. "COMECON Reform Depends on Trade with World Markets." Columbia Journal of World Business, Vol. 4, No. 4, pp. 51-58.

Hirschman, Albert O. 1969. National Power and the Structure of Foreign Trade. Berkeley: University of California.

Holzman, Franklyn D. 1976. International Trade under Communism-- Politics and Economics. New York: Basic Books.

Hudson, Michael. 1972. Super Imperialism: The Economic Strategy of American Empire. New York: Holt, Rhinehart and Winston.

Hufbauer, G. C. 1970. "The Impact of National Characteristics & Technology on the Commodity Composition of Trade in Manufactured Goods." In The Technology Factor in International Trade: A Conference of the Universities—National Bureau Committee for Economic Research, ed. Raymond Vernon, pp. 145-231. New York: National Bureau of Economic Research.

Huff, David L., and Lawrence A. Sherr. 1967. "Measure for Determining Differential Growth Rates of Markets." Journal of Marketing Research, Vol. 4, No. 4, pp. 391-95.

Hveem, Helge. 1973. "The Global Dominance System: Notes on a Theory of Global Political Economy." Journal of Peace Research, Vol. 10, No. 4, pp. 320-40.

Ingram, James C. 1966. International Economic Problems. New York: John Wiley & Sons.

Jansen, F. P., and L. H. Janssen. 1969. "Imports from Developing Countries: A Comparison between EEC, EFTA, AND USA." In Towards Balanced International Growth: Essays Presented to J. Tinbergen, ed. H. C. Bos, pp. 129-56. Amsterdam: North-Holland.

Johnson, Harry G. 1967. Economic Policies Toward Less Developed Countries. Washington, D.C.: Brookings.

Johnson, Leland L. 1965. "U.S. Business Interests in Cuba and the Rise of Castro." World Politics, Vol. 17, No. 3, pp. 440-59.

Jones, Ronald W. 1970. "The Role of Technology in the Theory of International Trade." In The Technology Factor in International Trade: A Conference of the Universities—National Bureau Committee for Economic Research, ed. Raymond Vernon, pp. 72-92. New York: National Bureau of Economic Research.

Katrak, Homi. 1973. "Human Skills R and D and Scale Economies in the Exports of the United Kingdom and the United States." Oxford Economic Papers, New Series, pp. 337-60.

Kaufman, Robert R., Harry I. Chernotsky, and Daniel S. Geller, 1975. "A Preliminary Test of the Theory of Dependency." Comparative Politics, Vol. 7, No. 3, pp. 303-30.

Keesing, Donald B. 1968. "The Sources of Change in Export Performance: The United States and Canada." In <u>The Open Economy: Essays in International Trade and Finance,</u> Columbia Studies in Economics, 1, eds. Peter B. Kenen and Roger Lawrence, pp. 175-89. New York: Columbia University.

──────. 1967. "The Impact of Research and Development on United States Trade." <u>Journal of Political Economy</u>, Vol. 75, No. 1, pp. 38-48.

──────. 1966. "International Economics: Progress and Transfer of Technical Knowledge: Labor Skills and Comparative Advantage." <u>American Economic Review</u>, Vol. 56, No. 2, pp. 249-58.

Kegley, Charles W., Jr., and Eugene R. Wittkopf. 1976. "Structural Characteristics of International Influence Relationships: A Replication Study." <u>International Studies Quarterly,</u> Vol. 20, No. 2, pp. 261-99.

Kelly, Regina K. 1977. "The Impact of Technological Innovation on International Trade Patterns." Paper read at the Geneva Conference on Government-Industry Cooperation in Technological Innovation, June, Geneva.

Kendrick, John W. 1973. <u>Postwar Productivity Trends in the United States, 1948-1969.</u> New York: National Bureau of Economic Research.

Kindleberger, Charles P. 1970. "Comments." In <u>The Technology Factor in International Trade: A Conference of the Universities—National Bureau Committee for Economic Research,</u> ed. Raymond Vernon, pp. 280-86. New York: National Bureau of Economic Research.

Krasner, Stephen D. 1976. "State Power and the Structure of International Trade." <u>World Politics,</u> Vol. 28, No. 3, pp. 317-47.

Krause, Lawrence B. 1973. "European Economic Integration and the United States." In <u>The Economics of Integration: A Book of Readings,</u> ed. Melvyn B. Krauss, pp. 104-17. London: George Allen & Unwin.

Kravis, Irving B. 1970. "Comments." In <u>The Technology Factor in International Trade: A Conference of the Universities—National</u>

Bureau Committee for Economic Research, ed. Raymond Vernon, pp. 286-95. New York: National Bureau of Economic Research.

Kuznets, Simon. 1964. "Quantitative Aspects of the Economic Growth of Nations: IX. Level and Structure of Foreign Trade: Comparisons for Recent Years." Economic Development and Cultural Change, Vol. 13, No. 1, pp. 1-106.

Leamer, Edward E. 1974. "The Commodity Composition of International Trade in Manufactures: An Empirical Analysis." Oxford Economic Papers, New Series, Vol. 26, No. 3, pp. 350-74.

Leontief, Wassily. 1956. "Factor Proportions and the Structure of American Trade: Further Theoretical and Empirical Analysis." Review of Economics and Statistics, Vol. 38, No. 4, pp. 386-407.

Linneman, Hans. 1966. An Economic Study of International Trade Flows. Amsterdam: North-Holland.

Lipsey, Robert E. 1972. "The Current International Competitive Position of the United States." Conference Board Record, Vol. 9, No. 4, pp. 21-25.

Lloyd, Peter J. 1968. International Trade Problems of Small Nations. Durham, North Carolina: Duke University.

Lowinger, Thomas C. 1975. "The Technology Factor and the Export Performance of U.S. Manufacturing Industries." Economic Inquiry, Vol. 13, No. 2, pp. 221-36.

Lupton, Colina MacDougall. 1972. "Hong Kong's Role in Sino-Western Trade." In China's Trade with the West: A Political and Economic Analysis, ed. Arthur A. Stahnke, pp. 175-208. Praeger Special Studies in International Politics and Government. New York: Praeger.

MacFarlane, David L. 1971. "Commercial Trade in Temperate Farm Products." In Commonwealth Policy in a Global Context, eds. Paul Streeten and Hugh Corbet, pp. 98-110. London: Frank Cass.

Maizels, A. 1963. "Recent Trends in World Trade." In International Trade Theory in a Developing World: Proceedings of a Conference Held by the International Economic Association, eds. Roy Harrod and Douglas Hague, pp. 31-51. New York: St. Martin's.

Mandel, Ernest. 1970. *Europe vs. America: Contradictions of Imperialism.* New York: Monthly Review.

McGowan, Patrick J., and Klaus-Peter Gottwald. 1975. "Small State Foreign Policies: A Comparative Study of Participation, Conflict and Political and Economic Dependence in Black Africa." *International Studies Quarterly*, Vol. 19, No. 4, pp. 469-500.

Mikdashi, Zuhayr. 1974. "Cooperation among Oil Exporting Countries with Special Reference to Arab Countries: A Political Economy Analysis." *International Organization*, Vol. 28, No. 1, pp. 1-30.

Moran, Theodore H. 1974. *Multinational Corporations and the Politics of Dependence: Copper in Chile.* Princeton: Princeton University.

National Science Foundation. 1976. *Science Indicators*, 1974. Washington, D.C.: U.S. Government Printing Office.

Nye, Joseph S., Jr., and Robert O. Keohane. 1972. "Transnational Relations and World Politics: A Conclusion." In *Transnational Relations and World Politics*, eds. Robert O. Keohane and Joseph S. Nye, Jr., pp. 371-98. Cambridge: Harvard University.

Nystuen, J., and M. Dacey. 1961. "A Graph Theory Interpretation of Nodal Regions." *Papers of the Regional Science Association*, Vol. 7, pp. 29-42.

O'Conner, James. 1970. "The Meaning of Economic Imperialism." In *Imperialism and Underdevelopment: A Reader*, ed. Robert I. Rhodes, pp. 101-50. New York: Monthly Review.

Ojedokun, Olasupo. 1972. "The Changing Pattern of Nigeria's International Economic Relations." *Journal of Developing Areas*, Vol. 6, No. 4, pp. 535-54.

Okumu, John J. 1971. "The Place of African States in International Relations." In *Small States in International Relations*, eds. August Schou and Arne Olav Brundtland, pp. 147-55. Stockholm: Almqvist & Wikesell.

Ozawa, Terutomo. 1968. "Imitation, Innovation, and Japanese Exports." In *The Open Economy: Essays on International Trade and Finance*, Columbia Studies in Economics, 1, eds. Peter B. Kenen and Roger Lawrence, pp. 190-212. New York: Columbia University.

Pen, Jan. 1967. A Primer on International Trade. New York: Random House.

Pertot, Vladimir. 1972. International Economics of Control, trans. R. A. Clarke, N. Djurisic, D. J. I. Matko, K. Sidor, and A. White. Edinburgh: Oliver & Boyd.

Peterson, Peter G. 1971a. The United States in a Changing World Economy, Vol. 1: A Foreign Economic Perspective. Washington, D. C.: U. S. Government Printing Office.

_____. 1971b. The United States in a Changing World Economy, Vol. 2: Background Material. Washington, D. C.: U. S. Government Printing Office.

Pinto, Anibal, and Jan Knakel. 1973. "The Centre-Periphery System Twenty Years Later." Social and Economic Studies, Vol. 22, No. 1, pp. 33-89.

Posner, N. V. 1961. "International Trade and Technical Change." Oxford Economic Papers, New Series, Vol. 13, No. 3, pp. 323-41.

Prebisch, Raul. 1959. "Commercial Policy in the Underdeveloped Countries." American Economic Review, Vol. 49, No. 2, pp. 251-73.

Predohl, A. 1949. Aussenwertschaft: Weltwirtschaft, Handelspolitik, und Wahrungspolitik. Göttingen.

Quinn, James Brian. 1966. "Technological Competition: Europe vs. U. S." Harvard Business Review, Vol. 44, No. 4, pp. 113-30.

Rapkin, David P. 1976. "Trade, Dependence, and Development: A Longitudinal Analysis." Paper read annual meeting of the Southern Political Science Association, November, Atlanta.

Ray, David. 1973. "The Dependency Model of Latin America Underdevelopment: Three Basic Fallacies." Journal of Interamerican Studies and World Affairs, Vol. 15, No. 1, pp. 4-20.

Ray, James Lee, and Thomas Webster. 1977. "Dependency and Economic Performance in Latin America." Paper read at the annual meeting of the International Studies Association, March, St. Louis.

Reno, Philip. 1970. "Aluminum Profits and Caribbean People." In Imperialism and Underdevelopment: A Reader, ed. Robert I. Rhodes, pp. 79-88. New York: Monthly Review.

Richardson, Neil R. 1976. "Political Compliance and U.S. Trade Development." American Political Science Review, Vol. 70, No. 4, pp. 1098-109.

Richardson, Neil R., and Charles W. Kegley, Jr. 1977. "International Economic Dependence and Political Compliance: A Longitudinal Analysis." Paper read at the annual meeting of the International Studies Association, March, St. Louis.

Rosecrance, Richard, and Arthur Stein. 1973. "Interdependence: Myth or Reality?" World Politics, Vol. 26, No. 1, pp. 1-27.

Rostow, W. W. 1978. "Personal Communication." Austin, Texas: May.

Rubin, Leslie, and Brian Weinstein. 1974. Introduction to African Politics: A Continental Approach. New York: Praeger.

Rweyemamu, J. F. 1969. "International Trade and the Developing Countries." Journal of Modern African Studies, Vol. 7, No. 2, pp. 203-19.

Savage, I. Richard, and Karl W. Deutsch. 1960. "A Statistical Model of the Gross Analysis of Transaction Flows." Econometrica, Vol. 28, No. 3, pp. 551-72.

Senghass, Dieter. 1975. "Multinational Corporations and the Third World: On the Problem of the Further Integration of Peripheries into the Given Structure of the International Economic System." Journal of Peace Research, Vol. 12, No. 4, pp. 257-74.

Senghass-Knoblock, Eva. 1975. "The Internationalization of Capital and the Process of Underdevelopment: The Case of Black Africa." Journal of Peace Research, Vol. 12, No. 4, pp. 275-92.

Singer, Marshall R. 1972. Weak States in a World of Powers: The Dynamics of International Relationships. New York: Free Press.

Smith, Glen Alden. 1973. Soviet Foreign Trade: Organization, Operations, and Policy, 1918-1971. Praeger Special Studies in International Economics and Development. New York: Praeger.

Smith, Robert E. 1974. "Private Power and National Sovereignty: Some Comments on the Multinational Corporation." Journal of Economic Issues, Vol. 8, No. 2, pp. 417-47.

Spiegel, Steven L. 1972. Dominance and Diversity: The International Hierarchy. Boston: Little Brown.

Stallings, Barbara. 1972. Economic Dependency in Africa and Latin America. Sage Professional Paper in Comparative Politics, Vol. 3, No. 01-031. Beverly Hills: Sage.

Stehr, Uwe. 1977. "Unequal Development and Dependency Structures in COMECON." Journal of Peace Research, Vol. 14, No. 2, pp. 115-28.

Stryker, J. Dirck. 1968. "The Sources of Change in Export Performance: The United States and Canada." In The Open Economy: Essays on International Trade and Finance, Columbia Studies in Economics, 1, eds. Peter B. Kenen and Roger Lawrence, pp. 150-74. New York: Columbia University.

Sunkel, Osvaldo. 1973. "Transnational Capitalism and National Disintegration in Latin America." Social and Economic Studies, Vol. 22, No. 1, pp. 132-76.

_____. 1969. "National Development Policy and External Dependence in Latin America." Journal of Development Studies, Vol. 6, No. 1, pp. 23-48.

Teubal, Morris. 1976. "Threshold R&D Levels in Sectors of Advanced Technology." European Economic Review, Vol. 7, No. 4, pp. 395-402.

Thoman, Richard S. 1964. "Trade Relationships between the European Economic Community and the United States." East Lakes Geographer, Vol. 1, pp. 29-39.

Thoman, Richard S., and Edgar C. Conkling. 1967. Geography of International Trade. Englewood Cliffs, New Jersey: Prentice-Hall.

Tinbergen, Jan. 1962. Shaping the World Economy: Suggestions for an International Economic Policy. New York: Twentieth Century Fund.

Tulloch, Peter. 1973. The Seven Outside: Commonwealth Asia's Trade with the Enlarged EEC. London: Overseas Development Institute.

Tyler, William G., and J. Peter Wogart. 1973. "Economic Dependence and Marginalization: Some Empirical Evidence." Journal of Interamerican Studies and World Affairs. Vol. 15, No. 1, pp. 36-45.

Uri, Pierre. 1976. Development without Dependence. Praeger Special Studies in International Economics and Development. New York: Praeger.

Vital, David. 1971. The Survival of Small States: Studies in Small Power/Great Power Conflict. London: Oxford University.

―――. 1967. The Inequality of States: A Study of the Small Power in International Relations. Oxford: Clarendon.

Waehrer, Helen. 1968. "Wage Rates, Labor Skills, and United States Foreign Trade." In The Open Economy: Essays on International Trade and Finance, Columbia Studies in Economics, 1, eds. Peter B. Kenen and Roger Lawrence, pp. 19-39. New York: Columbia University.

Weinstein, Brian. 1967. "Leon Mba: The Ideology of Dependence." Geneve-Afrique, Vol. 6, No. 1, pp. 49-62.

Wilkenson, B. W. 1968. Canada's International Trade: An Analysis of Recent Trends and Patterns. Quebec [?]: Canadian Trade Commission.

Willey, H. David. 1968. "Growth Patterns and Export Performance: Britain and Germany." In The Open Economy: Essays on International Trade and Finance. Columbia Studies in Economics, 1. Eds. Peter B. Kenen and Roger Lawrence, pp. 127-49. New York: Columbia University.

Wolf, Charles, Jr., and David Wernschrott. 1973. "International Transactions and Regionalism: Distinguishing 'Insiders' from 'Outsiders.'" American Economic Review, Vol. 63, No. 2, pp. 52-60.

Woolley, Herbert B. 1966. Measuring Transactions between World Areas. New York: Columbia University.

Yates, P. Lamartine. 1959. Forty Years of Foreign Trade: A Statistical Handbook with Special Reference to Primary Products and Under-Developed Countries. New York: MacMillan.

Yeates, Maurice H. 1969. "A Note Concerning the Development of a Geographic Model of International Trade." Geographical Analysis, Vol. 1, No. 4, pp. 399-404.

Young, Lewis H. 1974. "Why U.S. Companies Can Compete." Journal of International Affairs, Vol. 28, No. 1, pp. 81-90.

DATA SOURCES

Annual Statement of Trade of the United Kingdom, various issues. Her Majesty's Stationery Office.

Australia Bureau of Census and Statistics. Monthly Bulletin of Overseas Trade Statistics, various issues. Canaberra.

East African Common Services Organization. 1962. Annual Trade Report of Kenya, Uganda and Tanganyika for the Year Ended 31st December 1961. Mombassa.

Foreign Trade Division, Bureau of the Census. 1953. Quarterly Summary of Foreign Commerce. Washington, D. C.: U. S. Government Printing Office.

International Monetary Fund and International Bank for Reconstruction and Development. Direction of Trade, various issues. Washington, D. C.

Marer, Paul. 1972. Soviet and East European Foreign Trade, 1946-1969: Statistical Compendium and Guide. Bloomington: Indiana University.

Ministry of Finance. 1971. Japan Exports & Imports.

Det Statistiske Department. Danmarks Vareindførsel og-udførse, various issues. København.

Societe d'Etudes Economiques Sociales et Statistiques. 1952. Bulletin Economique et Social du Maroc, Vol. 16, No. 56. Rabat.

Statistical Office of the United Nations. World Trade Annual, various issues. New York: Walker.

United Nations Statistical Office. Yearbook of International Trade Statistics, various issues. New York.

United States Bureau of the Census. 1965. Foreign Commerce and Navigation of the United States, 1946-1963. Washington, D. C.: U. S. Government Printing Office.

United States Department of Commerce. Survey of Current Business, various issues. Washington, D. C.

World Bank. 1975. World Bank Atlas: Population, Per Capita Product, and Growth Rates. Washington, D. C.: World Bank.

ABOUT THE AUTHORS

Robert T. Green is associate professor of international business and marketing at The University of Texas at Austin. He is a specialist in international marketing and international trade analysis.

Prior to joining the faculty of The University of Texas, Professor Green received his doctorate in business administration from the Pennsylvania State University with concentrations in international business, marketing, and political science. Although he has been affiliated with The University of Texas since his graduation, Professor Green has taken leaves of absence to teach and conduct research abroad. He has been a visiting professor at the Universidad de Carabobo in Valencia, Venezuela and at the Institut d'Administration des Entreprises in Aix-en-Provence, France.

Professor Green's publications include the monograph <u>Political Instability as a Determinant of U.S. Foreign Investment</u> which is based on his doctoral dissertation. He has also published more than twenty articles on international business and marketing in such professional journals as the <u>Columbia Journal of World Business</u>, the <u>Journal of International Business Studies</u>, <u>Management International Review</u>, the <u>California Management Review</u>, the <u>Journal of Marketing</u>, the <u>Journal of Marketing Research</u>, and <u>Public Opinion Quarterly</u>.

James M. Lutz is an Assistant Professor of Political Science at West Virginia University. His areas of interest are international relations and comparative politics with particular reference to Africa and the Middle East.

Professor Lutz received his Ph.D. from The University of Texas at Austin writing his dissertation on "The Diffusion of Political Phenomena in Sub-Saharan Africa." Professor Lutz has also co-authored a monograph, <u>Industrial Classification, Regional Market Structure and Divestiture</u> and has published in <u>Economic Geography</u>. He has also presented numerous papers at professional meetings in political science, geography and international studies.

LIBRARY OF DAVIDSON COLLEGE

regular loan may be checked out for   Book